Fictions of
Consciousness

Jonathan Loesberg

Fictions of Consciousness

Mill, Newman, and the Reading of

Victorian Prose

RUTGERS UNIVERSITY PRESS

New Brunswick and London

Copyright © 1986 by Rutgers, The State University

All Rights Reserved

Manufactured in the United States of America

Library of Congress Cataloging-in-Publication Data

Loesberg, Jonathan, 1950–
    Fictions of consciousness—Mill, Newman, and the
reading of Victorian prose.

    Bibliography: p.
    Includes index.
    1. English prose literature—19th century—History
and criticism.   2. Autobiography.   3. Narration (Rhetoric)
4. Mill, John Stuart, 1806–1873. Autobiography.
5. Newman, John Henry, 1801–1890. Apologia pro vita sua.
6. Consciousness in literature.   7. Philosophy in
literature.   8. Authors, English—19th century—Biography.
I. Title.
PR788.A9L63   1986   828'.808'09   85–30271
ISBN 0–8135–1173–9
ISBN 0–8135–1204–2 (pbk.)

British Cataloging-in-Publication Information Available.

For Gail Grella

Contents

Acknowledgments

Written over a number of years, this book has, in the process, accumulated for its author a number of debts. I would like to thank first Professors Dorothy Mermin and Roger Henkle. Dorothy Mermin's early direction of the project shaped many of the ideas that appear here. Roger Henkle, who first introduced me, when I was an undergraduate, to the study of Victorian literature, also, fittingly, played a central part in helping me find the proper form in which to express my ideas. Their confidence in the value of my work, at times when the profession was not always hospitable, gave me a less measurable but equally important form of support. At later stages, I have benefited from the helpful suggestions of Judith Ferster, Tzvetan Todorov, E. D. Hirsch, L. Perry Curtis, and Laura Tracy. Leslie Mitchner at Rutgers Press, Ed Kessler, and Kay Mussell made invaluable suggestions when I was doing my final revision.

I am also grateful to the School of Criticism and Theory and the National Endowment for the Humanities for financial and intellectual support during parts of this project. American University's Mellon grants for faculty development also offered financial support.

Earlier versions of parts of this book have appeared in *Interspace and the Inward Sphere*, edited by Norman A. Anderson and Margene Weiss (Macomb, Ill.: Essays in Literature, 1978), 87–106 and *University of Toronto Quarterly* 50 (Winter 1981): 199–220. I thank the editors for permitting their appearance in revised form here.

Fictions of
Consciousness

Introduction

This book uses autobiography as a transitional discourse to discuss some concepts of consciousness important to Victorian intellectual and literary history. It delineates a connection between nineteenth-century philosophic debate on consciousness and nineteenth-century narrative, which often shapes and is shaped by those articulations of consciousness. Approached by critics in various ways—as a literary genre, as a historical document, as the expression of a philosophy—autobiography is often an entry point for the literary analysis of nonfictional prose.[1] And so it is here. By seeing autobiography as a genre that transforms philosophy into narrative, this book shows how the tools we use to analyze fiction, informed by an awareness of philosophic context, may produce a fuller understanding of the literariness of Victorian prose. The purpose of my movement from works of logic, history, and theology through autobiography to a strictly formal analysis of narrative structure in autobiography is to suggest how the texts of Victorian intellectual history become Victorian narratives. The result of understanding that movement is, I believe, a more adequate methodology for reading Victorian prose in both its philosophic and its narrative aspects. That methodology I discuss extensively in the book's final part.

My use of the word *movement* is deliberate. Both the process that I argue occurs in Victorian prose and the process by which I show that transition, move with the characteristics of a logical progression. This organization contrasts with one normally found in books: a generalization followed by a series of examples. First, a few warnings are in order about what articulating such a movement entails. Although autobiographies are, ultimately, key texts in my argument, indeed the texts toward which the logical movement is directed, what follows is emphatically not a series of readings of nineteenth-century autobiographies. Rather, I trace twice, in the cases of John Stuart Mill and John Henry Newman, the role

autobiographies play in their philosophic works and the relationship between their philosophic arguments and their autobiographical narratives.
Thus, rather than analyze only autobiographies, I first discuss the body
of thought Mill and Newman produced in their nonautobiographical
works and how that thought relates to their autobiographies. The result
of my argument's dependence on logical progress is that this book will
not respond well to a skipping from the introduction to any one of the
readings of separate works. My analyses of the various works of Victorian prose, though I hope they are internally coherent and persuasive,
depend for their larger significance as much on their specific location
within the argument as they do upon their relation to the overriding
thesis.

The common thread in the movement nineteenth-century writers
made from philosophy through autobiography to narrative, and thus the
common thread in the movement of my argument, was the problematic
status of nineteenth-century theories of consciousness. Those theories
were both an intellectual problem and a series of models for narrative
structure; showing how one gets from philosophy to narrative thus involves delineating a logical progression from crux to structure.[2] Consciousness was a crux because nineteenth-century philosophy found it
logically inexplicable, a phenomenological event one experiences but
whose existence one can not quite verify. In such a situation, a writer
could formulate a paradoxical definition of consciousness that justified
and explained other paradoxes more central to his system. In Mill's case,
the ostensibly more central problem was how to show individual free will
could coexist in a philosophic system that rested upon an implicitly de-
terminist psychology. In Newman's case, that first problem was his claim
that religious doctrine has the same type of certainty as scientific theory
without being subject to the same rules of verifiability. Although these
problems are not necessarily autobiographical, they become intimately
and pervasively so when their paradoxical quality is ascribed to and explained by a writer's definition of consciousness. An argument over free
will, for instance, would not normally entail self-reference, but when that
argument is supported by a definition of self-consciousness, the status of
its proponent's own consciousness and will may suddenly become markedly relevant. The first point at which philosophy may start to impinge
upon autobiography, then, occurs when a philosophic problem is explained in terms of a paradoxical definition of consciousness. Although

these definitions of consciousness come ultimately to shape the auto-biographies of Mill and Newman, the explanations of the problems that lead to the paradoxical definitions are the most purely philosophic sections (Chapters II and VI) of my argument. There I discuss those works of Mill and Newman which explicitly constructed philosophic and epistemological systems: *A System of Logic* and *An Examination of Hamilton's Philosophy* in Mill's case, *The Development of Christian Doctrine* and the *Grammar of Assent* in Newman's.

My further discussion of Mill and Newman draws both the specific connections between their philosophic arguments and their autobiographical narratives and the general connections that obtain between philosophic argument and narrative. The first way in which philosophy leads to narrative is actually common enough in many texts. Frequently within philosophic argument there are short narratives that serve to explain or demonstrate a concept, for example, Socrates' account of the prisoners of the cave, used to explain how material reality, which seems so real, may actually be only a reflection of a higher reality. In more extended forms, such narratives may become exemplary tales, such as *Rasselas* or *Candide*, narratives that must be understood primarily as explaining a philosophic position. Most of these narratives well merit, as responses to their verisimilitude, Glaucon's complaining response to Socrates: "A strange image you speak of . . . and strange prisoners."[3] And yet, when autobiographies exemplify an author's philosophic position about consciousness, their claims about the reality of the events they narrate are far stronger than that of verisimilitude.

The paradoxical definitions of consciousness discussed in my chapters on philosophy are more acceptable to Mill and Newman than the original paradoxes from which they resulted because nineteenth-century philosophers saw consciousness as logically inexplicable—as understood through experience rather than through canons of logical coherence. When a writer had resolved his prior paradoxes in his paradoxical definition of consciousness, he could then argue that, paradox or not, his own experience of consciousness indicated that his own definition was empirically true; he could then recount that experience in his autobiography. When a writer uses autobiography as an empirical defense of a philosophy, he is making the first kind of connection between philosophy and narrative, writing an exemplary tale. By placing Mill's *Autobiography* and Newman's *Apologia* in their philosophic contexts, I argue the vital importance of understanding the accounts of the lives as examples of the philosophies. But exemplary tales, demonstrating, as they often do, abstract concepts, have a tendency to be strange in the way Glaucon complains about, that is, to be more comprehensible as allegorized ideas than as represented events. The exemplary tales within the *Autobiography* and the *Apologia* partake of this strangeness, and it of course undercuts the value, as empirical evidence, of the events narrated.

This first intersection between autobiography and epistemological theory is not only problematic but not inevitable; theoretically there are other ways of offering empirical evidence for a definition of consciousness than writing autobiographies. But autobiography is not simply convenient in showing a connection between philosophy and narrative. As a result of a structural homology between consciousness and narrative, autobiography is a model form in the enacting of such a connection. Both self-consciousness and narrative are terms that have two aspects in isomorphic relationship. Self-consciousness involves both a conscient mind and the events or experiences of which the mind is conscious; narrative involves both an act of narration and the events the narrative voice or stance narrates. Moreover, whatever relationship we hypothesize for the elements of consciousness can be transposed upon those of narrative, and the reverse is also true. For instance, if one says that experiences are all that make up oneself, one still has to posit, minimally, a passive, receptive sensorium. In the same way, one may see narrative as a mere sequence of events, but to construe an arbitrary collection of events as a narrative, one still has to posit, minimally, the shaping involved to select and form a sequence and thus, a separable narrative stance or voice. And, to take the opposing definitions, even a radical idealism would have its narrative cognates, perhaps in the modern fiction distinctive in its imperial narrative voices.[4]

This structural identity between consciousness and narrative is the basis for the second type of connection between philosophic argument and narrative. Since both consciousness and narration involve the same relationship between the parts that make them up, and since autobiographical narrative is necessarily an act of self-consciousness, the author of an autobiography is in a privileged position to shape his literary narrative structure as an empirical example of his definition of consciousness. In effect, the paradoxical definition of consciousness determines a narrative structure (and since structure is not thematic, the conceptual paradoxes of philosophy are not problems for it). This narrative structure in turn determines the events that comprise it, events that were originally offered as empirical evidence. My argument about the second connection between philosophy and narrative delineates, through a thoroughly formalist reading, the narrative structures of the *Autobiography* and the *Apologia*. It thus shows how the implicit definitions of consciousness shape the written lives.

I have chosen Mill and Newman as examples through which to show this movement from philosophy to narrative because their works embody particular structural intersections of consciousness and narrative, not because I think they represent any particular poles in Victorian intellectual history. Despite the one's agnosticism and the other's Catholicism, they responded similarly to the various issues that swept Victorian England. They do exhibit a structural if not a thematic opposition, however, in their definitions of consciousness and in the narratives that embody them. Mill's image for the events both of a life and of a narrative is of beads on a thread; he sees events and experiences as a potentially endless progression. Consciousness and narrative stance are each merely one more bead on its respective thread. But the particular beads of narrative and consciousness have a special status as completing or formative acts or events even while each is ontologically merely yet another act or event. They are the special end points to threads that theoretically have no ends. For Newman, both the conscient mind and the acts of narrative are primary rather than terminal. More than merely reflecting or recounting the events they perceive and narrate, their reflections and recountings create the significance of those events. They are thus a reproduction or reflection that is also an original significance. My discussion of each writer explains, I hope, both how they arrived at these definitions of consciousness and narrative and why each definition makes more sense as narrative than as epistemology. Here I merely want to note that these definitions are structural limits in the way consciousness and narrative may be defined. Although Mill and Newman may not appear as thematically central to Victorian studies as, say, Carlyle, they do have a real structural significance.

This movement I have been describing originates in certain general problems of Victorian intellectual history. First, why would the status of consciousness seem so naturally relevant an issue in, to us, not obviously related debates, or why would Victorian writers turn to autobiography in the course of philosophic discourse? Second, why would it feel relatively natural to place paradoxical definitions and narrative structures at the center of one's philosophy? My discussions of the movements Mill and Newman enact answer these questions in different ways for each writer. Although specific and individuated answers to these kinds of questions would seem to imply an underlying common answer of duplicity (the authors intending to take their audiences in, particularly in the case of the possible fictiveness in the *Apologia*), duplicity is the one common answer I would not want to imply, and this is because avoiding questions of intention in order to see the motive forces behind philosophic and narrative discourse is one of the purposes of my study. Such an implication would also be mistaken on historical grounds. There were good general reasons why Victorians would turn naturally to consciousness and autobiography in intellectual debate and why they would not be uncomfortable with paradox and connections to narrative in epistemological definitions. These general reasons, which comprehend Mill's and Newman's specific reasons, make suggestions of duplicity not simply inappropriate but misleading.

A first glance at nineteenth-century texts would not seem to make autobiography or consciousness particularly auspicious as form or subject for Victorian writers. Josiah Bounderby, the industrialist in *Hard Times* who justifies his ruthlessness by telling the story of his own rise from destitution to power, a story that is finally shown to be false, nicely embodies a Victorian suspicion that autobiography's self-justificatory opportunities had a distinct tendency toward hypocrisy. By making self-involvement its own end, one could perhaps avoid the perils of hypocrisy implicit in self-justification, but only to be confronted with a state of mind many Victorian poets and social critics feared just as much: a debilitating overinvolvement with self. Thomas Carlyle's work ethic and his concomitant insistence on self-forgetfulness were only the most extreme of Victorian reactions to an immobilizing self-consciousness.[5] Now morbidity does not necessarily result from a desire to understand oneself fully any more than justification necessarily involves hypocrisy, but Victorians were acutely aware of connections in both situations. And yet, despite this awareness, autobiography was by no means an unusual form of expression in the nineteenth century. Why were so many writers willing to face these alternative threats and write their autobiographies?

The Victorians wrote autobiography because it offered them a mediating position between philosophies claiming that all knowledge is experiential and others that tended to insist on the possibility and indeed central importance of an intuitional knowledge of a priori truths about the world. Moreover, since that compromise was formulated in terms of an autobiographer's definition of self-consciousness, the very quality that made self-justification and self-investigation threatening, autobiography seemed to have the possibility not merely of avoiding the threats of morbidity and inauthenticity in the quest of a philosophic mediation but of transforming those threatening qualities and making them part of that mediation.

By recalling the meeting of the British Association held at Oxford in June 1860, we can see both the importance a mediation between the claims of intuition and experience had for the Victorians and the way seemingly independent polemics could persistently involve those claims. There, Bishop Samuel Wilberforce and Professor T. H. Huxley, among others, discussed Charles Darwin's theory of evolution. Their interchange is famous. Wilberforce turned to Huxley and "begged to know, was it through his grandfather or his grandmother that he claimed descent from a monkey?" The audience laughed, and Huxley patiently waited his turn. When it came, he responded that he was not ashamed to be descended from a monkey but he would be "ashamed to be connected with a man who used his great gifts to obscure the truth." The effect is supposed to have been electric. As one critic put it, "Huxley had committed forensic murder with a wonderful artistic simplicity, grinding orthodoxy between the facts and the supreme Victorian value of truth-telling."[6]

The war between orthodoxy and fact is really an externalized version of the older war between intuitional knowledge and experiential knowledge.[7] Orthodoxy, depending on tradition, rests on our faith in the testimony of others or on our intuition of that testimony's truth. The existence of a fact, however, is apprehended through our experience, or our reasoning from our experience. If a debate over evolution could also entail problems of intuition and experience, it should hardly surprise us that Mill's concern to find a place for free will within the experientially determined economy of associationism and Newman's desires to claim for the truths of orthodoxy the status of facts could also be redirected toward that epistemological issue. Consciousness offers the possibility of mediating this conflict because it occupies an ideal middle ground in the dispute. One could honestly describe the facts of one's life, of one's experiences and intuitions. Moreover, if the intuitions were irrational, it might still be a fact that one had them. Autobiography, the embodiment of such a description, thus can become a narrative with implicit philosophic and polemic implications.

Not only does autobiography have a potential role to play in this philosophic debate, it will not operate easily unless its role is mediatory, unless it embodies a double position of consciousness as both experience and ontologically special knowledge. By looking at writers who approached autobiography but edged away from the form because of extremist positions in the debate between intuition and experience, we can see how necessary the formulation of this mediating position is to the writing of autobiography. Carlyle's *Sartor Resartus*, for instance, is so scornful of empirical reality's significance, and therefore of the value of experience as a way of learning truth, that it is doubtful whether the book can be called autobiography at all.[8] Here, for instance, is Teufelsdröckh on facts:

> What are your historical Facts; still more your biographical? Wilt thou know a Man, above all a Mankind, by stringing together beadrolls of what thou namest Facts? . . . Facts are engraved Hierograms, for which the fewest have the key.[9]

Facts have here no inherent value; nor may their meaning be ascertained by reasoning from their appearance or phenomenal aspects. As "Hierograms," they can only be deciphered by the initiate who has the key.

But when Carlyle discusses the intuition that perceives the significance of nature, the key to the Hierogram, he smuggles experience back into the picture in a way that suddenly allows for the possibility of autobiography. The relationship between intuition and experience that Carlyle outlines is implicit in his use of Kantian terminology in the following passage:

> Our Professor's [Teufelsdröckh's] method is not, in any case, that of common school Logic, where the truths all stand in a row, each holding by the skirts of the other; but at best that of practical Reason, proceeding by large Intuition over whole systematic groups and kingdoms. (*Sartor*, 52)

Even though practical Reason is here contrasted to Logic, it is not to be taken as an aspect of Kantian pure reason but as a form of Kantian "understanding," of phenomenal knowledge, as the chapter's headnote to this section, "Intuition quickened by Experience," makes clear. Intuition is the Carlylean cognate to Kant's pure reason; but by using that term, Carlyle makes distinct changes in Kant's philosophy.[10] Intuition was a part of Kant's understanding in the sense that there are certain aspects of phenomenal reality that we do not experience but the intuition of which is a condition of experience itself. The pure reason, which apprehends the Kantian "ideas," those supersensible truths closest in Kant to the kind of significance Carlyle has intuition obtaining from experience, was split from this process entirely. Kant insisted that we had no experiential or tangible knowledge of noumenal essence. By taking intuition to be the same as pure reason but maintaining its place in experiential perception, Carlyle effectively connects experience of material reality with an intuition of spiritual essence. In such a situation, a description of an author's experiences would clearly be relevant to a statement of his intuitions.

But Carlyle's connection between intuition and experience is a light, nearly an aleatory, one. Teufelsdröckh's knowledge develops not by logic, not by reasoning upon experience, but by "Intuition quickened by Experience." It is not the particular shape of experience that gives us intuitional knowledge but the simple act of experience that ignites our intuition of spiritual reality. With no very close connection between the type of experience and the intuition it sets off, no reason exists for a very close concern with the particular experience behind an intuition. The suggestion here that the specificity of experience is not relevant to the perception of the spiritual truth it lies behind draws Carlyle away from the need to offer reliable spiritual autobiography and toward the playfulness of *Sartor Resartus.*

Carlyle is enough of a mediator in the dispute between intuition and experience to see experience as a necessary aspect of apprehending truth, and *Sartor's* Editor frequently counteracts those of Teufelsdröckh's metaphysical declamations that seem to depart from all dependence upon empirical experience.[11] But, since experience can be fictionalized and different experiences interchanged and we can still arrive at the same intuitional truths, *Sartor* seems to be less concerned with presenting particularized autobiography than with archetypal versions of experience.

If Carlyle's sense of the interchangeability of experience and the unity of intuitional truth eliminates that need for sticking to the details of one's life upon which autobiography depends, Darwin so insists on a scientific approach that his *Autobiography* lacks cohesion. One critic characterized Darwin's work as "the evolution of Charles Darwin treated in a thoroughly scientific spirit."[12] Indeed, Darwin's own subtitle, "Recollections of the Development of my mind and character,"[13] puts it clearly within the body of the rest of his scientific work. As he has discussed evolution of the species, he will also discuss his own evolution.

The problem is that the particular experiences of life are not precisely the same as the external facts of biology that, as a scientific observer, Darwin can generalize into a theory. He may be empirical about the external world, may deny any integral status to the species, but he is not an associationist: "I am inclined to agree with Francis Galton in believing that education and environment produce only a small effect on the mind of any one and that most of our qualities are innate" (*Autobiography*, 43). This assertion would seem to place Darwin in league with Carlyle. We do not learn from experience but have an innate, integral self. Yet Darwin, unlike Carlyle, never tries to make his *Autobiography* a manifestation of his innate self. He simply and logically states that certain qualities of his, that he perceives he has, have no experiential basis and must therefore be inherent.

Darwin, in the *Autobiography*, never discusses explicit his withdrawal from intuition into science. The reasons for that withdrawal, though, may be implicit in the fate of his father. Robert Darwin is described as having an overwhelmingly comprehensive memory and an intuitive grasp of psychology so incisive that to Charles he seemed able to read minds. The result of this sensitivity and memory is not as positive as Darwin explicitly describes it, however: "I once asked him, when he was old and could not walk, why he did not drive out for exercise; and he answered, 'Every road out of Shrewsbury is associated in my mind with some painful event'" (*Autobiography*, 40). This passage anticipates Jorge Luis Borges's "Funes, the Memorious," in which the title character, so burdened by his ability to see reality in all its detail and remember everything he has ever experienced, lives out his existence in a carefully darkened room. Like Funes, Robert Darwin ends his life paralyzed by his ability to remember everything and by his sharp sensitivity to everything he remembers. Moreover, like Funes, who could not think, "my father's mind was not scientific, and he did not try to generalize his knowledge under general laws" (*Autobiography*, 42). The suggestion is clear: intuition, memory, and excessive sensitivity paralyze one's ability to think and act in the world.

In contrast to his father, Darwin insists on his own ability to generalize:

"From my early youth, I have had the strongest desire to understand or explain whatever I observed,—that is, to group all facts under some general laws" (*Autobiography*, 141). But scientific observation can be a very mechanical process. Indeed, Darwin laments that "my mind seems to have become a kind of machine for grinding out general laws out of large collections of facts" (*Autobiography*, 139). The facts of one's life, however, are not amenable to scientific generalization since, as innate, they are not in the realm of science. They can be understood only with the kind of intuition that paralyzes Robert Darwin and from which Charles withdraws.

Darwin's *Autobiography* may be seen as a machine constantly grinding to a halt. It is filled with detail after vivid detail, but the evolution of the mind as a whole never takes form. The poignant last lines are almost an avowal of the failure of the autobiographical project: "With such moderate abilities as I possess, it is truly surprising that I should have influenced to a considerable extent the belief of scientific men on some important points" (*Autobiography*, 145). Darwin cannot even manage to explain the first thing about himself, how he became a scientist. Both Carlyle and Darwin made autobiographical gestures to the extent that their theories pushed them away from their preferred position in the debate between intuition and experience. Carlyle's sense that intuition was grounded in experience influenced him to consider the connection between philosophy and autobiography; Darwin, to record the facts of his life correctly, had to mention his intuitions, his innate self. But Carlyle so stressed intuition over experience that even when he described experience, it was fictionalized, and Darwin so insisted on scientific method that when his method came upon an intuition, it broke down. His *Autobiography* remains simply recollections.

Mill and Newman were not as extreme as Carlyle and Darwin on this issue. Although they started from opposite poles of the debate, they both attempted to move toward the center. Mill started with an associationally inculcated belief in utilitarianism, but he tried to find a place within that rationalistic philosophy for emotion, unreasoned response, esthetic appreciation. Newman started with an intuitively accepted, essentially Calvinistic conversion, but he moved steadily toward delineating objective manifestations of the cause of his intuitions and attempted to explain philosophically how one may reliably travel from the empirical to the religious, from the visible to the invisible world. And at the core of their mediatory theories were their definitions of self-consciousness. In Mill's thought, self-consciousness, because of its special position in the thread of experience, was the one aspect of perception he claimed was inexplicable by an associational theory of psychology. It was therefore a port of entry for esthetic and emotional perception. In contrast, Newman made the reflection of self-consciousness the activity of reasoning upon our intuitions even as he insisted on the ontological priority of consciousness. Thus, for him, it served as a way to give intuition a reasoned basis without fully opening the propositions of intuition to logical inquiry. Starting from opposite ends in their move toward the center, each thinker used self-consciousness to create a mediating force between intuition and experience. And the comparison goes one step further. Since each man made self-consciousness the mediating force, each embodied his theory and expressed his thought in that most self-conscious of forms: autobiography.

Victorian autobiographers, and particularly and centrally Mill and Newman, were willing to risk passing between the Scylla and Charybdis of self-consciousness—hypocritical self-justification and morbid self-concern—because autobiography offered a special mode of discourse, a distinctly valuable form in which to construct a philosophy that mediated between the claims of intuition and experience. Modern critics have not seen the possibilities of autobiography in quite such optimistic terms. Though they have not explicitly concerned themselves with moral issues of hypocrisy and morbidity, they have used, to break down the Victorian theoretical structure of complementary opposition, precisely the stance of consciousness from which an autobiography is told. By looking at the nature of this breakdown and the reasons Victorians, though essentially aware of the logic behind it, were not bothered by it, we can see why they were not uncomfortable in turning to paradox and narrative in their philosophic disputes.

For many modern critics, autobiography can never be a completely honest and straightforward reflection on experience. John Freccero, for instance, outlines the problems of assuming honesty in his discussion of the special place that Augustine's *Confessions* has in the history of autobiography. Freccero argues that the form of the *Confessions* followed the Pauline model of conversion in which there was "a burial of the 'old man' and a putting on of the new." Such a model creates a straightforward explanation for self-detachment, and self-detachment is the first requirement for being able to see the self in unity, the basic activity of autobiography.

Modern psychology, however, allows no radical breaks in the personality: "only death can close the series, lock the door of the self so that inventory may be taken. Death being what it is, however, it is impossible for the self to 'take stock' of itself." This is to say that any position one finds or creates, from which one may draw firm conclusions about one's life, must be essentially fictional because no such position exists within a chaotic series of experiences that is terminated only by death.[14] I am not suggesting that there is no such thing as conversion or change, sudden or gradual. But, if one assumes that, prior to death, there is no ultimate change that sums up one's life and makes it whole, then any position one creates from which to see one's life whole is fictional, at least in the sense that it imposes an order upon the life that cannot be inherent in the life. Yet such a position of self-conscious reflection is obviously vital to an autobiography and particularly to the mediatory desires of Victorian autobiography. To call the stance fictional is, then, to say that autobiographies are fictional.[15]

Victorian autobiographies are not intended as fictions, though. If they did not exist *as factual evidence* for mediating positions in the dispute between intuitional and experiential theories of knowledge, they would be valueless in that dispute. Mill and Newman both, therefore, insist on their truthfulness and honesty. Even at the end of the Victorian period, when experiments in fictional form were starting to create questions about the distinction between autobiography and fiction, Edmund Gosse, in his autobiography, *Father and Son*, felt constrained to begin his work with the following reminder:

> At the present hour, when fiction takes forms so ingenious and so specious, it is perhaps necessary to say that the following narrative, in all its parts, and so far as the punctilious attention of the writer has been able to keep it so, is scrupulously true. If it were not true, in this strict sense, to publish it would be to trifle with all those who may be induced to read it. It is offered to them as a *document*, as a record of educational and religious conditions which, having passed away, will never return. . . . It offers, too, in a subsidiary sense, a study of the development of moral and intellectual ideas during the progress of infancy.[16]

Other autobiographies have, of course, begun with the claim of being strictly true. Noteworthy here, however, are the terms Gosse insists upon in describing the work: a "document," a "record," a "study." When we remember that almost immediately after this description, the author falls into the allegorical labeling of himself as the Son and his father as my Father—surely there were less suggestive ways of hiding the real names— the insistence upon the documentarity of the text is even more remarkable.[17] Gosse sees his life as exemplifying, most importantly, historical and religious development. If it is only "in a subsidiary sense" an exemplum of epistemological development, one starts to wonder how subsidiary are the actual details of the life that create such a universal emblem. Nevertheless, Gosse insists that his account is strictly evidential. He justifies the existence of *Father and Son* in a historical or theoretical context only by its literal truthfulness. Otherwise, he felt he would be trifling with his readers.

To say, then, with Freccero, that the self-concern that protected the validity of an autobiography presupposes a fictional narrative stance is to undercut the form's claims to arrive at and substantiate philosophic positions and discoveries (or for that matter positions or discoveries of any kind). What the autobiographies were supposed to demonstrate, though, was a mode of consciousness that had certain philosophic ramifications. Yet how can autobiography claim to demonstrate a mode of consciousness whose primary manifestation within the work, the position from which one views oneself, is a fiction? If verifying a philosophic position within autobiography depends on fiction, the autobiographer's philosophy is to that extent suspect, if not as Bounderby's self-justification, at least as inaccurate and faulty theory. I have been reversing cause and effect here. A thinker does not arrive at a flawed philosophy because he has fictionalized an account of his life any more than Bounderby was a ruthless hypocrite because he falsified his account of his childhood. One turns to the fictions of autobiography as a result of the flaws in the philosophy. One turns to autobiography to substantiate through narrative description what cannot be substantiated through philosophic discourse. In particular, Mill and Newman turn to a self-conscious narrative structure when a philosophy cannot adequately support a theoretical formulation of self-consciousness as a faculty mediating the claims of intuition and experience.

Victorians, however, would not see this turn as a fictive embodiment of a flawed philosophy but as a natural discursive shift. There were moments in Victorian philosophy, particularly the moment of discussing self-consciousness, when the models of narrative would make more sense than the informations of logic. By returning to Freccero's theory for a moment, we can see why. It is not a discovery of modern psychology, nor at all a scientific fact, that the self is only the sum of one's experiences, that therefore only death provides a vantage point from which to view a life whole. It is a theory datable to Hume's *Treatise of Human Nature*, which argued that there is no identity or self independent of one's sense perceptions, that there is no a priori relationship between those perceptions, that therefore one is merely the sum or "bundle" of one's chaotic sensations and there is no unified self.[18] This theory need hardly be taken as definitive. In one sense, it was not more widely believed in the nineteenth century than it was in Saint Paul's time, and certainly a writer who opposed to it his own definition of a unified self and a vantage point from which to view that self had as much reason to believe in the validity of his position as Saint Paul had to be sure about his model in which conversion divides the self into "old man" and "new man." In another sense, however, Freccero is right about nineteenth-century autobiographers. If Hume's labeling of any unification of the series of perceptions into a self as "fiction"[19] was not accepted as accurate, nevertheless it was generally believed that Hume's theory, like his other theories, was logically sound and its problem was that any theory that ran so obviously counter to the beliefs of common sense showed more the limitation of reason than the fallibility of common sense. Consequently, to define self-consciousness in the nineteenth century was both liberating and suspect: liberating because no definition was going to be subjected to logical inquisition if the very existence of the thing defined was unprovable; suspect because any likely definition could be offered since one could not easily dispute about a quality that no one could prove existed in any case. The only possible defense of a definition would be either simple assertion or the marshaling of empirical evidence. The empirical evidence for a definition of self-consciousness would be, of course, a narrative account of one's self-consciousness and therefore a self-conscious narrative. Moreover, the definition of consciousness and the narrative construct would mesh easily because of the structural likeness between them. In a sense, then, the Victorian philosopher became an autobiographer as soon as he tried to think about self-consciousness and what it was, and he would start to think about self-consciousness as soon as he thought of any one of a number of issues that raised problems of intuition and experience. It follows that the results of his thought were the results that narrative had to offer him. The autobiographical narrative shaped the philosophy at the moment that narrative was intended as evidence.

Here, something interesting happens. Up to now, I have been using the term *fiction* to mean an order imposed upon the world by man's mind. But there would seem to be no necessary problem about being factually and empirically accurate within the boundaries of the controlling fiction. In other words, we might allow that autobiographers necessarily select and shape without claiming that they necessarily falsify. But, if the formulation of self-consciousness with which one shapes one's life has an extra-autobiographical importance as the delineation of a philosophic mediation, the events one relates become valuable as an ostensibly empirical defense of one's theoretical position. For a writer concerned with supporting a particular formulation about self-consciousness, then, the next step was, through the fictional shaping of an autobiography, to create the empirical evidence that defended the theory. At this point both the controlling order and the events of an autobiography become fictional, and the way is prepared for a philosophy's embodiment as a narrative structure. When this formal embodiment occurs, the movement from philosophy to narrative is complete.

To show how this movement occurs, Parts One and Two first place, respectively, Mill's *Autobiography* and Newman's *Apologia* in the contexts of the author's philosophy. Opening chapters of each part pay close attention to the philosophic works of the respective authors; how they respond to the conflict between the demands of intuition and reason; the compromises they formulate; the definitions of self-consciousness these compromises involve; and finally, the dead ends, paradoxes, and bald assertions in which those compromises and definitions terminate. I then explain how the autobiographical attempt to defend empirically positions that are logically indefensible results in very real falsifications in the accounts of the lives, particularly in the accounts of Mill's mental crisis and Newman's conversion. These chapters often seem to diverge quite far from the subject of autobiography proper. They are devoted largely to Mill's social philosophy and metaphysics, to Newman's theology, historical theories, and epistemology. Only at the end do they explicitly return to a discussion of the autobiographies. But the departure is only apparent.

To be a defense of a philosophy, as well as a defense of truthfulness, and not merely an assertion of either, autobiography must present facts. Gosse insists that he offers a document. But the theories of self-consciousness that Mill and Newman espouse are supported by a narrative structure and accounts of conversions that are necessarily fictional. Autobiography remains different from fiction, though, not because it *is* true, but because its derivation from philosophic discourse necessitates that it claim to be true even at precisely the moment when it cannot be. To understand that insistence, we must understand the philosophy that creates a need for it. To understand why Mill and Newman turn to autobiography, we must understand why the philosophies behind the accounts of the lives will not stand on their own terms. Only with that understanding can we undertake the formal narrative analysis with which I end each part, because only then can we understand the full ramifications of narrative structure.

One of the results of reading autobiographies as narrative texts in response to other kinds of texts by their authors is a somewhat revisionary reading both of the philosophies and of the autobiographies of Mill and Newman. My emphasis on the centrality of Mill's often marginal comments about consciousness and my reading of Newman's epistemological theories are in various ways departures from received readings. One might think that, in principle at least, those revisions would not have been a necessary part of my theory about the discursive relationships of philosophy, autobiography, and fiction. Specific interpretations have a way of remaining disconcertingly stable in the light of the most widely varying esthetic and historiographic theories.[20] But I would argue that my revisions *are* a necessary consequence of my theory and my methodology. By seeing autobiographical narratives in relation to a series of philosophic works they derive from, we can begin to see the narrativity of philosophy and the philosophies of narratives.[21] My concluding Part Three and its discussions of Carlyle and Matthew Arnold try to generalize and make explicit the reading of Victorian prose that such a methodology would lead to and the particular value of that reading. But my rereadings of Mill's and Newman's works, nonautobiographical as well as autobiographical, can be taken as an implicit demonstration of that methodology as well as an explanation of the theory of discursive connections that lies beneath it.

Part 1
Free Association

Chapter I
The Philosophic Context of
Mill's *Autobiography*

Parts One and Two are about transformations, the transformation of philosophy into narrative through the linking discourse of autobiography. The link an autobiographer would like his reader to see between autobiography and philosophy is the one of empirical evidence. Recourse to empirical evidence occurs in a philosophic argument when proof or logical consistency are no longer available. Mill is explicit about this movement of argument in his discussion of first principles:

> To be incapable of proof by reasoning is common to all first principles; to the first premises of our knowledge, as well as to those of our conduct. But the former, being matters of fact, may be the subject of a direct appeal to the faculties which judge of fact—namely, our senses, and our internal consciousness.[1]

Mill is, of course, right. By definition, first principles cannot be proved, and our only evidence in arguing for their acceptance is empirical. Further, autobiography, a record of a life, as the sum of "our senses and our internal consciousness," does represent an acceptable, if not irrefutable, appeal to empirical evidence. But look again to those two terms, "our senses" and "our internal consciousness." One might easily see them as coordinates for the terms the Victorians were trying to bind together, experiential and intuitional apprehension. Further, taken together, the terms represent the two components of consciousness: our internal consciousness gives a self that is conscious and our senses give the self of which it is conscious, or at least an aspect of that self. Thus, the appear-

ance of first principles in philosophy seems to call automatically for autobiography inasmuch as it calls for the act of and the informations of self-
consciousness.

If self-consciousness is the mode by which we may produce ostensibly
accurate empirical evidence in support of first principles, it is also itself
the subject of first principles, in Mill and Newman as the reader will see
in these two parts and, as a result of Hume's dismantling of the concept of
self, in Victorian thought generally, as I argue in the introduction. As a
matter of first principles, the definition of self-consciousness is on the one
hand open to any assertion defensible in terms of the empirical evidence
only it can offer about itself. By that very openness, it is easily amenable,
on the other hand, to being defined in terms of the narrative structures
that, in autobiography, will reveal it. We have, therefore, a self-enclosed
system, a principle that provides evidence for itself and, more important,
a situation ideally suited to the formulation of philosophic principles in
the terms of narrative. The transforming effects of using autobiography
to demonstrate philosophy, then, the process by which philosophy becomes narrative, may be summarized as follows: First, what a writer takes
to be a first principle may actually be simply an assertion used to solve a
contradiction or a flaw that would otherwise threaten an important aspect
of a theory. In other words, if defining self-consciousness in a certain possibly paradoxical way can resolve a certain prior philosophic problem—in
Mill's case, a desire for a form of free will within associationism; in Newman's case, a search for a way to transform unreasoned intuitions about
the world into objectively certain knowledge about it—then that definition can be offered regardless of its paradoxicality. After all, first principles are not provable but merely a matter of experience. The definition
of self-consciousness, then, can both form and be formed by the exigencies of narrative structure, the narrative structure that in turn determines
the shape of the particular experiences an autobiography recounts. An
autobiographer may not, therefore, really offer the solution to a philosophic problem but, rather, assert the solution through the narrative
structure.

To look at an autobiography in this way changes the context in which it
is usually placed. By looking at it as a created defense of a theory, we can
see it more as a reflection of the author's ideas at the time he wrote and less
as a reflection of past ideas or ideas formerly held. We can regard the
claim to be telling the truth not as indicative of the accuracy of the events

narrated but as indicative of the stake an author has in the philosophy he offers, the very stake that will transform that philosophy into narrative. Finally, we can attend to the philosophic texts that surround the autobiographical one in an attempt to understand the ideas, the logical claims and logical breakdowns, that, I argue, determine the shape an autobiography takes as much as the life recounted does.

That Mill's *Autobiography* throws more light on his views when he wrote it in 1853–1854 than it does on the events he relates is a fact far too often ignored by his critics.[2] This might seem a relatively unpolemic and straightforward contention, yet such a recognition immediately undercuts, for instance, the very basis on which biographers and psychobiographers often attempt to analyze the significance of Mill's mental crisis. To analyze the language Mill uses in 1854 in order to uncover the subconscious significance of an event Mill dates as occurring in 1828, the psychological critic must assume that the choice of words at a later date tells us about the earlier state, and this assumption depends on a remarkable intellectual and psychological stability in the author.[3]

Looking at the *Autobiography* as a theoretical defense makes particularly good sense because, as often noted, it reads like a work of philosophy. There is, in fact, good evidence that Mill originally saw it as such. A letter to his wife Harriet, written during the composition of the *Early Draft*, shows both to what extent the work was a result of its time of composition and the hopes Mill had, at the time of the writing, for its effect:

> Two years, well employed, would enable us I think to get most of it [what they have to say] into a state fit for printing—if not in the best form for popular effect, yet in a state of concentrated thought—a sort of mental pemican, which thinkers, when there are any after us, may nourish themselves with & then dilute for other people. The Logic & Pol. Ec. may perhaps keep their buoyancy long enough to hold these other things above water till there are people capable of taking up the thread of thought & continuing it. I fancy I see one large or two small posthumous volumes of Essays, with the Life at their head, & my heart is set on having these in a state fit for publication quelconque, if we live so long, by Christmas 1855.[4]

The idea of the pemican may not be as grotesquely egocentric as some have suggested. Both Mill and Harriet were suffering from tuberculosis, and Mill doubted whether they would even last until 1856. One is almost not sure whether Mill intends the pemican as an *oeuvre* or a bequest. In either case, he intends it as a uniquely complete statement of their philosophy, and his *Autobiography* would stand at its head. Since he writes the *Autobiography* explicitly to explain his education and intellectual development (and judging from the letters he and Harriet exchanged, to justify their relationship as well as explain it), the suggestion is that that narrative account will somehow clarify and complete the philosophic works that will follow.

Having recourse to an account of one's life in order to clarify a philosophic position suggests that the position wilfully resolves rather than logically solves a philosophic problem of considerable personal importance. The list of candidates for the role of this central problem in Mill's work contains all the various contradictions critics find in Mill's philosophy.[5] But all the contradictions center on Mill's attempt to find a place for emotion and poetry within associationism and utilitarianism. It is true that in the *Autobiography* Mill describes this attempt as extremely important; but he felt confident of its philosophic success, as his discussion of qualitative value in *Utilitarianism* indicates (*Util*, 210–212). Whether or not we agree with his defense of the place he finds depends, I think, upon a prior problem, one that brings more to the center his frequently ignored theories of metaphysics and epistemology, and one that he never quite resolves logically and can only claim to have resolved experientially.

This problem is that of finding a place for free will within the unbreakable chain of cause and effect created by associationism. The problem has obvious psychological implications, given our knowledge of Mill's life. His father had, in effect, erased his own past and created himself anew, had "turned his back upon his origins so successfully that his famous son, who certainly had every opportunity of knowing anything his father considered of interest, was unable in later life to give any account of their early circumstances."[6] He had also, however, created his own son, in more than one sense of the word, and thus to assert his own selfhood, Mill had ample reason for wanting to believe that his choices were not predetermined by that education and that he had a will of his own.[7] The basis of the problem, however, may be as much one of ethical theory as of psychology. If Mill had merely wanted to defend a theory of free will, he could have accepted an intuitionist theory of knowledge, and with it an unmitigated theory of free will, thus breaking completely from his own past, as his father had done from his. Indeed, Mill came close to this solution in his early essays on poetry. To accept such a theory completely, however, would have been the end of his career as a reformer. In a passage from the latter part of the *Autobiography*, he rejects Sir William Hamilton's philosophy because, he argues, if all aspects of human character were innate and indelible, rather than caused by experience and changeable by experience, then the improvement of mankind would be impossible (*Auto*, 270).[8] A psychology based entirely on external causation, however, is equally unacceptable since, as one critic of Mill has put it, "to advocate reform presupposes that people have a certain amount of choice about what they do, enough at any rate to make it worth encouraging them to make certain choices and not others."[9]

In *A System of Logic*, Mill claims to have resolved the problem and to have found a place for free will within associationism. Taken by itself, his claim is not very convincing, for reasons that become clear. To validate his position, he had to make what he pretended were minor adjustments, but what I argue were vital revisions, in his father's theory of associational psychology. These revisions are implicit in certain passages of *A System of Logic*, but they are most clearly worked out in the *Examination of Sir William Hamilton's Philosophy* and the footnotes he wrote to his father's *Analysis of the Human Mind*. These may seem rather dusty and arcane byways to travel in order to find a central contradiction that would demand an autobiographical response; yet, I argue, the faults and fissures in these byways send tremors through the rest of Mill's theories, finally leading him to the *Autobiography*.

One of the fascinations of reading Mill and Newman is precisely that their theories can be treated this way: each writer's texts respond to his own earlier and later texts; theories develop from earlier versions, commenting upon and revising those versions. Looked at in this way, their works become an unofficial autobiography against which we can measure the *Autobiography* and the *Apologia*, watching how the narratives of the official autobiographies remake the development of ideas that led to the final theories as well as watching how the theories lead to and demand the narrative that in turn both remakes and unmakes those theories. I wrote at the outset that each of these two parts would be the account of a transformation. To each account of transformation may be added two more accounts: first, the account of the theory that exists after the transformation (the *Autobiography* and the *Apologia*, respectively), and second, that of the theory itself, an account we can begin to see as an account only when we start to see the account of the transformation.

The movement from philosophy to narrative, defined in the introduction, breaks down in Mill's case as follows: First, in Chapter II, Mill's attempt to define a mode of free will consistent with his associational theories leads him to formulate a paradoxical theory of consciousness and claim that paradox as a necessary first principle within associationism. The emergence of that paradoxical first principle leads Mill's philosophy toward narrative in two ways. Chapter III shows how the theory of consciousness Mill developed became central to his thinking in the 1850s, central, at least, I argue, to the way he perceived his relationship with Harriet. His *Autobiography*, particularly the account of the mental crisis, was constructed as a description of the form of consciousness he posited, both as an example of it and as the empirical evidence that his consciousness worked that way. That construction leads to the second form of philosophical narrative. In Chapter IV, I analyze the narrative structure of the *Autobiography* as an expression of Mill's theory of consciousness and thus how that theory, transformed into narrative, shapes and constructs the account of the life that the *Autobiography* offers.

Chapter II

Associationism, Will, and Consciousness

The problem of consciousness is not usually considered a central one in Mill's *oeuvre* just as his strictly metaphysical works, *An Examination of Sir William Hamilton's Philosophy* and his footnotes to his father's *Analysis of the Human Mind*, are not considered his most important works. I have no particular stake in altering traditional evaluative hierarchies, but Mill's definition of consciousness, I think, can be shown to be far more important than has been generally recognized. The roots of that definition are in the theory of free will that Mill himself discusses as vital, both in his *Autobiography* and in his letters—the theory he articulated in *A System of Logic*. The same definition plays a central role in the writing of the *Autobiography*. It is, in fact, a turning point, a paradoxical definition whose paradox creates the potential for philosophy to transform itself into narrative.

Free Will and Associationism

Although the importance of free will to Mill's theories can be easily related (too easily, I think) to the problem of his education by his father, the need for a specific form of will that was both free and yet coincident with associational theory may more logically be explained by the exigencies of Mill's desires for political reform. I mentioned the connection between reform and an associational theory of free will in broad terms in the previous chapter: For people to be able to reform, they must be reformable; hence their psychologies must be associational and therefore educable rather than innate and therefore fixed. On the other hand, if a person is to be able to enact his will to reform when he sees the need, he must first have a will to act on. These two requirements are more than just glib and potentially paradoxical generalizations for Mill. Despite the melodrama of some its language, indicating psychic desires at work, a letter written to Alexis de Tocqueville in 1843 strongly suggests Mill's own sense of the general social and philosophic importance of his theory as well as the importance it has had for him, saying that with the ideas written in the chapter "Of Liberty and Necessity" in *A System of Logic*,

> je puis dire que j'avais trouvé la paix, puisqu'elles seules avaient satisfait pleinement chez moi au besoin de mettre in harmonie l'intelligence et la conscience, en posant sur des bases intellectuelles solides le sentiment de la responsabilité humaine. Je ne crois pas qu'aucun penseur un peu sérieux puisse jouir d'une vraie tranquillité d'esprit et d'âme jusqu'à ce qu'il ait accompli quelque solution satisfaisante de ce grand problème. Je ne desire pas imposer ma propre solution à ceux qui sont satisfaits de la leur, mais je crois qu'il y a beaucoup d'hommes pour qui elle sera, comme elle a été pour moi, une veritable ancre de salut.[1]

If Mill felt that the theory had given him peace, that feeling derived from his sense of having satisfied his intellect and his conscience, by grounding on a solid intellectual basis—one assumes, the basis of his associational theory—his sense of human responsibility. In other words, articulating a connection between free will and associationism is necessary in order to give the social category of responsibility an intellectual or philosophic standing. Thus he can claim that no serious thinker can avoid coming to some solution of his own to the problem of the will. Since it is only a problem, in Mill's terms, because of his belief in associationism, his following disclaimer that he does not want to impose his solution on those who already have their own lacks some persuasiveness. The theory's importance to him, however, is only too clear. To see how satisfactory this theory is, we must turn to "Of Liberty and Necessity."

A discussion of probability that occurs earlier in the *System of Logic* reveals the barrier Mill must breach in order to maintain the existence of free will:

> We must remember that the probability of an event is not a quality of the event itself, but a mere name for the degree of ground which we, or some one else, have for expecting it. . . . Every event is in itself certain, not probable: if we knew all, we should know positively

that it will happen, or positively that it will not. But its probability, to us, means the degree of expectation of its occurrence, which we are warranted in entertaining by our present evidence.[2]

Chance, or rather the impression of chance, is the result of a percipient's ignorance, not an event's uncertainty, and this definition applies to human actions as well as to natural events. Since any human personality is experientially caused, it follows that one's actions will be certain and theoretically predictable. They will result from the interaction of certain and theoretically predictable motivations with certain and theoretically predictable external experiences, events, and sensations. And that would seem to be the end of free will. If everything one does is caused by motivations that are in turn caused directly or indirectly by sensations and chains of sensations, then there would seem to be no place for any purely self-ordained activity. Mill admits all the premises of the above sentence and yet attempts a consistent definition of self-ordination. His argument falls into three parts. The first two, strictly speaking, simply try to take the sting out of necessitarianism by arguing that causation is not really an external constraint. The third, and central, argument then delineates how a motivationally caused will can still be free.

Here, then, is the line Mill draws between predictability and necessity:

> We do not feel ourselves the less free, because those to whom we are intimately known are well assured how we shall will to act in a particular case. We often, on the contrary, regard the doubt what our conduct will be, as a mark of ignorance of our character, and sometimes even resent it as an imputation. The religious metaphysicians who have asserted the freedom of the will, have always maintained it to be consistent with divine foreknowledge of our actions; and if with divine, then with any other foreknowledge. We may be free, and yet another may have reason to be perfectly certain what use we shall make of our freedom. (*Logic*, 837)

The first two sentences of this passage are true but not obviously pertinent. We expect someone who knows us well to be able to predict our actions because he is familiar with how we have acted in similar circumstances, not because he understands the causal bases of everything we think and feel. Consequently, our expectation of the friend's knowledge is distinctly limited to events of a certain magnitude and action. We would expect him to know if we would be likely to, say, plagiarize a paper (even here, the "be likely" is a recognition that we do not expect him to be absolutely certain about it) but would be extremely surprised if he were able to predict with absolute accuracy an extended train of thought. The analogy that follows in the next sentence is pertinent but less persuasive. Divine foreknowledge does not contravene free will because the knowledge is not based on logical induction or deduction. As divine, the knowledge is not contingent, and thus God may know an event without there being a presumption that the event was caused and the cause known. It might be argued that there is a type of human knowledge that is equally uncontingent, but Mill could certainly not so argue, and if he did, there would be no need for the torturous attempt to define a freely willed yet logically contingent act. The last sentence, then, simply is not true. To the extent that another's certainty of what we shall do is not based on any special form of knowledge such as divine revelation or innate capability of foresight, that other person's certainty must derive from knowing what causes our actions, in other words, what contravenes our freedom.

Mill's whole argument here is based on blurring the line between immediate external constraint and indirectly operating constraint. Obviously, it is not the friend's knowledge per se that binds our actions. Rather, his having the knowledge implies that we are already bound. Break the bonds of cause and effect, and the knowledge implies nothing. That is precisely what Mill tries to do in the second part of his argument, by erasing the link between cause and effect:

> There are few to whom mere constancy of succession appears a sufficiently stringent bond of union for so peculiar a relation as that of cause and effect. Even if the reason repudiates, the imagination retains, the feeling of some more intricate connexion, of some peculiar tie, or mysterious constraint exercised by the antecedent over the consequent. Now this it is which, considered as applying to the human will, conflicts with our consciousness, and revolts our feelings. We are certain that, in the case of our volitions, there is not this mysterious constraint. We know that we are not compelled, as by a magical spell, to obey any particular motive. We feel, that if we wished to prove that we have the power of resisting the motive, we could do so, (that wish being, it needs scarcely be observed, a *new antecedent*;). . . . But neither is any such mysterious compulsion now supposed, by the best philosophical authorities, to be exercised by any other cause over

its effect. Those who think that causes draw their effects after them by a mystical tie, are right in believing that the relation between volitions and their antecedents is of another nature. But they should go farther, and admit that this is also true of all other effects and their antecedents. (*Logic*, 837–838)

Psychologically acute as an explanation of why we feel free, this argument remains irrelevant to a defense of a real power of ordination. It is undeniable that psychological determinism carries with it an aura of concrete constraint that it need not imply. It is equally true that our imaginative perception of cause and effect insists on binding the two links by something more than the inevitable succession that is all that Mill's empirical philosophy supposes. Moreover, terms like "mysterious constraint" and "magical spell" give the argument the added rhetorical strength of suggesting that we need only free ourselves from medieval superstitions to see the innocence of the necessitarian doctrine. One of Mill's critics has described necessity as the dragon at the gate of the social sciences.[3] It would seem that Mill does not want to vanquish the dragon, however, but to show it to be a pussycat.

This argument goes a good deal farther than the first, but not really in the right direction. Mill has perhaps explained our *impression* that we are free agents, but he has not proved that we can be causally determined and still remain truly free agents. In effect, the argument opens up a space between cause and effect and slips the agent's will into that space. Both this argument and the last seem to be based on a willed forgetfulness. If we remember that certain knowledge of our future actions does not create constraint and then forget that it presumes the existence of constraint; if we remember that cause and effect imply merely temporal succession, and then allow ourselves to believe that the fact of the intervening space, in some way, replaces the existence of the prior cause; then we may believe we are both caused and free. Forgetfulness of the attachment between cause and effect also forms the basis of Mill's central argument for freedom:

Now a necessitarian, believing that our actions follow from our characters, and that our characters follow from our organization, our education, and our circumstances, is apt to be, with more or less of consciousness on his part, a fatalist as to his own actions, and to believe that his nature is such, or that his education and circumstances have so moulded his character, that nothing can now prevent him

from feeling and acting in a particular way, or at least that no effort of
his own can hinder it. In the words of the sect [the Owenites] which
in our day has most perseveringly inculcated and most perversely
misunderstood this great doctrine, his character is formed *for* him and
not *by* him; therefore his wishing that it has been formed differently
is of no use; he has no power to alter it. But this is a grand error. He
has, to a certain extent, a power to alter his character. Its being, in the
ultimate resort, formed for him, is not inconsistent with its being, in
part, formed by him as one of the intermediate agents. (*Logic*, 840)

Again, this argument is acute but not quite to the point. It is true that
resignation is a logically inconsistent reaction to the concept of necessity.
One can no more choose not to act than one can choose to act. Also, a
wish to change is potentially a very potent cause of our character. But to
take the wish as an indication of freedom, one must again forget that it
is as much caused by experience as is the fatalist's spurious pose of
resignation.[4]

Needless to say, commentators have not been very well satisfied with
Mill's handling of the problem. Even his biographer, Michael St. John
Packe, finds the argument equivocal.[5] The real question, however, is how
Mill could have been satisfied with such an argument. Had his aim been
to explain the psychological impression of freedom, to find a place for the
generally experienced sensation called free will, his position would have
been fairly strong. But the theory is, rather, Mill's "ancre de salut,"
which, as he informs Tocqueville, he offers to the world as a solid intellectual base for the sentiment of human responsibility. These are large
claims, and if Mill is less insistent in "Of Liberty and Necessity," he is no
less certain: "The free-will doctrine . . . has given to its adherents a practical feeling much nearer the truth than has generally (I believe) existed in
the minds of necessitarians" (*Logic*, 841–842).

The reason for Mill's confidence lies, I think, in a particular ripple in his
argument that has gone relatively unnoticed. To Mill's argument that we
may be intermediate agents in forming our character by wishing to
change, the Owenite necessitarian can obviously respond by stepping
back one link in the chain and arguing that external forces cause the wish
to change. To this, Mill responds:

But the wish which induces us to attempt to form [our character]
is formed for us, and how? Not, in general, by our organization, nor

wholly by our education, but by our experience; experience of the painful consequences of the character we previously had: or by some strong feeling of admiration or aspiration, accidentally aroused. (*Logic*, 840–841).

The reader will want to keep this passage in mind when I discuss Mill's definition of his relationship with Harriet and again when I examine his discussion of his mental crisis. At the moment, though, I want to note the strategy Mill uses to break the infinite regression of the causal chain. First, free will seems to be limited to actions we take to form our own character. Mill does not take into account externally directed acts, possibly because they ultimately derive from our own character. More important, the motivation of a freely willed action is of a very special kind: dissatisfaction with oneself because of either personal inadequacy or the superiority of an external example. Either way, a dissatisfaction with self arises from self-consciousness. If self-consciousness can be defined in such a way as to free it from associational causation and if that definition would not necessitate an acceptance of intuitional knowledge, then freely willed activity will have a place within an associational psychology. In other words, Mill must now open a space for uncaused self-consciousness directly within standard associational theory. So, in finding the room for himself that he needs to justify his equivocal version of free will, Mill turns to that terminal point in Victorian philosophy, self-consciousness.

The Paradox of Consciousness

To discuss Mill's definition of a paradoxical form of self and self-consciousness, I have to investigate texts written much later than *A System of Logic*, the book in which he offered a definition of free will that he had first developed earlier still. These later texts also postdate the first two drafts of the *Autobiography*. But the *Logic* states, in condensed form, views close enough to those of *An Examination of Sir William Hamilton's Philosophy* that the final editions of both books cite each other for further elucidation of arguments. Here, for instance, in the *Logic*, Mill defines the mind:

There is a something I call Myself, or, by another form of expression, my mind, which I consider as distinct from these sensations, thoughts, &c.; a something which I can conceive to be not the thoughts, but the being that has the thoughts, and which I can conceive as existing for ever in a state of quiescence, without any thought at all. But what this being is, though it is myself, I have no knowledge, other than the series of its states of consciousness. As bodies manifest themselves to me only through the sensations of which I regard them as the causes, so the thinking principle, or mind, in my own nature, makes itself known to me only by the feelings of which it is conscious. (*Logic*, 64)

This passage is the basic outline of the paradoxical formulation of consciousness that Mill wants to create. He posits an independent mind, but where is it since all thought is sensation? Possibly Mill wants here simply to shift his discussion to the status of sensation by saying that that is the only possible area of logical inquiry, without either polemically denying or really admitting the validity of the concept of a self independent from sensation. With that tactic, he shifted the discussion earlier from the problem of noumena and phenomena to an interest solely in phenomena. But in an earlier article on Samuel Taylor Coleridge, in denying intuitional knowledge, Mill again implies the paradoxical formulation, only there without the same contextual reasons: "There is no knowledge *a priori*; no truths cognizable by the mind's inward light, and grounded on intuitive evidence. Sensation, and the mind's consciousness of its own acts, are not only the exclusive sources, but the sole materials, of our knowledge."[6] By allowing the mind consciousness of its own acts, Mill seems to have allowed the mind a status outside experience. This description of consciousness stands out because, at the point in the essay at which Mill offers it, he does not argue its truth but puts it in the mouths of Locke and other prior empiricists. In effect, he silently amends associational theory in order to agree with it. His emendations become less silent later on.

Before I place Mill's theory of mind within his philosophy as a whole, I want to stress its centrality at least to his metaphysics, a centrality we can see by turning to his theory of matter. That theory, as we might expect, rests firmly in the empirical tradition. Using a catchphrase, Mill defines matter as the permanent possibility of sensation. In other words, when we say that a thing exists, we mean that if we place ourselves in the appropriate position, we will receive the bundle of sensations we have come to associate together as defining that "thing." Further, if we leave and return and the thing has remained stable, we will be able to experience the sensations again. This theory has troubled Mill's commentators because, while its definition of matter places matter outside of the mind (the possibilities of sensation, being permanent, exist independently of the mind), that independent existence nevertheless depends on the concept of a possible percipient. Sensations, after all, cannot exist without someone to sense them.[7] His picture of external reality appears therefore rather shadowy and unreal at times,[8] but it will hold philosophically, on one condition. The possible percipients of possible sensations must be conceived of as having both memory and expectation;[9] without these qualities, the concept of a sensation's duration breaks down. A bundle of sensations that we neither remember as having occurred in a certain situation, nor expect to occur again if we return to the situation, does not have the substantial duration demanded by our experience of matter.

The result of these two qualities is a staggering admission of a paradox. In accordance with his definition of matter, Mill defines the mind, as he has done earlier, as the series of its sensations, thoughts, and ideas, accepting the metaphor of it as a "thread of consciousness." Such a theory is obviously necessary to an associational psychology since, if we suppose there to be something involved in the makeup of the mind besides the sum of experiences or acquired ideas of experiences, we also suppose some form of a priori knowledge or identity. The concepts of memory and expectation, however, bring Mill to a crashing halt:

> The fact believed [in memory and expectation] is, that the sensations did actually form, or will hereafter form, part of the self-same series of states, or thread of consciousness, of which remembrance or expectation of these sensations is the part now present. If, therefore, we speak of the Mind as a series of feelings, we are obliged to complete the statement by calling it a series of feelings which is aware of itself as past and future: and we are reduced to the alternative of believing that the Mind, or Ego, is something different from any series of feelings, or possibilities of them, or of accepting the paradox, that something which *ex hypothesi* is but a series of feelings, can be aware of itself as a series.[10]

Neither memory nor expectation is itself paradoxical here. Memory, for instance, is definable as the mind's representation of a past sensation, expectation as its representation of a future, anticipated sensation. But each of these representations, Mill argues, depends upon the concept of a self, even if only as the sum of sensations, to which to refer these representations. The representations of memory are, then, dependent upon a consciousness of a self that is not any single event in the series of sensations, but the whole series itself. That self-consciousness cannot be part of the series unless we accept as part of the series the paradoxical quality of being aware of itself as series. Only by relegating the paradox to the status of ultimate fact does Mill even attempt to recuperate it. He then claims that much of its difficulty arises from the limitations of language: "one mode of stating [the nature of consciousness] only appears more incomprehensible than another, because the whole of human language is accommodated to the one, and is so incongruous with the other, that it cannot be expressed in any terms which do not deny its truth" (*Hamilton*, 194).

Commentators have frequently been surprised that Mill does not realize the damage that the admission of this paradox does to his theory.[11] Indeed, it would seem that to avoid Mill's paradox, an acceptance of an intuitional self-consciousness split from the series of sensations would be desirable. In fact, by making the paradox an ultimate fact, Mill effectively does just this. The mistake here is not Mill's, however, but that of his critics in assuming he is making an innocent and ingenuous admission. *Hamilton's Philosophy* may have been Mill's first extended foray into the woods of metaphysics, but he was no babe there. He had been trained early in the questions he was dealing with and knew the implications of what he was saying. Consider for instance what this "admission" achieves for him. The infinitely regressing chain of cause and effect that gave him so much trouble in his attempt to validate free will has been effectively snapped at a link only one step removed from the willing of action. Free will, after all, begins in a self-conscious dissatisfaction with one's character. Now self-consciousness is an ultimate fact and, thus, a place where uncaused, freely ordained action may occur. Nevertheless, the "admission" is restricted enough so that it will not allow any form of intuitional knowledge arrived at independently of experience. Even knowledge of oneself is accreted. The fact of self-consciousness is ultimate, but the object of the consciousness remains the series of sensations, and one's judgment of that series is therefore available for logical inquisition. One could hardly imagine a more convenient paradox.

Formulations about the self and self-consciousness are, of course, generally fraught with difficulty in nineteenth-century English discourse as a result of the English acceptance of empirical language and methodology coupled with a distaste for the conclusions of that language and methodology. Newman, who was certainly not particularly concerned about squaring his ideas with the main body of associational thought, ventures a definition as equivocal as Mill's paradox turns out to be arbitrarily assertive. Mill enacts here, indeed, the standard response to self-consciousness described in my introduction. Not all nineteenth-century philosophers, however, wrote autobiographies. Mill's formulation, though (as I argue in Chapter IV), defines one way to structure narrative as much as it defines self-consciousness. In the *Autobiography*, Mill describes his development and learning as capped by a self-consciousness and the events of his life as capped by a narrative, both of which are completions as well as, themselves, developmental experiences. Mill, writing of himself, then, is "a series of feelings . . . aware of itself as a series." The philosophic definition enables the autobiographical narrative even as the narrative intends to demonstrate the empirical validity of the definition.

But Mill has some further steps to make in his philosophic discourse before he can turn to narrative. We can only suffer the existence of a paradox within logical argument if we are indeed in the face of an ultimate fact, a first principle that we must accept as a result of experience. By looking at the way Mill arrives at the necessity for his ultimate principle, we can see how he creates rather than accepts that necessity. In the footnotes he wrote to his father's *Analysis of the Human Mind*, an extended discussion of the problems of memory and identity offers him the opportunity to justify his addition of a new ultimate fact to associationism.

We find the first hints of a trap Mill sets for his father in the chapter titled "Consciousness." The body of the chapter itself is brief since James Mill does not distinguish between being conscious of a feeling and having a feeling: "the word Conscious is applicable to the feeler, and Consciousness to the feeling: that is to say, the words are GENERICAL *marks*, under which all the names of the subordinate classes of the feelings of a sentient creature are included" (*Analysis*, I:225–226).[12] This statement is not so baldly and polemically assertive as it sounds since James Mill discusses the other activity often referred to with this term, the pure activity of awareness, in his chapters titled "Reflection" and "Will" (though not in a manner any more satisfactory to Mill). Here, he is simply restricting the definition of the word. Nevertheless, the chapter ends with a long footnote by Mill that says in part:

> The notion of a Self is, I apprehend, a consequence of Memory.
> There is no meaning in the word Ego or I, unless the I of to-day is

also the I of yesterday; a permanent element which abides through a succession of feelings, and connects the feeling of each moment with the remembrances of previous feelings. . . . A slight correction, therefore, seems requisite to the doctrine of the author laid down in the present chapter. There is a mental process, over and above the mere having a feeling to which the word Consciousness is sometimes, and it can hardly be said improperly, applied, viz. the reference of the feeling to our Self. (*Analysis*, I:229–230)

So far there seems little problem. James Mill would hardly argue with the contention that memory demands the concept of an identity between the self remembering and the self remembered, and such an identity implies a reference of feeling to the self. Mill's "slight correction" might indeed be merely an argument over terms. Nevertheless, that innocent correction is a trap set for his father.

The next stage of Mill's rectification occurs in the note to the chapter "Memory." James Mill defines memory as made up of three ingredients: "1, the point of consciousness called the remembering self; 2, the point of consciousness called the percipient self; 3, the successive states of consciousness which filled up the interval between these two points" (*Analysis*, I:335). Mill objects in his footnote, "But (apart from the question whether we really do repeat in thought, however summarily, all this series) explaining memory by Self seems very like explaining a thing by the thing. For what notion of Self can we have, apart from Memory?" Mill holds back from further comment at the moment, however, since "the author admits that the phenomenon of Belief, and the notions of Time and Personal Identity, must be taken into account in order to give a complete explanation of Memory" (*Analysis*, I:340). Mill's objection here is based not on anything inherent in what James Mill says of memory but on his own early footnote, cited above. To spring this trap, therefore, he must wait for the chapter titled "Identity."

James Mill begins his discussion of identity by defining our knowledge of the existence of external identity. We may believe that a man at point x in time and a man at point y in time are the same man either by virtue of observation or by virtue of reliable testimony. We may have seen the man at both point x and point y and, if we know him well, in numerous intervening moments and thus conclude from the constant similarity of sensations that it is the same man. Or someone whose testimony we have reason to believe is reliable may inform us that the man we see at point y was also previously at point *x*. Our sense of our own identity is, then, our belief in another connection of a series of sensations, with this difference:

> In the case of Evidence by memory and sensation, we have observed a peculiarity, necessary to be remembered, that the Evidence and the Belief are not different things, but the same thing. The memory which I have of my own existence, that is the memory of a certain train of antecedents and consequents, is the Belief of them. (*Analysis*, II:168)

I believe in myself as a unified series, then, for the same reason as I believe in other unified series, except that I have better reason for the belief since the evidence, which is my memory, is also the belief, which, as a product of association, is also the result of memory.

In Mill's footnote, the trap, in the form of a vicious circle, now springs shut:

> These considerations remove the outer veil, or husk, as it were, which wraps up the idea of the Ego. But after this is removed, there remains an inner covering, which, as far as I can perceive, is impenetrable. My personal identity consists in my being the same Ego who did, or who felt, some specific fact recalled to me by memory. So be it: but what is Memory? It is not merely having the idea of the fact recalled: that is but thought, or conception, or imagination. It is, having the idea recalled along with the Belief that the fact which it is the idea of, really happened, and moreover happened to myself. . . . The phenomenon of Self and that of Memory are merely two sides of the same fact. (*Analysis*, II:173–174)

The first thing to note here is the language. James Mill once claimed that if he had time, "I would make the human mind as plain as the road from Charing Cross to St. Paul's."[13] The *Analysis of the Human Mind* is the map he drew up, and it is written in the clear, concise terms of a man giving directions. In this footnote, however, we are suddenly in the presence of outer veils, husks, inner coverings that are impenetrable, and even a translated "amen," language not any more typical of the son than of the father. Mill might be allowed, of course, a little rhetorical expansiveness since he has finally arrived at that ultimate principle of self-consciousness. Memory depends on a concept of self-identity, and self-identity can only be defined by memory. To break the circle we must raise the concept of self-consciousness out of experience to the status of a given.

Mill's emendation is not a minor one. It posits that to some extent the mind, particularly in its knowledge of itself, constitutes more than simply a train of sensations, embodies more than merely the result of experience. Self-consciousness is here a given, an intuitional part of the self, even if its informations result from experience. But everywhere else in his writing, Mill goes to the same length as his father does to argue against the necessity or desirability of ever supposing any knowledge or belief to be intuitional. I return, therefore, for a space to James Mill's argument because if it is consistent and not vicious, one would expect it to be his son's argument as well.

In the aspect of James Mill's theory of memory that Mill attempts to dispense with in a parenthesis, there lies, I think, the solution to the problem of circularity that Mill raises. In addition to a remembering and a remembered self, James Mill posits a complete recalling of all intervening moments and states of consciousness. Nor is this a thoughtless slip in the passage quoted above. The definition is repeated three pages later: "we have found the association [of memory] to consist of three parts: the remembering self; the remembered self; and the train which intervened" (*Analysis*, I:338). This third aspect removes the need of positing an idea of self prior to defining memory. It is true that the normal act of memory already includes a knowledge on the part of the self at one end of the train of events that it is identical with the self at the other end. But let us suppose an originating act of memory in which no concept of self-identity is operating. If we use Mill's theory of memory as a representation of a discrete past event, then indeed there would be no reason for the rememberer to presume identity with the remembered percipient. If we presume with James Mill, however, the memory of the intervening train, then the concept of self-identity is an obvious result of this ur-memory: one sees a series connected by involving the participation of the same percipient at each moment leading up to the moment of remembrance, and one naturally concludes an identity. Since James Mill defines identity as the result of "the memory of a chain of states of Consciousness" (*Analysis*, II:169), there seems little doubt that he had such a moment as I have described in mind. That he felt that a definition of memory was only provisionally dependent on a concept of self is evident in his referring the reader to the "Identity" chapter: "the analysis, then, of SELF, or the account of what is included in the state of consciousness commonly called the *idea of personal identity*, is still wanting to complete development of Memory" (*Analysis*,

I:338–339). It is true that we normally think of memory as including a concept of self-identity, and so a definition of such a concept is needed to "complete" the account of memory. The concept nevertheless grows out of memory and is not presupposed by it.

The only possible objection to James Mill's theory is that it seems unlikely in its unwieldiness. Our impression, at least, is that we do not remember all intervening moments when remembering a past event. Mill evidently felt that such an objection was sufficient, the parenthetical "apart from the question whether we really do repeat in thought, however summarily, all this series" being the extent of his remarks about that aspect of the theory. This objection should not have been persuasive for Mill, though, if the alternative was the acceptance of an intuitive explanation. In *Hamilton's Philosophy*, he stated that "an intuitive cognition of Deity, like every other doctrine relating to intuition, can only be disproved by showing it to be a mistaken interpretation of facts; which, again, as we shall see hereafter, can only be done by pointing out in what other way the seeming perceptions may have originated, which are erroneously supposed to be intuitive" (*Hamilton*, 59). For Mill, as for his father, if the problem can be explained experientially, it should be. If unwieldiness were a proper criticism, then Mill's own arguments in *A System of Logic* for the empirical development of mathematical first principles would be a shambles. Nor is even the criticism of unwieldiness that strong in itself if we take into account Mill's Laws of Obliviscence: "it is one of the principle Laws of Obliviscence, that when a number of ideas suggest one another by association with such certainty and rapidity as to coalesce together in a group, all those numbers of the group which remain long without being specially attended to, have a tendency to drop out of consciousness" (*Hamilton*, 257). In other words, we need only suppose a few early acts of complete memory to establish firmly by association the concept of self. The necessity for a complete intervening train would then be over and we might cease to take the effort to make complete connections. Whether or not James Mill supposed such a process, the concept was certainly available to Mill to help him with the difficulty of unwieldiness, and he had used it often enough in the past.

What is the motivation then for Mill's unnecessary revision? Why does he carry on this guerilla warfare in the footnotes to his father's text, especially if the task of editing was taken on as an act of "filial vindication"?[14] The process of footnoting a father's text, placing oneself as a minor commentator to the longer work of one's predecessor, is naturally fraught with ambiguities. Nevertheless, by 1868, Mill had long ago resolved, if not solved, the problems of his relationship to his father, as his preface to the *Analysis*, in its remarkably even-toned yet generous praise of James Mill, amply shows; and his footnotes generally are minor corrections intended to bring the theory up to date. What value, then, does his intuitive self-consciousness have, what quality that an associationally caused concept of self would lack? The answer is, I think, that Mill needs a concept of an active self-consciousness to put into motion the act of self-reform or education that is the model for him of a freely willed moment. James Mill's concept of identity involves no more than a passive recognition of an abstract, nominalistic unification of a series of sensations, a knowledge of self that would not result in any particular actions. Further, by making self-consciousness an ultimate given, Mill terminates the infinite regression of cause and effect that threatened his free-will theory.

At this point, the purely philosophic section of my analysis of Mill's uses of philosophy and narrative is complete. As a part of creating both the ability to reform, an ability that depends on an associationally formable psychology, and the ability to ordain reform, free will, Mill defined a mode of free will consistent with a theory of a psychology based on causal necessity. And, finally, this theory of free will comes to rest on an ultimate form of inexplicable intuition, self-consciousness. This self-consciousness is not creative of higher truths as one within an intuitional theory might be; its choices must be logically confirmed. But it offers us the ability to make meaningful choices about our own actions. I have traced here, then, the process by which tangential issues become central. Mill stated in many places the importance he gave to his solution of the problem of free will. That solution, however, rested on the argument that self-consciousness had to be a psychological given. Now the position on consciousness by itself is hardly one of great import, a metaphysical curiosity perhaps in the work of an ethical philosopher. Because of its relationship to the problem of the will, though, which Mill did see as a moral and ethical one, the formulation of an intuitive principle of self-consciousness within associationism takes on considerable significance. First principles may be justified by empirical evidence of their existence even if that existence may not be logically demonstrated, and an autobiography would logically contain empirical evidence that one's self-consciousness manifested itself in a certain way. This understanding of Mill's paradoxical definition of consciousness and his justification of that paradox as an ultimate fact, or first principle, then, brings me, in the next chapter, to the effects of Mill's philosophy on his narrative in his *Autobiography*, and finally, in Chapter IV, to the merging, in that work, of philosophy and narrative.

Chapter III

Examples in Narrative:

Harriet and the Mental Crisis

Psychobiographers usually try to show how a subject's psychological character and problems, as manifest in biographical events, express themselves in that subject's ostensibly objective theorizing. On the face of it, the procedure is sound, even by the standards of Mill's associationism (perhaps especially by those standards). Theories do not result from spontaneous generation; and to the extent that we do not believe they are inspired by God, we are logically committed to a connection between who we are and what we think. The connection operates in both directions, however. Whether the desire for self-change is an act of free will or is associationally caused, Mill is at least correct in holding that we can indeed influence our own actions. It follows that, in addition to forming theories that may assuage psychological wounds or explain psychological problems, a thinker may shape the events of his life to support or validate theories that he feels particularly bound to. Biographical events may explain theories, but theories may also explain biographical events.

The assertion that a life may be shaped according to theory is less controversial in some contexts than in others. For a philosopher to try to live his subsequent life in terms of one of his theories (to the extent to which such a project is conceivable) and to see his subsequent life in terms of that theory should not surprise us if we assume that that philosopher has any stake at all in the theory. An autobiographer's account of that segment of his life might then reasonably read like a manifestation of his theory and still refer straightforwardly to events in the life. But if theory can determine how the later life is lived and seen, surely it might determine how the earlier life is seen and interpreted, particularly that part of the life that ostensibly led the writer to develop the theory. This second possibility vexes the situation of autobiography considerably, however. For a theory to be consistent it must be able to account for its development on its own terms; but if the development comes prior to the theory, it cannot, at least in the intention of the philosopher, have occurred in the theory's terms. Nor can we resolve the situation easily by supposing a set of determinate, early biographical events that are shaped but not falsified by a theoretically determined later interpretation. Events whose importance is defined as their leading up to a theory have no status except as parts of the theory that determines their interpretation. Their existence is irrelevant except as evidence, but their evidential purpose is determined after the fact. Thus, to understand an autobiographical event so determined, we must assume an autobiographer's primary reference to the theoretical context at the time of writing rather than to any determining psychology at the time of the event described. Since most interpreters of autobiography do not even analyze the relatively straightforward first case, it is not surprising that the second one is even more rarely considered.[1] Offering events of one's life as evidence for a theory is the first way in which narrative may support philosophy, and this chapter discusses the ways in which that evidencing may occur. In the theoretical sources for Mill's definition of his and Harriet's relationship, we can see the way in which a life can be a lived-out theory and thus (since the *Autobiography* was written partly with their relationship in mind) the relevance of Mill's definition of consciousness to his autobiography. Then, in the *Autobiography's* construction of the mental crisis, we can see how a theory can turn an autobiography into an example in narrative of how that theory works.

Harriet Taylor's Embodiment of Mill's Theory

Using this reversal of the normally asserted relationship between biographical event and theory, we can formulate an alternative approach to the vexed problem of Harriet Taylor's place in Mill's life and thoughts. Mill's estimation of Harriet has generally been explained, or explained away, by some estimation of Mill. This procedure has ranged in its results from the early comment that Mill's praise of Harriet represents simply a hallucination,[2] to Bruce Mazlish's recent assertion that, in praising Harriet, Mill both praised himself and justified "his terribly complicated

Oedipal 'sin' to himself and the world."[3] One of the few recent favorable estimations of Harriet's role accepts Mill's definition of that role in order to create a foundation for his theories of sexual equality: "the idea of complementary skills and knowledge, such that each spouse can be both leader and follower, teacher and student, on a firm basis of shared values and goals, reads like a description of the Mills' own marriage."[4] But this estimation uses the same method of analysis, merely reversing the evaluation. Either the marriage, based on their accurate estimates of each other, provides evidence for a theory of sexual equality, or the marriage, based on psychological needs that shape its structure, produces a theory that supports those needs. Rather, I think, it is Mill's theories of free will and self-consciousness that produce his estimation of the marriage.

Nor is this reversal in cause and effect arbitrary. As the next chapter shows, Harriet's importance in the *Autobiography* is essentially to insure Mill's freedom from his father. By enrolling himself under her tutelage, he assures himself that he has terminated his father's influence. The autobiographical method of freeing himself, in turn, from Harriet, creating his own creator in the narrative, is determined by a complex act of self-liberation enacted in the *Autobiography* and other texts written in the 1850s. There Mill creates, in his panegyrics to Harriet, a figure that simply cannot exist in the world of his philosophy and psychology. Thus, by praising her beyond human recognition, paradoxically, he frees himself from human influence.

When Mill describes his relationship to Harriet, both within and outside of the *Autobiography*, he formulates a theory more than he recounts a series of events. The centrality of the relationship to the *Autobiography*, in Mill's view of the work as well as in the work itself, is very clear. Writing the first draft of the work in the 1850s, when he thought he was dying of tuberculosis, Mill was concerned to record and preserve his philosophy and to record and explain his relationship with Harriet. The two aims were connected obviously through his sense that Harriet's contribution to his intellectual development was such that he could not describe his development without describing her contribution. More important, perhaps, as the *Autobiography* finally depicts Mill both as associationally caused and as the creation of his own will and intellect, it depicts the relationship with Harriet both as one of the strongest causes of his thought and work and as a locus of his freedom, indeed virtually as paradigmatic of the kind of situation in which associational free will can arise. The relationship with Harriet, then, is lived and perceived in accordance with the theory that, through that relationship's centrality to the life as recorded, also shapes the *Autobiography*.

The language Mill uses to describe Harriet outside the *Autobiography* is often even more revealing than that in it. One of the metaphors that recur in the letters is that of a machine. In 1850, Mill writes to Harriet, "I am but fit to be one wheel in an engine not to be the self moving engine itself,"[5] clearly implying in context that she is the self-moving engine. Again, just after her death, Mill says in a letter that "the spring of my life is broken."[6] This reverses the earlier metaphor in an inconsequential way: Mill is the machine, Harriet the part. But Harriet is the spring that moves the machine. In each case, Mill is dependent upon an external motive force. This is the nearest Mill gets to picturing himself as entirely caused, entirely without choices of his own. The image is one from Dickensian nightmare: Pip in *Great Expectations* dreaming himself a cog in an engine of destruction, Esther in *Bleak House* dreaming herself a bead on a flaming necklace.

Mill is rather more pleased than disturbed by the image, however. Nor need we look far for the reason he might comfortably speak of himself in this way. Around 1832, he and Harriet had exchanged essays on marriage and divorce, evidently as an attempt to help each other clarify their situation and their relationship. In his essay, Mill writes, "A woman ought not to be dependent on a man, more than a man on a woman, except so far as their affections make them so, by a voluntary surrender, renewed and renewing at each instant by free & spontaneous choice."[7] This is not quite a picture of a marriage of equal partners. Rather, a partner freely chooses not to be free, remaking the decision moment by moment as long as the relationship lasts. Mill could easily speak of himself as a cog operated by Harriet's force since each moment that such a relationship lasted was a moment in which he freely chose his position. Actively choosing *not* to change oneself is an aspect of free will left out of Mill's chapter in the *Logic*, but it is an aspect that is justifiable in the same terms: as long as one self-consciously ratifies the externally caused decision, one remains free even while being moved externally.

Asserting freedom by either changing oneself or self-consciously not changing oneself is only fully an act of freedom if the self-conscious act cannot be associationally explained. In his account of his mental crisis, Mill describes his self-consciousness in just that manner (as associa-

tionally inexplicable). In describing his relationship with Harriet, however, something analogous to that account, but with a strange difference,
occurs. Mill consciously chooses to be influenced by Harriet and then
embodies *in her* the associational inexplicability of consciousness. Harriet
becomes like those prisoners in Socrates' cave, a representation of a theoretical concept. Mill makes Harriet the equivalent of self-consciousness
by giving her the one quality he denies to all other members of the human
race, characterizing her as a woman "of penetrating and intuitive intelligence" (*Auto*, 193) and speaking of her "moral intuition," (*Auto*, 97). Intuitive intelligence is, for Mill, oxymoronic, and moral intuition a concept little short of blasphemy. Nor does one have to go to other works to
find Mill's condemnation of the idea of intuition; his commitment to
associationism permeates the *Autobiography*. Effectively, Mill makes Harriet the living embodiment of the Romantic concept of the beautiful soul.
He might be attracted to this concept as a metaphor, but its dependence
on psychological tenets that he would never allow made it impossible for
him to give that image a concrete existence. He has praised Harriet into
the state of living metaphor, and in doing so he has removed from his
descriptions of her influence any sense of constraint in any meaning of the
term that would make sense to him. I am not saying that Mill is being
ironic here. His feelings about Harriet were such, however, that he could
never possibly have felt her to be a threat to his freedom in the way he felt
his father was. By representing all that was perfect, Harriet gave him an
example to inspire change; and we should remember that his formulation
of free will posited such an example as a possible motive for change. But
despite his speaking of indebtedness to her originating mind, there was
never a real question of causation or constraint because she did not exist
as an associationally explicable natural agency but rather as a trope of
Mill's own making.

In fact, the whole overworked problem of joint authorship takes on a
different light in this context. Mill never claimed that Harriet had any
part in the actual composition of the works, implicitly admitting the contrary when he writes that when two minds form their ideas in unison, "it
is of little consequence in respect to the question of originality, which of
them holds the pen; the one who contributes least to the composition
may contribute most to the thought" (*Auto*, 251).[8] And, except in the
case of the chapter on the future of the working classes, Book IV, chapter
vii, of *Principles of Political Economy*, the evidence shows her participation

to be only of the most tangential kind, hardly amounting to anything that might be reasonably called joint authorship.[9] Mill does state about *On Liberty* that "there was not a sentence of it that was not several times gone through by us together" (*Auto*, 257). But if her editing of the *Early Draft* is any indication—and it is the only evidence—her contributions were probably only in the direction of minor stylistic emendations.

Mill sees joint authorship, though, not in terms of who put the words on the page, but in terms of inspiration:

> During the greater part of my literary life I have performed the office in relation to her, which from a rather early period I had considered as the most useful part that I was qualified to take in the domain of thought, that of an interpreter of original thinkers, and mediator between them and the public. (*Auto*, 251)

Mill follows this statement with a list of all the other people who influenced him. If Harriet is a more important influence, Mill's description of her importance sounds rather like a description of inspiration than of direct participation. Mill calls this joint authorship rather than inspiration because his philosophy cannot allow this second form of "collaboration" any more than it can allow intuitional knowledge. Still, Harriet's relation to his writing seems, finally, like that of God to Milton's. One is not willing to say absolutely that God did not have a part, but *Paradise Lost* is still attributed to Milton.[10]

The *Autobiography* makes Mill's and Harriet's relationship central in a way that accords with his theory of free will and self-conscious choice. Harriet first represents an alternative to James Mill, an alternative to which Mill may aspire, feeling his own inadequacy. She then becomes an inspirational figure that, by being outside of associational causation, allows that alternative to become Mill's free choice. In 1861, Mill added a paragraph to the *Autobiography* that summed up Harriet's influence:

> At the present period [1830–1835], however, this influence was only one among many which were helping to shape the character of my future development: and even after it became, I may truly say, the presiding principle of my mental progress, it did not alter the path, but only made me move forward more boldly and at the same time more cautiously in the same course. (*Auto*, 199)

Harriet's role was, finally, benevolent indeed, according to Mill. She helped him to become more himself than he might have been.

Mill's and Harriet's marriage was a relationship that was constantly being consciously defined as it was lived. Thus, as Mill defines the relationship as one of self-consciously accepted direction on his part that extended rather than terminated his freedom, and as this definition becomes the paradigm for the numerous lesser cases of influence upon him recounted in the work, the interaction of caused development and consciously willed autonomy becomes the central subject of the work. The marriage that was constantly defined in the 1850s in accordance with earlier theoretical problems and solutions thus creates, more than the events of the life prior to composition, the subject and form of the *Autobiography*.

The Making of a Mental Crisis

Explaining Mill's definition of his relationship with Harriet and how that definition influenced the shaping of the *Autobiography* does not completely undermine that text's documentarity since the theories preceded or were contemporaneous with the relationship the *Autobiography* recounted. It is a rather different matter, however, to argue that Mill constructs his mental crisis to provide empirical evidence of a theory of consciousness that postdated the crisis but predated the *Autobiography* that describes/constructs the crisis. Such an explanation of the crisis does undercut the text's documentarity quite thoroughly. I should specify that I do not deny the existence of an internal event to which Mill gives the name mental crisis, but I doubt this admission will much pacify potential critics of the following account. That existence, which as internal event is both undeniable and unprovable, was, I think, so absolutely trivial in significance as to be completely negligible until its interpretation as mental crisis. That interpretation, moreover, was entirely in terms of theories Mill did not hold until years after whatever occurred occurred.

This situation is analogous to Richard Rorty's explanation of how Thomas Kuhn's depiction of scientific theory as paradigm shift can be held without resorting to idealism. Rorty allows that in a scientific experiment there *is* an external event. That event is the response of whatever measuring device the experiment sets up, "needle red, here, now," for instance. But the meaning of that event is entirely determined by the experiment that constructed its possibility.[11] The situation of marking out internal events within an associational theory of psychology is perhaps even more slippery. Sensations, of course, occur constantly as long as one is alive and awake. Even marking one as an "event" will not involve anything inherent in the sensation but will be the act of that paradoxically placed sensation, consciousness. In other words, seeing a sensation as an event worth marking off is an interpretation of consciousness prior even to that more massive interpretation of giving it the name "mental crisis." But Mill's mental crisis is offered as empirical evidence of the structure of the consciousness that interprets it as event and names it "mental crisis." This is the circularity we saw earlier in which one evidences a first principle of consciousness with "our senses, and our internal consciousness." By explaining the shape of the mental crisis in terms of Mill's theory of consciousness, I am, accordingly, explaining the *Autobiography* as the construction of that circularity of empirical evidence deriving from the first principle it ostensibly demonstrates.

The documentary status of autobiographies has frequently been called into question, even on occasion by historians who want to use literary texts as historical evidence.[12] But calling into question the documentarity of Mill's mental crisis perhaps feels more daring than it ought because that mental crisis is the one significant bit of information about Mill that the *Autobiography* alone offers; consequently, it has become one of the work's most famous moments. Every critic of the *Autobiography*, every biographer or psychobiographer, almost every commentator on Mill's writing as a whole rather than on any selected topic, has had to confront that account and interpret its significance. Yet the results of such widespread attention have not been impressive. There have been basically only three psychological theories: Bain's utilitarian view that it was due to overwork, Levi's Freudian analysis, and Durheim's argument that Mill was trying to break through an internal censor. Of these, only Levi's has had real influence (although Bain's is usually mentioned).

This paucity is not, of course, an inherent problem since it might indicate the accuracy of Levi's early formulation. I suspect, though, that it is, rather, a response to a narrative that is more complexly structured than a psychoanalysis of the text as a reference to the original event can account for. To begin with, there are really two crises being recounted in the work, an emotional one and an intellectual one. Both are perforated with chronological problems; and although the existence of the intellectual crisis has partial support from texts outside the *Autobiography*, the emotional crisis does not. These problems are caused by the construction of the earlier emotional crisis to give a particular kind of support to the later intellectual one, which is accordingly redefined. And the whole process of construction and redefinition is determined by the theory of consciousness outlined in the last chapter.

Though Mill goes to great lengths to bind the intellectual and the emotional crises together, there are some marked separations. Mill's emotional breakdown of 1826 is essentially resolved with the reading of Jean François Marmontel. His original theoretical indifference to poetry (*Auto*, 115),[13] which is an intellectual crisis because it is symptomatic of the general narrowness of the philosophy into which he was educated, is rectified with his reading of Wordsworth in 1828. He connects the two crises through his discovery of self-conscious emotion during the breakdown and his consequent appreciation of Wordsworth and poetry in general as a means of cultivating those feelings.

The discrepancies in Mill's description of his intellectual conversion are readily evident when we compare the views he attributes to himself in 1853–1854 with the notes he wrote in 1829 for the speech he gave in answer to John Roebuck, "Wordsworth and Byron." In those notes, he defends Wordsworth from the charge of mysticism by saying that that is "charging Wordsworth the poet with the faults of Wordsworth the metaphysician," and he goes on to direct himself to

> show the difference between describing feelings and being able to analyse them—the tendency of a man who by a long indulgence of particular trains of association, has connected certain feelings with things which excite no such feelings in other men, if he then attempts to explain is very likely to go into mysticism.[14]

In the *Autobiography*, Mill also charges Wordsworth with bad philosophy but good poetry; the value assigned to good poetry, however, differs here from the value the *Autobiography* gives it. In this speech, there is a truth inherent in poetry not available to logic, the truth of the feelings created by the poetic association. Bad philosophy here constitutes the attempt to explain those feelings, unsuccessfully, in analytic language. In the *Autobiography*, bad philosophy is again inadequate explanation of emotional phenomena; good poetry, however, is not the expression of a different kind of truth but the creation of a deeper, emotional attachment to truths that are also logically available.

One might possibly defend Mill's account of his intellectual transformation as an allowable form of telescoping. After all, the position he was moving toward in 1828 did give way in the course of the 1830s to the position he describes in the *Autobiography*. Still, for reasons that become clear, Mill wants to make a change that was part of a gradual and continuing development appear to be a radical conversion completed in an instant. He insists, describing the influence of Harriet, that when he met her in 1830, "the only actual revolution which has ever taken place in my modes of thinking was already complete" (*Auto*, 199);[15] and this desire indicates an attempt to give the mental crisis a significance it will not bear. Moreover, if there are problems with the intellectual section of the crisis, the emotional section contains problems even more difficult to explain.

One manifestation of the problem of taking the emotional section of the mental crisis as an accurate record is that Mill's chronology is extremely faulty.[16] In the first place, Mill states that "of four years' continual speaking" at the debating society, 1826 "is the only year of which I know nothing" (*Auto*, 143). But only a few pages earlier, in the preceding chapter, he gives a reasonably detailed account of the 1826/1827 season (the autumn and winter of his mental crisis):

> In the season following, 1826/7, things began to mend. We had acquired two excellent Tory speakers, Hayward and Shee (afterwards Sergeant Shee): the radical side was reinforced by Charles Buller, Cockburn, and others of the second generation of Cambridge Benthamites; and with their and other occasional aid, and the two Tories as well as Roebuck and me for regular speakers, almost every debate was a *bataille rangée* between the "philosophic radicals" and the Tory lawyers; until our conflicts were talked about, and several persons of note and consideration came to hear us. (*Auto*, 131, 133)

To explain how Mill could give such an account of a year of which he remembered nothing, we must suppose either the absurd situation of his taking copious notes of events that were making no impression on him at all, or the even more absurd occurrence of a case of amnesia that comes and goes with remarkable convenience.[17]

Mill is also not quite sure about the termination of his mental crisis.

The 1861 version of the *Autobiography* concludes the account of reading Marmontel with the following sentence: "Thus the cloud gradually drew off, and I again enjoyed life: and though I had several relapses, some of which lasted many months, I never again was as miserable as I had been" (*Auto*, 145). This sentence is unobjectionable; it even accounts for Mill's omission of the description of his nearly complete breakdown at his father's death. His original version, however, had the limitation "during the next few years" before the admission that he had relapses (*Auto*, 144).[18] This would seem to indicate that relapses had terminated with the mental crisis itself around 1830. It seems unlikely that in 1853–1854 Mill had simply forgotten his experience of his father's death. The question was whether to connect that event with the mental crisis and if so, how explicitly. The problem does not end there, however. At the end of his reading of Wordsworth, Mill claims, "The result [of the reading] was that I gradually, but completely, emerged from my habitual depression, and was never again subject to it" (*Auto*, 153). Only a few pages before, it was Marmontel who had terminated the habitual depression; only relapses occurred after that. Now it is Wordsworth who is given that signal value.

This may seem like too much attention paid to trivial detail, but it is indicative of a larger fact: Mill certainly changed some of his philosophic positions around the years 1828–1830, but his insistence on tying that intellectual change to an emotional conversion experience of substantial duration gives him chronological problems of which even he was evidently aware. And there are other indications that the emotional crisis is being seen through the grid of the intellectual crisis. Mill's biographers have had a notoriously hard time with his mental crisis. Bain notes that except for the *Autobiography*, he has no documents for the years between 1820 and 1830. He thus accepts, with misgivings, Mill's description of the subjective importance of the events, adding only his comments about the amount of work in which Mill was engaged in 1826.[19] Packe complains of the confusion surrounding the incident, attributing it to Mill.[20] Mazlish claims that the mental crisis "lights up Mill's life like a flare,"[21] but his psychoanalysis adds nothing to Levi's earlier account except a melodramatized version of Mill's details. The resistance of the account to biographical explanation, despite its obvious biographical significance might be due, as I have suggested, to the complex structuring of only barely visible events.

I am not suggesting that nothing at all happened to Mill in 1826. Rather, I am saying that what did happen, drained of the essentially intellectual significance that he later gave it, was, indeed, simply "a dull state of nerves." This was a state that, according to a letter he wrote to Comte, was not unusual for Mill:

> je suis tombé . . . depuis quelques temps dans une sorte de langueur intellectuelle, pour ne pas dire morale, qui tient, à ce que je crois, surtout à des causes physiques. Sans aucune maladie bien définie, j'éprouve une faiblesse nerveuse et une affection quasi-fébrile chronique que j'ai du reste, ressentie à diverses époques antérieures de ma vie, et que je connais assez familièrement pour savoir qu'elle ne durera pas longtemps.[22]

The symptoms of an intellectual and emotional languor, tied to a state of fevered nervousness, are not substantially different from the specific symptoms of the mental crisis that Mill connects to the more generalized emotional depression. Yet they are here taken lightly as a common and passing state. They are not nearly as serious as the eye tic, the stomach and lung disorders, and the baldness that afflicted Mill upon the death of his father in 1836. There seems a real likelihood that the nervous breakdown of 1826 was actually a minor event that would have gone unnoticed had it not been for its fortuitous placement just prior to an intellectual event of some significance.

We can explain both the status given to the event of 1826 and the particular literary shape it takes by seeing that event as both support and justification for Mill's theories of free will and self-consciousness. To shape the event so that it would fit those theories, Mill faced three exigencies. First, he could not describe the movement in the late 1820s as an entirely intellectual one. In the first place, such an entirely intellectual movement is, within associational theory, an entirely caused one. If it is caused, on the one hand, by the proper demands of a theoretical inconsistency in the ideas Mill had been educated in, then there is no radical break involved in the mental crisis. The theories Mill arrived at would have been implied by the theories he held. He was, as I argue in the next chapter, concerned to show that his change did involve adding to his father's theories rather than dropping any part of them; but he could not accept any implication that his addition was entirely caused, and perhaps even intended, by his father's education. In 1832, he wrote to Carlyle that "I was not *crammed*; my own thinking faculties were called into strong though partial play; & by their means I have been enabled to *remake* all my opinions."[23] Mill's education was the basis for his change, but it was not constitutive of it. He was not made but was enabled to remake all his opinions. On the other hand, if an entirely intellectual change is not caused by a prior theoretical inconsistency, it can only be ascribed to a perverse willfulness. Since that kind of willfulness could not be ascribed to a consciousness of a personal lack, far from being free, it would be the result of motivations caused by some unknown, unfortunate, and undesirable prior association of experiences.

Second, if Mill's change of thought cannot be entirely motivated by intellectual demands and still be free, neither can it be entirely a result of internal causation. To ascribe to the self the power of unilaterally originating activity would be to relinquish not merely some aspect, but the whole body, of associational theory. Mill would no longer be making minor corrections, or even large-scale revisions. He would be accepting an overwhelmingly definitive form of innate personality. His theory of free will, however, does nothing so radical; supposing the presence of an external cause, either the experience of one's own inadequacy or the experience of another's superiority, it leaves to the self only the consciousness of either the inadequacy or the superiority. Third, because of the delicate demands of his theory, Mill is, then, faced with the difficult task of defining his mental crisis in such a way that it is externally caused but possible only because of internal responses. He must delineate a change that is implied by his father's theories yet marks a distinctive turning away from them.

To see how Mill treads this theoretical tightrope, we turn to the account of the onset of the emotional crisis:

> It was in the autumn of 1826. I was in a dull state of nerves, such as everybody is occasionally liable to; unsusceptible to enjoyment or pleasurable excitement; one of those moods when what is pleasure at other times, becomes insipid or indifferent; the state, I should think, in which converts to Methodism usually are, when smitten by their first "conviction of sin." In this frame of mind it occurred to me to put the question directly to myself: "Suppose that all your objects in life were realized; that all the changes in institutions and opinions which you are looking forward to, could be completely effected at

this very instant: would this be a great joy and happiness to you?"
And an irrepressible self-consciousness distinctly answered, "No!"
(*Auto*, 137, 139)[24]

The passage opens with a purely physical, associational explanation. Dull states of nerves are easily attributable to minor physical malfunctions and the consequent sensations. Further, they are not distinctive in any way: "everybody is occasionally liable to" them. The comparison to the religious experience of conviction of sin is an odd note, however. If the analogy is meant to elucidate convictions of sin, it is a mere sociological aside. If, however, it elucidates the "dull state of nerves," it adds a clear element of uncontingent choice. The conviction of sin itself is not willed. One is "smitten" by it. But the resulting Methodist conversion was a freely willed one in deliberate contradistinction to any antinomian concept of election. Even if Mill was unaware of or unconcerned with such a basic aspect of Methodist theology in his use of the comparison, the phrase "conviction of sin," drained of purely religious significance, is very close to the sensation of one's own inadequacy that was so important to the *Logic*'s definition of free will.

The mere suggestion of an aspect besides external causation becomes a sharper presence in the next sentence: "In this frame of mind it occurred to me to put the question directly to myself. . . ." The initial use of the passive voice returns us to an associational reading of the moment. Mill did not decide, but it occurred to him, as, effectively, associational chains of thoughts cause other thoughts. Nevertheless, he puts the question directly to himself. We are now clearly within a self-conscious moment. The self-consciousness becomes explicit and active in the final moment: "And an irrepressible self-consciousness distinctly answered, 'No!'" The answer Mill receives is caused in the sense that it is a response to a situation. But it is overwhelmingly a response from the self to the self, in a moment that seems entirely independent. There is only one final limitation of his independence.

Self-consciousness is irrepressible. As a result of an internal moment, Mill may choose to change; but he cannot choose to remain precisely the same. In the same way that the information given by self-consciousness is subject to logical inquisition, the occurrence of self-consciousness is subject to associational causation. Only the moment itself, in its psychological inexplicability, is entirely free. And yet, that one slight moment is enough. To create that moment, he opened a space in his father's psychological theory, a space to be filled by an ultimate principle that he supports by the supposedly empirical evidence of the event he describes here.

As with the microcosm of this passage, so with the macrocosm of the mental crisis as a whole. Cause is followed by effect, which becomes a further cause to be followed by a further effect. And yet there are constant moments of self-consciousness that edge Mill into responses. He expresses the value of Wordsworth in a solidly utilitarian appreciation of poetry, and yet he reads himself into every poem. The original crisis is assuaged by a book, Marmontel's *Memoires*, yet, again, he reads himself into the passage, noting the "sudden inspiration" that Marmontel feels. And this brings us to the most extraordinary act of balance in the whole account. Mill never describes any explicit moment of rebellion. He never places himself in the role of the romantic rebel (Byron was never Mill's favorite poet). He dispenses tribute after tribute to his father's theories and his father's education of him. Yet he quietly places the shadow of his father over the whole affair, making the declaration of freedom muted but present.

That Mill had long seen the mental crisis in terms of the 1836 crisis upon the death of his father, consciously rather than subconsciously, is a possibility for which there are at least two strong indications. First there is an odd, amusing, and hitherto unnoticed biographical discrepancy: there are two accounts of when Mill lost his hair. In 1836, soon after James Mill's death, Carlyle visited the Mills at their summer house, writing back to his wife a rather frightening picture of Mill's physical condition, saying in part: "His eyes go twinkling and jerking with wild lights and twitches; his head is bald, his face brown and dry—poor fellow after all." [25] Biographers have generally followed Carlyle's account. There are other descriptions of the development of Mill's eye tic, and it seems likely that the baldness would coincide. Mill, however, talking to Caroline Fox, dated his baldness to a much earlier period. Fox recounts Mill's account of the baldness while describing a ride with Mill's sister Clara: "Took Clara a ride. Spoke much of her father and how he had entirely educated John and made him think prematurely, so that he never had the enjoyment of life peculiar to boys. He feels this a great disadvantage. He told us his hair came off 'when you were quite a little girl and I was two-and-twenty.'" [26] Mill was twenty-two in 1828. His mental crisis, then, followed from his education, and his baldness followed from his mental crisis. Ordinarily, Mill would, of course, be the better source for this kind of fact. Carlyle was often a notoriously unreliable narrator. Nevertheless, it seems staggeringly improbable that he would describe to his wife Mill's baldness as part of his physical decay in 1835 if his wife had known Mill to be bald or even balding from the first time that they ever met, which would have been the case had his baldness dated from 1828. Was Mill then lying to Caroline Fox, or was his mistake a Freudian slip? Neither supposition is necessary. If Mill constantly thought of his father's death and his mental crisis as related, his statement might simply be a symptom of that tendency to connect them.

The second reason for supposing Mill to have made conscious connections between his mental crisis and his father's actual death has to do with the passage on reading Marmontel, or rather, a startling echo of it. Describing his attitude upon his father's death, Mill—in the place of the *Early Draft*'s final "I had now to try what it might be possible for me to accomplish without him"—had originally written, "I had now to try how far I might be capable of supplying his place" (*Auto*, 212). The *Early Draft* concludes the description of the scene from Marmontel with "He, then a mere boy, by a sudden inspiration, felt & made them feel that he would be everything, would supply the place of everything to them" (*Auto*, 144). Even if we suppose that the original echo of the phrase was not a conscious one, the fact of the revision indicates that at some point Mill realized what he was doing with his use of Marmontel. The clear implication is that he wanted to retain but moderate the father-replacement overtones of the Marmontel passage.

I am not by any means suggesting that Mill was conscious of wishing his father's death. I am suggesting that the account of the mental crisis, rather than faithfully representing an abreaction that at the time of the writing was twenty-seven or twenty-eight years in the past, consciously means to suggest a rebellion against the father without making that rebellion explicit. One of the most serious difficulties of the abreaction theory is Mill's actual reaction to the death of his father. An abreaction, the acting out through representation of a guilty and repressed desire in a supposedly innocent form, serves to alleviate the guilt by allowing the abreactor to experience the desired activity innocently. If Mill had been reconciled in such a way with his wishes for his father's death, it would follow that the actual death should have evoked from him no more than the usual expressions of grief. In fact, as we know, he went through a very real crisis at that time, obvious to all those around him. Yet *that* crisis the

Autobiography barely discusses at all. It is possible, then, that Mill never truthfully described his equivocal reactions to his father's death because that was the event he could never consciously face. Moreover, the emotional crisis of 1836, in the absence of any significant intellectual revision of thought, could have no theoretical importance. The 1826 crisis, then, was given the full emotional significance of 1836, connecting the intellectual with an emotional conversion while relieving the latter crisis of its weight of guilt.

If we were to read the account of the mental crisis not as an accurate record of a past event but as a short story, the effect of that story would be to support the psychological and philosophic theories at which its protagonist arrives. The story Mill tells supports his theoretical position by giving to the first principles of his philosophy the empirical evidence of emotional events. But of course that evidence is no evidence at all, for as I have shown, it is largely the creation of Mill's language. Of the content of the moment itself, prior to its construction through interpretation, we have little hard knowledge, and much of that is contradictory. What we do have are the depiction and description of self-consciousness in terms of Mill's theories. Seeing Mill's account as a short story also prepares us, of course, to move from an analysis of narrative as an example of a philosophic concept to an analysis of narrative as the embodiment of a philosophic concept, to look at the narrative structure of the *Autobiography* as that structure derives from the work's philosophic context.

Before proceeding to that final analysis, it is worth summarizing the argument so far to see clearly Mill's movement from philosophy to narrative. This summary has a special place here because these past two chapters have concerned movements within a philosophic discourse, while the next marks a break into a more formal analysis of narrative, albeit a formal analysis that could not exist without the prior discussion of the philosophy. We started, then, with a political philosophy that demanded a theory of free will coincident with associationism. That theory in turn created a paradoxical theory of consciousness as both a moment within an associational train of sensations and yet a terminal, ontologically separate moment. To justify this formulation of consciousness, Mill claimed he rectified, when actually he opened a hole in, his father's theories, filling that hole with a newly minted ultimate principle. Then, to support this theory of self-consciousness posing as an ultimate principle, Mill offered the only kind of support to which ultimate principles of consciousness are amenable, empirical evidence in the form of an autobiographical account. In the *Autobiography*, he claims to recount an experiential discovery of a theoretical need, but actually he opens a hole in his life (and the chronological ragged edges remain as indications of the violence of that opening) and fills it with an interpretation determined by the theory that interpretation ostensibly supports.

But this philosophic debacle is an esthetic triumph. Mill's mental crisis has become a *locus classicus* of the liberal imagination.[27] It is the task of this book to outline a method for arriving at an understanding of the power of this moment and moments like it in Mill's *Autobiography* and in other works of Victorian prose. These past chapters have shown, I think, that that understanding will not emerge from a treatment of the prose—Mill's at least—as purely referential, philosophic discourse. Neither will that understanding come from a literary analysis that is not able to accommodate the works' philosophic intents. By recasting philosophy into narrative through Mill's definition of self-consciousness, though, the following chapter shows how philosophic discourse can be coincident with narrative and how an analysis of philosophic theories that is essentially literary can reveal the connection between the discourses. That connection is, I think, the cause of moments like the mental crisis whose importance is not quite a matter of intellectual history, not quite a matter of literary history, and yet a matter of both.

Chapter IV

Consciousness as a Narrative of Completion in the *Autobiography*

T he tendency to consider autobiography as a form of fiction, though relatively recent, is so healthy that often those who want to draw distinctions between the genres seem not the conservative and more traditional but the rebellious, modern, less traditional critics.[1] The reasons for connecting autobiography with fiction are not far to seek. It has become one of the commonplaces of Anglo-American definitions of fiction that the novelist must find a form that makes sense of the shifting and various world of experience without distorting that world.[2] But of course such a commonplace applies also and obviously to autobiography, which, to make a book out of a life, must shape the experiences of the life without (at least most autobiographers claim) falsifying that experience. To a certain extent, the preceding chapter could be taken as exemplifying the fictionalizing process in the case of Mill's account of his mental crisis.

It is not fictionalization per se that is my concern, however, but narrativization, the narrativization of philosophy within Victorian prose. In this process, Mill's description of his mental crisis exemplifies the first moment in which philosophy connects with narrative, the moment in which one uses a narrative account, an autobiography, as empirical evidence for a philosophic theory about the workings of consciousness. But for Mill, this connection is not momentary at all, for his philosophic theory constitutes his narrative form, and his narrative form is the final expression of his philosophy. Thus the discussion of Mill's philosophy leads here to a literary analysis of his *Autobiography*, but equally that literary analysis must also be a discussion of his philosophic contentions since those contentions shape the form of narrative under analysis. Part Three constructs from this connection between consciousness and narrative a methodology for reading Victorian prose that accommodates equally well both its intellectual content and its literariness. The formal analysis in this chapter, in addition, then to showing how the connection first works thoroughly in autobiography, is also an example of the kind of reading of Victorian prose such a methodology encourages.

Autobiography is a particularly useful genre in articulating the jointure between consciousness and narrative because consciousness is central to its narrative regardless of any philosophic issues or contexts. After all, self-consciousness shapes any autobiography. In considering his life and searching for the shape that informs it or may encapsulate it, the autobiographer so clearly enacts self-consciousness that the fact almost seems to go without saying. Almost, but not quite, because this self-consciousness does not simply plan or imagine before the writing; it *is* the act of autobiography. Autobiographical narrative is itself an act of self-description, self-consideration, self-consciousness. But consciousness is also the subject of autobiography, its vital and necessary content. The autobiographical subject's awareness of his life, his response to what he does and what is done to him, must interest the autobiographical narrator at least to the extent that he cares about recounting himself and not merely external events. The subject's self-awareness is a necessary condition of being a self to be narrated, just as the narrator's self-awareness is a necessary condition of there being a narration. Subject and narrator in autobiography are therefore uniquely bound up in each other. And the definition an autobiographer gives to self-consciousness in order to narrate will naturally influence the experience of self-consciousness he attributes to the self who is narrated.

Indeed, consciousness and narrative mesh so thoroughly in autobiography that we might question generalizing from the situation to any larger theory about a connection between philosophy and narrative, were it not for the peculiarities the form assumes when it also participates in the genre of Victorian prose. After all, even if the concept of consciousness is necessarily central to the form of autobiography, the autobiographer might be concerned with his own experience of consciousness without necessarily attending to the philosophic ramifications and contexts of that experience, certainly without intending that experience as evidence for any particular theory with extra-autobiographical, polemic significance. But the synonyms we use to describe the great writers of Victorian prose—sage, prophet—indicate the polemical and argumentative nature of that prose (if any particular reminder is needed). Sages and prophets are particularly concerned with the intellectual content of what they write and its argumentative effect upon their audience. It should not surprise us, then, that Victorian autobiographies share with other forms of Victorian prose an argumentative intent, a concern with intellectual and theoretical contexts and implications of the experiences recounted. Moreover, I have already stressed in the introduction the importance of philosophic definitions of consciousness in nineteenth-century intellectual discourse, particularly their importance to the debate over intuition and experience as ways of knowing, and the broad ramifications that debate had for Victorians. The shaping of nineteenth-century autobiographies by their philosophic and theoretical contexts may, in such an intellectual and literary context, be less a matter of a group of writers, for more or less individual reasons, intending to use the form in that way than a matter of a form that, in that period, made theoretical and philosophic concerns intrinsic to itself.

I note the importance of polemical and philosophic concerns within Victorian autobiography via its connection with the larger category of Victorian prose, not simply as an exercise in deductive logic, however. The peculiar importance of polemic and philosophy to Mill's *Autobiography* and Newman's *Apologia* is more a presenting symptom than an analytic conclusion. Part Two shows the importance of polemical context to the *Apologia* and the particular problems that that importance creates for a literary analysis of it. And even without the philosophic context of Mill's other works fresh in mind, critics have often found his *Autobiography* a failure even as an intellectual autobiography because of the book's relentlessly abstract and intellectual concerns and style.[3]

In fact abstract intellectuality is completely thematized in the book. Early in the work, for instance, Mill describes his childhood walks with his father: "In these walks I always accompanied him, and with my earliest recollection of green fields and wild flowers, is mingled that of the account I gave him daily of what I read the day before" (*Auto*, 11). From the beginning, Mill's account, his thoughts, his words, superimpose themselves over nature, which itself remains in the above passage an abstraction. Mill deals with abstraction, rather than that over which it is superimposed, because abstraction *is* the primary experience. Even this abstraction about the importance of intellectual abstraction to Mill's narrative and its account of his life becomes a matter of central concern to the narrative in its account of the mental crisis. A literary analysis that does not accommodate this insistent intellectuality and the philosophy it aims to articulate not only has ignored one of the work's most obvious and literarily problematic stylistic features but has failed to comprehend in their entirety both the emplotment of the work and the aims both literary and philosophic of that emplotment.

To go back, now, to what the preceding chapters bring to bear here: philosophy becomes particularly available to narrative when one defines self-consciousness because of the homology between the elements that make up the concepts of both consciousness and narrative. As a definition of consciousness must comprehend both a conscient mind and an object of which the mind is conscious, so a narrative must comprise both a narrator and at least one event narrated. Mill's associationism denied existence to any innate self prior to experience and defined the self as solely the thread of sensations experienced by a passive sensorium. An act of consciousness was, at one level, simply another experience on this thread. Still, Mill argued that the experience of consciousness was an associational paradox in that it was an experience on the thread that was particularly definitive of the self the thread comprised. In the *Autobiography*, we now find the consequent definition of narrative, which sees the awareness that constitutes the narrative act in autobiography as both simply another event in the life and in the narrative and yet as an event that uniquely determines both the value and the meaning of the life and the narrative. The act of narrative in Mill is an act of self-freeing and of completion.

A narrative structure that imbeds within itself a theory of consciousness entails at least the possibility that that structure, through the theory, will determine the themes and plot lines of the narrative, particularly in the case of autobiography. Given Mill's definition of self as comprised solely of accreted experience, the thematization of education as constitutive of the self in the *Autobiography* should hardly surprise us. Moreover, given that the associational process is one of binding and possibly entails as a corollary the absence of free will, a drama in which this education threatens to imprison the self it creates will seem to follow. Finally, Mill's paradoxical definition of consciousness as a series of experiences aware of itself as a series, a definition that created the possibility for a free will within associationism, also affects the *Autobiography*. There Mill frees himself from his education through an act of both consciousness and narration. So far, my account of the *Autobiography* does not differ much from normal readings of the work. The awareness of the full theoretical context of the *Autobiography*, however, does create shifts in the handling of the issues of education, consciousness, and self-freeing that result in a reading that is, I think, more adequate to the work both formally and intellectually.

Probably because they do not really accept Mill's associational epistemology, most critics, in short, define his early education as a warping, rather than a creation, of the self and consequently see the mental crisis as romantic rebellion against the father, a rediscovery, more or less successful, of the emotional roots of the self. Those critics who notice that Mill remains, as before the mental crisis, both a utilitarian and an associationist generally take this consistency to be a sign that the mental crisis was a rebellion incompletely achieved and then either attempt to recuperate the life as standard romantic spiritual autobiography by psychoanalyzing Mill through the text or simply describe the *Autobiography* as in some way inadequate or contradictory. To begin to see how consistently and coherently Mill's philosophy structures and is structured by the narrative in the *Autobiography*, we must start by taking seriously the picture of the mind and its workings that Mill's epistemology and narrative create. The reading that follows thus begins with an account of what a self made up only of experience, not experience imposed upon an innate personality, looks like, how education and learning in this system can only be constructive of a self, not by definition, warping. The next section discusses how Mill's two moments of coming to awareness, his discovery of Benthamism as a worked-out philosophy and his mental crisis, define the self by completing it through consciousness and narrative, even as Mill insists that these acts are carried out in the terms of the original philosophy. The final section details how this form of consciousness—an experienced paradox in, but not a denial of, associationism—in the form of narrative, becomes the method of Mill's self-freeing. Through self-consciousness, he claims his various makers in the same way that his theory of free will earlier did not deny, but claimed to exist within, a system of causal necessity.

A Made Self

Like many other autobiographies, Mill's offers early on a version of a first memory. But this originating moment differs from most others precisely because it does not originate anything, is in effect a claim not to be able to reach a first moment:

> I have no remembrance of the time when I began to learn Greek. I have been told that it was when I was three years old. My earliest recollection on the subject, is that of committing to memory what my father termed Vocables. (*Auto*, 9)

This passage is not simply the opening of a section on Mill's education; it is the first mention in the *Autobiography* of an event in his life. The earliest event he can remember is of already being in the middle of an education, of being changed without any reference to a stable first self prior to the change. Learning Greek at the age of three may be extraordinary, but the learning of Greek per se is in no way defining. The act of learning itself, though, prior to any development of an innate personality, does make the *Autobiography's* opening arresting. And that act of learning, with other acts of learning, completely determines Mill's personality, at least at first.

Moreover, Mill has no memory of an original, defining moment, not because he cannot remember back far enough but because the moment itself never existed. He begins—at least he and his father suppose he begins—as a tabula rasa. Theoretically, he might be able to remember the first sensation that made an imprint on the blank tablet of his mind, but that first sensation would not be defining. It would simply be followed by a second and third sensation, the mind being formed by that sequence. This theory of association was the "fundamental" principle behind Mill's education:

> In psychology, his fundamental doctrine was the formation of all human character by circumstances, through the universal Principle of Association, and the consequent unlimited possibility of improving the moral and intellectual condition of mankind by education. (*Auto*, 109–110)

The fundamental doctrine is that there is no distinctive fundament. The personality results from either planned or unplanned additions, from either indiscriminate sensations or sensations connected with ideas. Within this system, the notion of an education as a warping of the self is simply incoherent. An education may be beneficial or not, but either way, it will be equally as constitutive of the self as any other experience, and only experience, only sensation, is constitutive.

Nor do we ever see the younger Mill waver in his adherence to this theory. Although when he describes his "mental crisis," he uses the past tense to refer to his belief in the theory, the tense clearly does not indicate a change in his opinions. He goes on to criticize his father's associational education not on a theoretical but on a methodological basis: his father had not built up strongly enough the son's prejudicial defenses against self-analysis. Near the end of the *Autobiography*, Mill's belief in associationism, and his enmity to any form of intuitional psychology, is restated in strong terms:

> In particular, I have long felt that the prevailing tendency to regard all the marked distinctions of human character as innate, and in the main indelible, and to ignore the irresistible proofs that by far the greater part of those differences, whether between individuals, races, or sexes, are such as not only might but naturally would be produced by differences in circumstance, is one of the chief hindrances to the rational treatment of great social questions and one of the greatest stumbling blocks to human improvement. (*Auto*, 270)

The slight reservation implied in the phrase "by far the greater part" needs some further specification. James Olney traces what he sees as a contradiction between Mill's cold, rational style and his highly emotional life story to the conflict between his associational psychology of the intellect and his sense of the power and value of irrational emotions.[4] But Mill's associationism does accommodate the emotions. In a passage on analysis, he remarks,

> [Analytical habits] are therefore (I thought) favorable to prudence and clear-sightedness, but a perpetual worm at the root both of the passions and of the virtues; and, above all, fearfully undermine all desires, and all pleasures, which are the effects of association. (*Auto*, 143)

To deal with this problem, Mill changes his beliefs in this way:

> I, for the first time, gave its proper place, among the prime necessities of human well-being, to the internal culture of the individual. I ceased to attach almost exclusive importance to the ordering of outward circumstances, and the training of the human being for speculation and for action. (*Auto*, 147)

Both thought and emotion are inherent capacities here and, to that extent, innate—hence the reservaton of "by far the greater part." Further, the degree to which one contains both intellect and emotion may vary inherently, as indicated by the fact that Mill feels himself "by nature" deficient in both intellectual and emotional capabilities. But thought and emotion, as general qualities, are not in any sense definitive of the individual personality. The distinctiveness of a personality arises from the differing ways intellect and emotion may be expressed and this difference, in both cases (as the first of the above two citations shows), results from the principle of association. Individuality also, to a lesser extent, manifests itself in the degree of expression of intellect and emotion, but here training can make up for an inherent deficiency, as Mill claims was so in his case. Therefore, degree is also connected with association. But here Mill draws a distinction between thought and emotion. Intellect or thinking can be encouraged by exterior and artificially contrived stimuli, by "outward circumstances." The emotions must be "internally cultivated." The expression or suppression of emotions can be externally encouraged, as Mill's father encouraged Mill to suppress his emotions, but the cultivation of the emotions themselves, and the augmentation of their intensity, is internally controlled, an act of self-consciousness. One intensifies and cultivates one's emotions by developing one's awareness of them.

I stress this distinction rather than Olney's for two reasons. First, we must constantly be careful not to accuse Mill of a contradiction because we do not like the way his theory works. Mill's formulation of association is comprehensively thought out, and its shape is integral to the shape of the *Autobiography*. The concept of internal cultivation brings us to the second reason for my distinction. Although emotion is not associationally inexplicable, internal cultivation, an act of self-consciousness, does enter that area in which associationism, for Mill, must embody paradox as first principle. The opposition between emotion and intellect that Olney worries is thus reducible to the opposition between experience and that particular form of experience called consciousness. This opposition becomes an actively important one because education, which, as a form of experience, does not warp but constructs the self, cannot complete that construction. Because self-consciousness is radically separate from all other experiences in Mill's association, it is needed, in the form of an act both outside the education and yet in terms of the education, to complete the self. Within the theme of education, this completion is formulated as an act of knowing what one has learned in order to become whole, a recognition that also becomes self-knowledge. The opposition between learning and knowing entails that other opposition between the intellect and the emotion, because just as emotions result from that form of self-consciousness Mill labels internal cultivation, so self-consciousness will be defined as an inherently emotional act.

We see the incompleteness of learning in the formation of the self in a series of remarks Mill makes about the end of his education's preliminary stage:

> I was not at all aware that my attainments were anything unusual at my age. . . . I never thought of saying to myself, I am, or I can do, so and so. I neither estimated myself highly or lowly: I did not estimate myself at all. . . . I have a distinct remembrance, that the suggestion thus for the first' time made to me, that I knew more than other youths who were considered well-educated, was to me a piece of information, to which, as to all other things which my father told me, I gave implicit credence, but which did not at all impress me as a personal matter. (*Auto*, 35, 37)

Mill's learning has given him a unique personality but his inability to recognize that personality makes the job unfinished. He is, but he does not know who he is. Because knowledge is tied both to emotion and to consciousness, however, the act of completing the self becomes a chancy business for Mill, and he finds the sensation of self-knowledge an extremely ambiguous one.

Knowing the Self

Mill's mental crisis has generally been dealt with in terms of the psychological version of sin coming home to roost, the return of the repressed.[5] In terms of this model, the crisis was both a result of the warping of the education and an attempt to cure that warping and return to a healthier psychological state. Since Mill, through the crisis, also discovered the value of poetry, a critic's psychological evaluations are often also deeply bound to his literary evaluations, and estimations of the completeness of the crisis's breakthrough also become estimations of the literary value of the *Autobiography*. These psychological discussions would not concern us here were it not for the literary evaluations to which they are tied. The treatment of the mental crisis in terms of the model of the romantic spiritual conversion rather than in terms of Mill's own philosophy turns out, I think, to be not simply a philosophic choice or error but also a flaw in literary analysis.

To understand both the consistency and the content of the mental crisis, we must begin with the recognition that it is not the sole conversion experience in the *Autobiography* but is preceded by the utilitarian conversion of reading Bentham and that whatever the difference in the content of these two experiences, they are structurally very similar. By analyzing both accounts and the movement from the one to the other, we can see a number of things about the workings of conversion, crisis, and change in Mill's narrative and his philosophy. First, a completely utilitarian logic controls both the movement from one conversion to another and the movement within conversions, and Mill never really calls into question the utilitarian basis on which he reasons, even when he defines the value of poetry. Second, only the act of recognition in these events, not the events recognized, only the moment of self-awareness, is associationally inexplicable; and even so, Mill explains the necessity of the act associationally. Finally, the second, if not the first, conversion seems a revolt of the emotion only because the self-consciousness that knows what one has learned is persistently described as an emotional experience. But the *Autobiography* never describes emotion per se as associationally inexplicable.

Their interiority is the real paradox behind Mill's conversions and crises. Up to the point of reading Bentham, Mill's personality was formed by experience of the external world, controlled or otherwise. While Mill allows the event of consciousness to have associational causation, the content of that event is carefully preserved as an associationally inexplicable, interior space. Thus, as he goes through his crisis, he tells no one, and no one recognizes his situation. Conversely, the reader is told virtually nothing of any of Mill's social activities at this time since they become wholly subsidiary to the activity occurring between the self and its consciousness of itself. This situation follows directly from the fact that the process of self-completion for Mill—knowing what he has learned—is entirely an internal one.

The reading of Bentham is not generally attended to as an event of the same order as the mental crisis. Yet the *Autobiography* places particular stress on it as a defining and completing moment in Mill's education.

Moreover, the mental crisis itself responds as much to the stable state created by the Benthamite conversion as it does to the education that preceded it. Mill begins the record of his 1826 crisis with this summary:

> From the winter of 1821, when I first read Bentham, and especially from the commencement of the *Westminster Review*, I had what might truly be called an object in life; to be a reformer of the world. My conception of my own happiness was entirely identified with this object. (*Auto*, 137)

The reading of Bentham is the first moment in which Mill defines to himself who he is, gives himself an "object in life," ceases to be merely his father's pupil. The activities surrounding the *Westminster Review* become the outward manifestation of that change—Mill's ability to think for himself—and a further process of self-education.

It is not the reading of Bentham, which according to the chapter title was the last stage of his education, that is the interesting moment here. Nor is it the political activity that follows the first stage of self-education. It is, rather, the intermediary stage, at the moment the young Mill puts down Bentham and the narrating Mill declares of his earlier self:

> I had become a different being. The "principle of utility," understood as Bentham understood it, and applied in the manner in which he applied it through these three volumes, fell exactly into its place as the keystone which held together the detached and fragmentary component parts of my knowledge and beliefs. It gave unity to my conception of things. I now had opinions; a creed, a doctrine, a philosophy. (*Auto*, 69)

The language of conversion is unmistakable here. Mill becomes a different being. He now has a philosophy. Yet the philosophy he is reading is the one upon which his whole education up to this point has been based. Mill becomes a different person here, not by discovering a new philosophy, but by discovering precisely what his philosophy has been all along, to what knowledge and actions his learning has been leading him. It can hardly be said that this discovery is a turn away from his education. Indeed his father "put into [his] hands" (*Auto*, 67) the book that causes the discovery. And yet the quality of discovering is not something the education can create. It occurs in an interior moment, after the book has been put down, between education and self-education; it is a moment of consciousness that completes the education, that is prepared for by the education and that is yet not part of it.

But his education does not create this moment. Nor does the form the self-knowledge takes really accord with the philosophy it had discovered:

> What thus impressed me was the chapter in which Bentham passed judgment on the common modes of reasoning in morals and legislation deduced from phrases like "law of nature," "right reason," "the moral sense," "natural rectitude," and the like, and characterized them as dogmatism in disguise imposing its sentiments upon others under cover of sounding expressions which convey no reason for the sentiment, but set up sentiment as its own reason. It had not struck me before, that Bentham's principle put an end to all this. The feeling rushed upon me, that all previous moralists were superseded, and that here indeed was the commencement of a new era in thought. (*Auto*, 67)

In one sense, the careful narrative past tense is deceptive here. Mill never lost his distrust of intuitional morality any more than of intuitional psychology, as both the end of the *Autobiography* and the *Examination of Sir William Hamilton's Philosophy* show. In another sense, however, it is an extraordinarily adept indication of Mill's awareness of the contradiction in his own earlier reactions. Even as he accepts Bentham's scorn of assenting to a philosophy on bases other than reason, we find that his acceptance is in terms of a "feeling" that "rushed upon" him. I have said earlier that for Mill self-knowledge is an emotional act. His discovery of his belief in Bentham's rationalism is surely emotional in that way and thus carries with it the roots of its own breakdown.

The problem here is of course that the emotional force of this moment of knowledge, of coming to consciousness of his own philosophy, does not match the philosophy that is the object of his consciousness. Thus when his consciousness explicitly questions the emotional content of his philosophy, the response he gives to himself is hardly a surprise:

> It occurred to me to put the question directly to myself, "Suppose that all your objects in life were realized; that all the change in institutions and opinions which you are looking forward to, could be completely effected at this very instant: would this be a great joy and happiness to you?" And an irrepressible self-consciousness distinctly answered, "No!" At this my heart sank within me: the whole foundation on which my life was constructed fell down. (*Auto*, 139)

I have already discussed this passage in the previous chapter as an embodiment of the epistemology Mill worked out in his other metaphysical texts and claimed that this embodiment may be taken for a microcosm of the mental crisis as a whole. Here I want to verify and expand upon that claim by showing how the philosophy becomes a narrative's series of events. This passage essentially sets that series off by putting to work the system of oppositions I have already been discussing—experience and consciousness of experience, learning and knowing, and intellect and emotion—and giving the first indication that it is the first opposition, experience and consciousness, that must be associationally accommodated for the others to operate smoothly.

Again, in this passage, self-knowledge is not a controllable intellectual entity. It is, like an emotion, "irrepressible." The point is worth stressing. The reason for Mill's despair is not that he does not feel. If that were the case, he would not feel the despair. In fact, as has been noticed before, Mill feels very acutely during the depression; but what he feels is barrenness of self.[6] The emotion of self-consciousness is unsatisfied with the self of which it has become conscious. He not only knows what he has learned but knows a lack in that knowledge. In the first act of consciousness, the knowledge of Benthamism, he learned knowledge's tie with emotional response. Putting into play the same mental event, a coming to consciousness not of his earlier education but of his consciousness of Benthamism, he finds the emotional response tied with that second act to be one of dissatisfaction with the original object of knowledge and consciousness.

He responds to this problem by taking the act of consciousness one step further and discovering in himself some emotions. He then concentrates on cultivating them through becoming conscious of them, in accordance with the method described earlier in the chapter when I was discussing Mill's psychology. He first discovers emotions in himself when he reacts tearfully to a reading of Marmontel's *Memoires*, an intensely convoluted moment I will pass over now and return to further on. In 1828, he discovers Wordsworth's poetry (although he had read the *Excursion* earlier, he explains, with no effect), the reading of which essentially ends the mental crisis. The poetry becomes valuable because Mill can see himself in Wordsworth's mourning over the loss of his youth. By reading of the compensation Wordsworth finds in the "tranquil contemplation" of the problem, Mill, since he "gradually but completely, emerged from my habitual depression" (*Auto*, 153), evidently also finds compensation. Thus, reading Wordsworth, Mill sees a version of himself and counteracts a despairing moment of consciousness with a consoling one.

Having pictured self-consciousness as the emotion that confirms and completes the self developed by learning, I must now deal with two passages that seem directly to contradict this reading. The first is the one on Mill's reservations about his habit of analysis. He complains that while analysis is valuable in dissecting external principles, breaking up the prejudicial association of value with a social structure that does not really have that value, analysis turned in upon the self—and that is a form of self-consciousness—tends to dissolve internal emotional associations as well and is, thus, like a version of the snake in the garden, "a perpetual worm at the root both of the passions and of the virtues" (*Auto*, 143). His first response is, therefore, to develop a theory that he explicitly connects with Carlyle's "anti–self consciousness principle." While it is still right to strive for happiness, Mill argues in a second passage that one should turn one's attention to subsidiary goals since if you "ask yourself whether you are happy . . . you cease to be so" (*Auto*, 147).

To resolve this contradiction, we must first differentiate between analysis, which may or may not be self-analysis, and the emotional act of self-consciousness. Analysis turned outward causes no despair in its capacity to break things down. It is only when turned inward that it becomes attached to the emotion of despair. Thus, "for all those who have but a moderate degree of sensibility and capacity for enjoyment" (*Auto*, 147), Mill does indeed espouse the avoidance of self-analysis since the slight joy that is possible unconfirmed by a consciousness of the joy is still better than despair. Even this conscious avoidance of self-analysis, we could argue, is a form of self-consciousness since one must consciously forget one's final goal, happiness, in order to achieve it. But Mill's second method of overcoming this problem, "internal cultivation," is neither unselfconscious nor even anti–self-conscious; he evidently considers it a far more satisfactory solution, at least the one he chooses, in that the very passages criticizing self-analysis are highly self-analytic and yet not despairing. It is, further, Mill's internal cultivation, his reading of Wordsworth, that makes him immune to the dangers of analysis and thus open to the pleasures of self-consciousness: "And the delights which these poems gave me, proved that with culture of this sort, there was nothing to dread from the most confirmed habit of analysis" (*Auto*, 153).

At this point, it might be argued that while Mill's reaction to his read-ing of Bentham is a straightforward act of self-recognition that confirms the self made by learning, Mill's mental crisis is a rather different experi-ence, a turning away from his education, particularly since Mill feels he cannot tell his problems to his father because "I saw no use in giving him the pain of thinking that his plans had failed, when the failure was prob-ably irremediable, and, at all events, beyond the power of *his* remedies" (*Auto*, 139, 141). Certainly, Mill's crisis, his discovery of Wordsworth, of the value of poetry and emotions, marks a radical modification of what he had been taught to believe. Associationally paradoxical moments of consciousness, which perceive the need of and largely constitute those modifications, do occur. But the process or changes they set in motion and the explanations for the new values Mill accepts—even the poetic values—are entirely in terms of the philosophy away from which he was supposedly turning.

The first effects of the crisis, for instance, reproduce the associational process by which experience constructs the self. His preliminary act of despair at first changes Mill to a tabula rasa. His remark "The fountains of vanity and ambition seemed to have dried up within me, as completely as those of benevolence" (*Auto*, 143) is more than just an assertion that Mill had lost undesirable as well as desirable emotions. Vanity and benev-olence are forms of the two emotions with which Rousseau and Hobbes endow primitive men and infants. Mill goes back to a state prior to those emotions, however, a state neither of those philosophers recognized but one on which James Mill had based his educational theory, the moment prior to experience in which there is no self. Since one cannot, of course, have a memory of a state in which there is nothing, Mill adds, "of four years' continual speaking at that society, this is the only year of which I remember next to nothing" (*Auto*, 143). Mill's despair at this point leads him to conclude: "There seemed no power in nature sufficient to begin the formation of my character anew, and create in a mind now irretriev-ably analytic, fresh associations of pleasure with any of the objects of hu-man desire" (*Auto*, 143). Mill's real despair is not simply that he does not feel, since in normal cases that can be corrected by the principle of associ-ation. Rather, it is that this return to the state of blankness prior to expe-rience has made him less than human, "a stock or a stone," he implies a page later on, at best a reasoning machine, in either case unreachable by association.

The rebuilding process occurs through his reading of Marmontel and then later of Wordsworth, which create in him enough emotion to make him feel that he is capable of pleasure. As a result, Mill, who had been taught to avoid passion and to undervalue poetry, proceeds to "internal cultivation" and a reading of the Romantic poets. But this change as well is explained in terms of the philosophy he had learned and not of any new one to which he might be supposed to have converted:

> I never turned recreant to intellectual culture, or ceased to consider the power and practice of analysis as an essential condition both of individual and social improvement. But I thought that it had consequences which required to be corrected, by joining other kinds of cultivation with it. (*Auto*, 147)

Mill does not forego Benthamism but simply corrects and improves on it, a possibility that any theory that posits the infinite improvability of mankind can easily envision for itself. The method of improvement itself is associational, an act of joining one form of valuable experience, intellectual culture, to another, the more general cultivation. Moreover, the principle of improvement by addition and joining allows Mill to claim that associational psychology shows the potential intelligence and social value of all people. It is also the only principle that would have made Mill's education necessary, since to be more than merely a follower of Bentham, a spreader of his word—for which role such an education as Mill had been given would hardly have been needed—implies that Mill will change Bentham's thoughts for the better. Thus, even the mental crisis, like the Benthamite conversion that preceded it, culminates Mill's education rather than denying it. The crisis forms a moment whose internal space is beyond the purview of the education but whose existence the education both causes and needs in order to be complete.

Indeed, Mill's summary of his education early in the book belies the standard notion of it as a mechanical exercise in information drilling:

> Mine, however, was not an education of cram. My father never permitted anything which I learnt, to degenerate into a mere exercise of memory. He strove to make the understanding not only go along with every step of the teaching, but, if possible, precede it. Anything which could be found out by thinking, I never was told, until I exhausted my efforts to find it out for myself. (*Auto*, 35)

Obviously James Mill is not the Gradgrind critics sometimes find him.[7] By demanding of Mill understanding, he makes the act of understanding the self, recognizing what was lacking, possible. And by demanding thought rather than mere memory of fact, he gives Mill the method for constructing a revised philosophy of self that would include emotion. The education effectively gives Mill the tools for its own reconstruction.

Finally, not only are the concept and method of revising his utilitarian and associational philosophy entirely in terms of that philosophy's system, but Mill even justifies the added value he discovers in terms of the old system. Mill defines the value of poetry and emotions in a relentlessly utilitarian way. He calls part of Wordsworth's "Intimations Ode" "bad philosophy," but if he does not accept Wordsworth's philosophy of natural compensation, neither does he oppose to it an inherently valuable poetic form:

> What made Wordsworth's poems a medicine for my state of mind, was that they expressed, not mere outward beauty, but states of feeling, and of thought colored by feeling, under the excitement of beauty. They seemed to be the very culture of the feelings, which I was in quest of. In them I seemed to draw from a source of inward joy, of sympathetic and imaginative pleasure, which could be shared in by all human beings; which had no connexion with struggle or imperfection, but would be made richer by every improvement in the physical or social condition of mankind. From them I seemed to learn what would be the perennial source of happiness when all the greater evils of life shall have been removed. (*Auto*, 151)

On a first reading, the evaluation in this passage sounds very much a felt rather than a reasoned one. Yet, at each important moment the verb "seemed" takes the place of "was" or "were." Is the value of poetry, therefore, illusory? No, because "the delight which these passages gave me proved that with culture of this sort, there was nothing to dread from the most confirmed habit of analysis." The "seeming" of the above passage leads to an objectively existent "delight" that analytically "proves" the value of the seeming. Mill has thus succeeded in making poetry and emotion, not bases for a new philosophy, but valuable entities in the eyes of the old one.

The drama I have been outlining here (of conversions and crises that are nevertheless not radical changes but rectifications and revisions) entirely coincides with the claims we saw Mill make, in the previous chapters, for the role of his theory of consciousness. Indeed the relationship between the general body of associational theory and Mill's special theory of consciousness that is associationally inexplicable but necessitated by associational theory is directly thematized in the *Autobiography* in the relationship between the educational process of learning and the moment in which one knows what one has learned, a moment that stands outside the education and yet is necessary for its completion. Moreover the system by which events are linked into a narrative sequence also reproduces this relationship: each moment of self-conscious knowledge sets off a chain of events linked by associationally explicable responses to the stimulus of that knowledge, as revision or rectification responds to perceived flaw. But each of these moments is itself narratively abrupt and separate, prepared for in some way by the education or experience that precedes it but, in its associationally inexplicable interior space, unlinked from the narrative sequence.

This separation leads us to the final binding of epistemology and narrative. Although each of the acts of consciousness I have been discussing is in some way an act of self-completion, because there are a number of these acts, none of them can be absolutely definitive; each must be integrated, however loosely, into the narrative sequence. But the concept of consciousness being embodied is of an event coming at the end of a series of events, at the end of a thread of experiences, of an event that sums up all events into a whole. That role Mill reserves for the consciousness that narrates the entire *Autobiography*, thus shaping his narrative as a whole in accord with the theory of consciousness that its themes and sequence embody. This definitive act of narrative consciousness, moreover, takes part in the *Autobiography*'s thematization of Mill's theory of free will and thus completes the process of narrativizing Mill's philosophy by pulling within the circle of the narrative the entire sequence of philosophic issues connected to it. It is to this narrative completion and freeing that I now turn.

Consciousness and Narrative Freedom

Within most of the psychological analyses I have discussed in earlier chapters—and the literary analyses that in one form or another derive from them—the theme of Mill's declaration of his own freedom plays an obvious role as part of the activity of the mental crisis and the consequent rebellion against his father's education. If the reading of the previous sections of this chapter is persuasive, then whatever the status of the psychological readings as an analysis of Mill, they are manifestly inadequate as formal analyses of the text of his autobiography. James Mill does not appear in it, at least explicitly, as a Blakean Urizen figure, and Mill justifies the revisions of his father's philosophy that he makes because of the mental crisis through the terms of that philosophy. Nevertheless, the issue of freedom does play a central role in the *Autobiography*, not as a result of James Mill per se but as a result of the implications of the associational epistemology to which both he and his son subscribe.

I have discussed in Chapter II the way in which associationism normally entails a causally determined rather than a free will. Mill tried to hold on to both causal necessity and freedom of the will by ascribing certain acts to internal causation resulting from moments of self-consciousness and by freeing the act of self-consciousness from associational causation, thus making its internal space, its nature, if not its occurrence, associationally inexplicable. The pertinence this argument has to my reading of Mill's discussion of his Benthamite conversion and mental crisis, and to their relation to the education from which they derived and yet changed through moments of consciousness, should be fairly clear. The issue of freedom, however, is not solved by but encompasses the mental crisis and extends more significantly to the host of figures who in some way or another make or influence Mill, not only his father but Harriet and, to a lesser extent, such subsidiary mentors and teachers as Sterling and Carlyle. And although Mill discusses his theory of free will explicitly—and rather cursorily—in the *Autobiography* (on page 177), the work's solution to the problem is embodied in its final and comprehensive act of completion through self-consciousness, the act of narration.

The fact that one of Mill's makers is his father is not the problem for him we might presume because within the rationalism in which he was trained, natural fathers have no particular metaphysical or metaphorical status. Indeed in many ways, the rationalistic world offers space for the widest possible freedom. In convincing Mill of the logical impossibility of proving the existence of God, James Mill states that

the manner in which the world came into existence was a subject
on which nothing was known: that the question, "Who made me?"

cannot be answered, because we have no experience or authentic information from which to answer it; and that any answer only throws the difficulty a step further back, since the question immediately presents itself, Who made God? (*Auto*, 45)

In this countercatechism, the world like the beings that inhabit it starts as a tabula rasa, free of any ordaining maker. Any given being, therefore, can be subject only to intermediary makers or chains of makers since there exists no known original and determining maker of the self. At first this view presents Mill with extraordinary freedom. In a world with no constraints of essence, Mill may choose who he will become by choosing who will influence that becoming. Nor does the first maker thrust upon him determine his choices irrevocably since his mind is "always pressing forward, equally ready to learn and to unlearn either from its own thoughts or from those of others" (*Auto*, 5).

Nevertheless, one must be made. Because one starts in blankness, obviously the first experience that sets up the associational process of personality construction must occur from the outside. That first moment sets off the causal chain that can encompass even later self-ordained moments. This is less a matter of philosophic logic in the *Autobiography* than of dramatic embodiment, as we can see in the critical moment in which Mill reads Marmontel:

> I was reading, accidentally, Marmontel's *Memoires*, and came to the passage which relates his father's death, the distressed position of the family, and the sudden inspiration by which he, then a mere boy, felt and made them feel that he would be everything to them—would supply the place of all that they had lost, A vivid conception of the scene and its feelings came over me, and I was moved to tears. (*Auto*, 145)

This passage is of course central to Levi's reading of the mental crisis as an abreaction on Mill's part, an acceptable working out of his wish for his father's death.[8] But we need not posit an unconscious reaction involving such a wish to see that Mill's obvious identification with Marmontel results from that author's ability to replace his father with full adequacy, thus indicating that he does not depend upon the father as sole maker of the self.

The difficulty is that one must "replace" the father; one does not create oneself anew, totally from the inside. The self thus becomes split. And

Mill's tears, in fact, do not identify him with Marmontel in that passage, since Marmontel went through the incident "sans verser un larme, moi qui pleure facilement."[9] Mill, who did not cry easily, identifies himself, through his tears, with the relief of the family, who, on hearing Marmontel's declaration of replacement, are described as letting flow "des ruisseaux des larme, mais des larmes biens moins amères,"[10] than those of their despair at the father's death. Thus Mill is the grateful spectator of Marmontel's replacement of his father as well as the son who replaces; and those vital tears of his, in gratitude for his ability to feel, connect him with the passive family as well as with the active Marmontel. Further, Mill specifically identifies the emotions as "passive susceptibilities" and intellectual powers as "active capacities." Thus, if the Mill who is self-made may move away from his father, the movement is severely limited by the fact that the Mill who is the actor in the self-making is the Mill made by the father. This fact does not merely follow from the reading of Marmontel and Mill's division between active capacities and passive susceptibilities, however. It is manifest in my earlier argument that the process of Mill's change is in precisely the terms of his father's psychology, and the valuing of new qualities is achieved through the evaluating methods of the old psychology.

Logically, of course, this problem has already been resolved in terms of the associationally unlinked interior space of self-consciousness discussed above. But a series of these moments, as I said, is not a completing moment. The theme of making and self-making, which encompasses the education and the mental crisis because it extends beyond them, allows Mill to create a definitive moment out of narrative consciousness. The next step in the process that leads to this moment posits an alternative to the act of making oneself; and it is an alternative that still exists within an associational sequence. This alternative is to choose other makers and to allow them to influence oneself in a way that, by the choice, implies one's approval, but in a way not bound to one's prior making. Thus Mill puts himself under the influence of Harriet Taylor. The balancing positions of Harriet and James Mill have been noticed by many readers of the *Autobiography*.[11]

Again, although this maneuver makes a certain logical sense, narratively it simply works to place Mill in the same position vis-à-vis Harriet that he was in vis-à-vis his father. Of his earlier propagandism he states,

It was my father's opinions which gave the distinguishing character to the Benthamic or utilitarian propagandism of that time. They fell singly scattered from him in many directions, but they flowed from him in a continued stream principally in three channels. One was through me, the only mind directly formed by his instructions. (*Auto*, 105)

Later he says of Harriet's influence on his writings,

During the greater part of my literary life I have performed the office in relation to her, which from a rather early period I had considered as the most useful part that I was qualified to take in the domain of thought, that of an interpreter of original thinkers, and mediator between them and the public. (*Auto*, 251)

In each case, Mill finds himself a conduit for someone else's thought, an intermediary. That Harriet's role is chosen by him does not change the essential passivity of his position as an effect in a sequence of causes and effects.

The solution to this entrapment within a narrative sequence does not occur explicitly within the text but is effected by the role of the narrator. We can approach this solution in terms of the formulations recent critics of the *Autobiography* have offered in order to escape from the difficult task of having to put Mill's eulogies of Harriet in some relation to the historical figure: what is important in these passages is less how true they are than what they tell us about the kind of figure Mill wanted to imagine for himself.[12] I would only add that the fact of the imaginative creation also makes Mill more than an interpreter of Harriet's thoughts. By creating the world's knowledge of Harriet, he literally makes his maker through his narrative.

Certain moments of play between narrator and agent significantly ratify this implication of the text's formal existence. These moments are infrequent and subtle in the work, yet self-estimations often occur, even if delicately made and buried beneath prose that attempts, ostensibly, to be an objective record of an experiment: "I conceive that the description so often given of a Benthamite as a reasoning machine, though extremely inapplicable to most of those who have been designated by that title, was during two or three years of my life not altogether untrue of me" (*Auto*, 111). It is in that present-tense conjugation of "conceive" and its contrast with the past "reasoning machine" that Mill completes himself. The Benthamite who had learned reasoning was not capable of conceiving himself as anything. Mill thus completes his reasoning with conception, with the ability to conceive himself, to make himself within the narrative.

We can see the effect of this narrative self-consciousness upon the associational sequence of the narrative events in the sentences that introduce the final chapter of the *Autobiography*:

> From this time, what is worth relating of my life will come into a very small compass; for I have no further mental changes to tell of, but only, as I hope, a continued mental progress; which does not admit of a consecutive history, and the results of which, if real, will be best found in my writings. I shall therefore greatly abridge the chronicle of my subsequent years. (*Auto*, 229)

This gesture of declaring the life thematically complete before the autobiography ends is not that uncommon a one. The *Apologia* makes the same claim upon Newman's conversion to Catholicism. What is odd about that statement here is that it does not seem to fit well with the claim of constant growth that has been the leitmotif behind the *Autobiography*'s themes of education and the movement from learning to knowledge. Nor will the opposition between "mental change" and "mental progress" as an explanation for the coexistence of completion and growth bear very close examination in and of itself since, as we have seen, changes are not easily distinguishable from simple developments in the accounts of the Benthamite conversion and the mental crisis. The paradox of Mill's claiming to have reached the end of a "consecutive history" still remains. Somehow, though the life still has growth, it no longer has temporal extension; the growth is now available for definition within a synchronous account. Nor does the resolution of this paradox occur within the events of the life that the *Autobiography* describes. There may have been a moment in the life when its course changed from consecutive history to continued progress, but the only moment in the *Autobiography* in which this occurs is in this statement by the narrative voice.

That statement, though, is essentially self-verifying. The claim to have grasped the life whole is borne out in the only way it can be: by the success of this passage in having done so. Moreover, the status of the sentences transforms the paradox into a dual function that is a formal possibility of narrative. On the one hand, these sentences are a summing up that stands separate from the events of the life recounted. They make statements about the shape the account has and will take: it was a history; it will be an abridged chronicle. On the other hand, this narrative moment itself is still considered to be, and is referred to, as an event in the life—what happens happens "from this time." And growth, if not change, will continue not only past whatever time is referred to but past the moment of writing this sentence. Mill will write later additions to the *Autobiography* describing later events in his life, in particular describing his political career, almost, we suspect, as a test to see if the sequence can still continue within the terms of the formulated completion.

This dual function is, of course, the narrative embodiment of consciousness as a series of events aware of itself as a series, as an act within the series that changes the nature of the series from entrapping sequence to self-ordained growth. Here the identification of philosophy with narrative is complete in Mill. The philosophic formulations of the space for free will and the structure of consciousness receive the narrative embodiment that is their final defense. Conversely, one can completely analyze the paradoxical nature and the formal status of this moment in a narrative ostensibly about constant growth only in terms of the philosophy from which it derives and that it encodes.

Part 2
Knowing Belief

Chapter V

The Philosophic Context

of Newman's *Apologia*

In addition to the *Apologia*, Newman wrote a series of different kinds of autobiographies at various points during his life, once even writing a few chapters as if he were his own future biographer, referring to himself as "Mr. Newman." The shortest of these documents is, more than any nineteenth-century autobiography, a purely meditative, self-justifying text and as such, provides a glimpse at the reason why standard Victorian autobiography reaches out toward the kinds of treatment as narrative and as philosophy that I give it in this book. In this half-page document, the events Newman records actually coincide precisely with the moments of recording:

> John Newman wrote this before he was going up to Greek on Tuesday, June 10th, 1812, when it only wanted 3 days to his going home, thinking of the time (at home) when looking at this he shall recollect when he did it.
>
> At school now back again.
>
> And now at Alton where he never expected to be, being lately come for the Vacation from Oxford where he dared not hope to be—how quickly time passes and how ignorant are we of futurity. April 8th 1819 Thursday. And now at Oxford but with far different feelings—let the date speak—Friday February 16th 1821—
>
> And now in my rooms at Oriel College, a Tutor, a Parish Priest and Fellow, having suffered much, slowly advancing to what is good and holy, and led on by God's hand blindly, not knowing whither He is taking me. Even so, O Lord. September 7, 1829. Monday morning. 1/4 past 10. And now a Catholic at Maryvale and expecting soon to set out for Rome May 29, 1846.

> And now Priest and Father of the Oratory, having just received the degree of Doctor from the Holy Father. September 23, 1850. And now a Cardinal. March 2, 1884.[1]

Because each entry records its own moment of writing, the problems of structuring one's life into a narrative out of the information and form of one's self-consciousness do not exist here. We have pure chronological progression, almost the record of pure experience. Moreover, as the first entry shows, we have in operation a consciousness whose experience of itself is almost the sole motivation for the act of recording. If we want an autobiography that avoids the trammels of narrative and philosophic motivation, that operates as pure and accurately recorded self-expression, surely this list of entries would be ideal—except that it communicates nothing either as experience or as consciousness. To avoid any undue explanation or interpretation of his recorded moments, Newman insists, "Let the date speak." But to us the date is silent, the experience a mystery. It speaks only to Newman. He had done poorly in his examination for a Trinity degree in November 1820. He would not receive the Oriel fellowship until over a year later than the recorded date, in 1822. Whatever happened in February 1821 left no external traces, and that is only the most opaque of the dates. He records not when he became an Oriel fellow, a Catholic, a doctor of divinity, a cardinal, but when he already was what he recorded. The recorded dates are at least months, and often years, late (he received the notice of his doctorate on 22 August, not 23 September, and he became a cardinal in 1879, not 1884).

This lateness of course is a necessity of writing. Writing is the only act one can describe and perform at the same moment. By recording the date of remembering to write about the event rather than the date the event occurred, Newman avoids the normal fiction of autobiography that it is the event recorded and not the act of recording that the text directly communicates. He also drains the event itself of any intrinsic significance. The issue in 1846 is not being a Catholic but writing about being a Catholic, and even about that issue, the writing tells us nothing. Writing about the act of writing is as hermetically closed as it is infinitely self-reflexive. We know Newman reflects upon himself, but what is he reflecting about? What does he think of the fact that "now" he is a cardinal? To make his reflections comprehensible to an external audience, he would have to write about their content in a way that divided the act of writing from the event written about and made that division a matter of attention.[2]

Once we attend to that division, though, we must also attend to the narrative it makes, by implication if not by explication. Why are certain events and not others told in a given order? Why are they seen as comprising a life? How is that seeing part of the life comprised, and what kind of act of seeing is it? These are all questions about how a narrative is structured and why it is structured in that way, questions of interpretation and intent. Without them, without any sense of the motivation for writing or any explanation and interpretation of the events recorded, we have nothing. Given interpretation and intent, however, the attempt to see the life as a whole and to explain the necessity for reseeing, we have the type of autobiography I have been trying to delineate, a mediating genre in which philosophic discourse (the why of the narrative) and narrative form (the how of the narrative) become aspects of each other, in which philosophic theory is transformed into narrative form even as that form can only be explicated through the theory it embodies and transforms.

The near opacity of Newman's autobiographical fragment has, then, just led us backward through autobiography's transformation of philosophy into narrative: we see the necessity of separating narrative stance from events narrated in the inability of a text to enact purely the moment of writing without disappearing into a void of self-reflexiveness. That separation constitutes the narrative structure of autobiography. Once given that structure, the attempt to explain the various shapes and meanings it can assume in specific autobiographies leads us, at least in the case of those autobiographies that participate in Victorian prose, back to the philosophic underpinnings and motivations of structure. My reading of the *Apologia* takes us once again through this connection between philosophy and narrative.

It takes us through, however, in a way very different from the way Mill's *Autobiography* did. The first difference—and for my general theory, the most important one—is the one outlined in my introduction: the structural opposition between Mill's and Newman's narrative forms and the definitions of consciousness those forms embody. For Mill, both consciousness and narration were acts within a sequence that completed that sequence without ever quite exiting from it or transcending it. Accordingly, the *Autobiography*, constructed by that system, operated through various thematizations of sequence—the life as an education, as a movement from one mentor to another—as a constant progression. For Newman, both consciousness and narration operate, not as completing acts, but as simultaneous reflections and embodiments of the essence within event sequences. The fragment we have just seen is only an exaggerated manifestation of the primary place both consciousness and narration play in Newman's work. Newman's embodiment of an epistemological and narrative opposition to Mill indicates the formal nature of the relationship between philosophy and narrative in Victorian prose by reproducing it in terms of an entirely different content.

A second difference—the considerable one between the kinds of philosophic issues that hover behind Mill's and Newman's differing epistemologies and narrative structures—may be less theoretically important, but it affects the shape of the next chapters far more obviously. The movement from philosophy to narrative in Mill was in many ways a fairly direct one since the philosophic problems discussed in the previous chapter were all intimately connected with autobiographical concerns. Mill's considerations about the problems of free will and self-conscious ordination, although they arose and were arrived at in ways different from the one the *Autobiography* suggests, had clear pertinence to his account of his mental crisis and of his relationship with his father and with Harriet Taylor. The paths from philosophy to autobiography, however, are not always so direct. The following chapter concerns areas of discourse and problems of theology and epistemology that seem, at first, very far from autobiographical concerns. The *Apologia* is very much the autobiography of a philosophy, but the philosophy whose development the autobiography narrates centers on issues that may not seem autobiographical: the relationship between faith and reason, the status of historical development, and finally, the ways in which self-conscious reason can support instinctive intuition. My chapters dealing with Newman's philosophy consider precisely these issues, but this seeming divergence from the autobiographical focus into very unautobiographical and unliterary areas of philosophic discourse is very significant for my theory. It suggests the voraciousness with which Victorian narrative, through its structural correspondence with definitions of consciousness, devoured Victorian philosophies of the most diverse kinds. Autobiographies transformed into narrative not only already amenable philosophies but ultimately all philosophies.

Indeed, that transformation, in another way, makes the issues in Newman's theology far more deeply autobiographical than those in Mill's case. For Mill, the definition of consciousness was a distinct and separate moment in his philosophic project; if one does not attend to its implications, it can even seem a tangential moment. For Newman, both the experience of consciousness and the definition of consciousness are omnipresent in his philosophy, and so all the issues raised in these chapters, as they connect to Newman's concepts of consciousness, are as autobiographically relevant as any theory of consciousness must be to its expression within an autobiographical narrative.

To understand how Newman's persistent concern with consciousness both motivated and determined the shape of his movement from philosophy to narrative, we must begin by noting the problematic aspects of that persistence and the originally unphilosophic nature of that concern. We can approach the problems created by the persistent concern with consciousness by considering the source of Newman's famous statement in the *Apologia* that his mind rested in "the thought of two and two only absolute and self-evident beings, myself and my Creator."[3] Newman intends to describe here his own primal act of consciousness. The description is also, though, a theological statement traceable back to John Calvin, who wrote: "The whole sum in a manner of all our wisdom, which only ought to be accounted true and perfect wisdom, consisteth in two parts, that is to say, the knowledge of God and of ourselves."[4] In this connection between Calvin and consciousness lies the problem that was to exercise Newman throughout his career, the problem whose solution was to determine the narrative structure of the *Apologia*. Newman's first conversion in 1816 was Calvinist, and so there was, at the time, no more problem for him than for Calvin with his perception of God within the self. Since Christianity here is first and finally a dialogue between God and the individual soul, any external ritual or regulation is in the nature of an obstruction, and any demand for argument or proof for one's contentions about the invisible world in terms of the visible world would simply be impertinence. If this formulation leads to an extreme position on the rights and prerogatives of individual intuitions, well, most Protestants were quite content to sanctify private judgment.

But the Newman who returned from Sicily as a Tractarian was not. As a Tractarian and as a Catholic, he still held that religion was based on an intuitional consciousness, but he came to believe that it was also an objective truth with authoritative demands on everyone. This position looks very contradictory, however. How can one reasonably claim that one's own subjective intuition leads to an objective truth that all people ought to acknowledge? On what basis can one demand that one person ought to assent to the conclusion of another's subjectivity? By echoing Calvin's sense of the priority of individual consciousness even as he explains, in the *Apologia*, his adherence to a faith embodied in an external authority, Newman indicates the persistence and importance of this contradiction in his thought.

Newman's pre-Tractarian, simultaneous consciousness of God and self was prior to logic and therefore also beyond argumentation or even explanation. Having introduced as a Tractarian and maintained as a Catholic, though, a belief in the necessity for an authority and a dogma binding on all men as objective truth, he had to make decisions about the status of this new belief. As a Catholic, Newman argued that the validity of a given external authority and even the necessity for such an authority were matters for reasoned intellection and not merely for intuition and even claimed for the propositions of religion the same status as the propositions of science. Having claimed an external validity for religion and religious authority and having given up pure intuition as a grounding for their claims, Newman had to articulate a philosophic discourse that provided such a grounding without opening religion to what he still realized were rationalism's fatal attacks.

This brief run-through of the philosophic dilemma confronting Newman indicates one of the revisions my theory leads to in the standard readings of his works. There are two usual readings of Newman's simultaneous claims that one intuits religious truths internally but that religious doctrines need embodiment in an external authority. The first argues that his life was a search for an authority properly constituted to serve as an external support for an internal belief.[5] The second interprets Newman as at heart a skeptic, doubting the validity of his own intuitions of God, and wanting an external authority to support his intuitions and doubts.[6] In these terms, Newman's movement toward Catholicism was simply a movement toward greater fideism and harsher repression of his skeptical intellect. These interpretations have, as their common ground, the contention that Newman's conversion to Catholicism represented an increasing attempt to affirm dogmatic religious authority while circumventing or transcending reason (depending on one's viewpoint). In contrast, my discussion of Newman's historiographic and epistemological theories shows that his conversion to Catholicism marked an attempt to find a reasoned, though not necessarily rationalist, basis both for personal knowledge and for the prerogatives of authority.

Mill's need to found political reform on both a flexible, associational psychology and the individual's ability to change himself led him to formulate his paradoxical definition of free will within associationism. Similarly, Newman's desire to claim for his beliefs about religion the status of knowledge led him, on his conversion to Catholicism, to articulate historical theory that would count as an argument for, rather than merely an intuition of, the truth of Catholicism. Because he could not finally claim that his theory demonstrated a case for Catholicism, however, he brought it to rest, if not on the intuitions it was meant to demonstrate, at least on an epistemological theory that attempted to give those intuitions the status of reasoned demonstrations. In his tentative and unpublished *Philosophical Notebook*, written mostly between 1859 and 1864, and in the final organized argument of *Grammar of Assent*, published in 1870, Newman described how one can attain a subjective certitude that is also objectively certain knowledge. In effect he argued there that while we can never demonstrate conclusively through logic or reason that any of our beliefs about the world are true, there are nevertheless certain modes of holding beliefs that occur only when the belief we hold is objectively true, and so if we hold a belief in this manner, then our belief is certain knowledge. Finally, he argued that one both recognized these beliefs as certain knowledge and transformed them into certain knowledge through a self-consciousness that has become both an intuitional given and a reasoning entity. Mill's contradictory attempt to affirm both associationism and free will came to rest in a paradoxical definition of consciousness. In the same way, Newman's contradictory desire, through historiography, to claim for religious beliefs the truth status of externally verifiable propositions, without opening those beliefs entirely to the depredations of reasoned inquiry, led him to a paradoxically doubled definition of consciousness as an unquestionable intuition and as a verifying process of reason. My explication of the philosophic situation exemplified in Newman's *Apologia* (Chapter VI) ends in this paradox.

The process, described in Chapter VII, by which Newman's autobiography operates as an exemplary narrative, explaining and evidencing his theory of consciousness, reproduces much the same process we have seen in Mill. Again, we can read an autobiography as an empirical demonstration of a theoretical construct, as a description of its writer's own self-consciousness operating in the way that writer's theory posits. The *Apologia* is perhaps particularly pertinent to Newman's epistemology because the only way to verify a belief in terms of Newman's theory of consciousness is to describe how one holds the belief, to describe one's own consciousness of one's beliefs. This situation becomes true not only of Newman's religious beliefs but also of his theories of how he holds religious beliefs since, as I argue, his theories about beliefs are finally tenable only in the way that the theory describes the beliefs themselves as tenable. To break out of this circularity, Newman constructs the empirical demonstration of autobiography, of his *Apologia*. As my reading of Mill's *Autobiography* focused on its importance to Mill's thought in the 1850s, here, again, to read the *Apologia* as a demonstration of Newman's Catholic theology turns its focus away from its putative subject—the history of his religious opinions up until 1845—to its role in the Catholic theories of the 1860s.

Like Mill, Newman uses theories held simultaneous to the writing of the autobiography to structure the narrative description of earlier events, and theories. Now, to defend philosophic theories, an autobiographical narrative must act out the construct of consciousness held by the theory in its finished form. But these theories of consciousness cannot account for their own past. Though a writer turns to consciousness as mediator when philosophic discourse breaks down, to the extent that the writer still claims to be writing philosophy, the breakdown that motivated the construction of a narrative of consciousness is precisely the thing the writer cannot make part of the theory as theory. Obviously, then, an autobiography that intends to demonstrate the empirical validity of a theory of consciousness by acting it out through a narrative structure, at the same time that it accounts for the theory's development in the narrative, cannot *accurately* account for the development since to do so would be to admit the fictiveness of precisely that which it is intended to validate as philosophy. So Mill's *Autobiography* had to construct the mental crisis in order to demonstrate the later theories of free will and self-consciousness. So Newman's *Apologia*, has to obscure Newman's early Anglican theories and redefine his conversion in order to demonstrate his later Catholic theories.

Having shown how the *Apologia* works as an exemplary narrative, I turn, in Chapter VIII, to an analysis of the working of Newman's philosophy within the narrative structure of his autobiography. That analysis returns us to a literary reading of Victorian prose in precisely the way Mill's did. Both Newman's theory of consciousness and his narrative form are in structural opposition to Mill's. Seeing consciousness as a reflection of self that develops the self of which it is conscious, Newman as narrator plays a far more evident role in the narrative structure of the *Apologia* than does Mill in the *Autobiography*, and Newman's themes and their working out follow accordingly. Despite thematic and structural differences between the *Autobiography* and the *Apologia*, however, my method for interpreting Newman's account follows exactly the method for interpreting Mill's. The knowledge of Newman's epistemology yields the structure of his narrative, and through that structure a formal, literary analysis of the *Apologia* becomes possible, an analysis that accounts for its philosophy as imbedded within its form, shaping and shaped by that form.

Chapter VI

From History to Consciousness

At first glance, Newman's historical justification of Catholicism seems a natural place to turn to find a theoretical context for the *Apologia*. The autobiography's subtitle (at one point its title) is, after all, "A History of My Religious Opinions," and using such a rubric to label one's life presents a clear opportunity to compare one's theological development with the pattern of doctrinal development one sees in church history. Moreover, Newman's historical theory represents his central attempt to justify the validity of Catholic authority in terms of an external, evidential discourse. As such, it could well play the kind of central role in his thinking that might make of it a structuring principle for his autobiography. Finally, Newman wrote his primary historical text, *An Essay on the Development of Christian Doctrine*, during the period of his conversion, effecting the conversion after he finished a draft of the book. Since an important aim of the *Apologia* was to explain and defend his conversion, the book on development and its theory clearly have both a logical and a chronological pertinence to the autobiography.

Indeed for all these reasons and in all these ways, Newman's historical thinking does bear significantly upon the *Apologia*. But it does not do so ultimately as a *historical* theory. In the first section of this chapter, I argue that at a vital moment Newman uses consciousness as a model for historical development, making changes in the status of the historical theory. Consciousness becomes more and more the primary concern and historical development more and more an example of a certain reliable mode of consciousness. Newman's necessary theoretic goal then becomes one of delineating this mode of consciousness and justifying its occurrence as evidence of the truth of the propositions of which it is conscious. And the structure of consciousness he delineates in *Grammar of Assent* becomes both the philosophical context for and the narrative structure of the

Apologia. So much are the two theories, in final form, a part of each other that, although it is helpful, it is also deceptive to separate them and write as if one superseded the other. Just as to understand Newman's concept of historical process, we have to understand its basis in Newman's model of the mind, to understand the claims Newman makes for that model and to understand how and why the model structures the autobiography, we have also to understand its historical extensions. In other words, if Newman's history is finally consciousness writ large, the consciousness he argues for is paradoxical precisely because it can claim to externalize itself into history.

The Development of a Historical Theory

We must separate Newman's historical and epistemological theories in the first instance to indicate the original role of the historical theory and thus the paradoxical role of the epistemological one. The historical theory derives from, and at times operates as support for, Newman's insistence as a Catholic that the content of religion is scientific and constitutes knowledge in the same way that science does. This assertion occurs again and again in *The Idea of a University*. The very basis for that work's claim that the teaching of theology cannot be ignored by any place of learning, that it constitutes knowledge as much as any science, is that it is true in the same way as science: "Religious doctrine is knowledge, in as full a sense as Newton's doctrine is knowledge."[1] But the claims of science rest on external evidence, not on the strength with which Newton or others held to their particular beliefs.

Consequently, in his first attempt to provide a basis for Catholic authority and to validate its claim of infallibility, Newman took one of the boldest steps of his intellectual career. He left the realm of personal faith and introduced the concept of history:

History is not a creed or a catechism, it gives lessons rather than rules; still no one can mistake its general teaching in this matter, whether he accept or stumble at it. Bold outlines and broad masses of colour rise out of the records of the past. They may be dim, they may be incomplete; but they are definite. And this one thing at least is certain; whatever history teaches, whatever it omits, whatever it exaggerates or extenuates, whatever it says or unsays, at least the Christianity of history is not Protestantism.[2]

The boldness of the maneuver consists both in the problems it seemed to solve and in those it seemed to create. History, as the record of material events, can indeed be used as a form of empirical evidence, a response to those who say that religious choice is a matter of opinion or sentiment.[3] If it does indeed present "lessons" and offer "bold outlines," then Newman would seem to have entered the realm of intellectual discourse. He would have found a basis for his claim that religious teachings ought to be accepted as information of objective fact. But there is also a threat. The inductive study of history is, after all, generally the practice of skeptics and atheists, of Gibbon and Hume. Newman would thus seem to have opened religion in general and Catholicism in particular to just the kinds of arguments he generally found impertinent and irrelevant, to the attacks of empirical reason.

The study of history per se would not, of course, present any threat to religion. To understand the nature of Newman's innovation, we have to turn for a moment to the beginnings of the debate between Protestants and Catholics over the issue of which church was an impure novelty and which offered pure, primitive doctrine. Although in both the *Apologia* and *Essays Critical and Historical*, Newman formulates the issue as one of Catholicity against antiquity, the terms of the original debate in fact differed slightly.[4] The argument at first was between primitiveness and perpetuity. The Catholics in the seventeenth century argued that Protestantism was prima facie a novelty, that there were no Protestants before Luther. The Protestants responded that Catholic doctrine was a novelty, that the gospels did not sanction its practices. Obviously, at this point, the argument was a simple standoff. Both sides had to turn to history. The Protestants tried to show that Catholic doctrines had been introduced in the Middle Ages; the Catholics, particularly Jacques Bossuet, took their stand not on development, but on continuity, using history to prove there had been no change.[5] Although both sides turned to history in this dispute, neither did so to understand or record a temporal process, for both were antihistorical, trying to show the absence of historical change.

Newman's redefinition of the debate, however, in his Anglican writings, changes its necessary grounds. He offers this hypothetical interchange between a Catholic and a Protestant:

Angl.—We go by Antiquity; that is, by the Apostles. Ancient consent is our standard of faith.

Rom.—We go by Catholicity. Universal consent is our standard of faith.

Angl.—You are cut off from the Old Fathers.

Rom.—And you are cut off from the present living Church.[6]

To reverse a Newmanistic formula, the Protestant is where he always was, defending himself on the basis of antiquity and primitive purity. The Catholic, however, no longer disputes change but, abandoning the defense of perpetuity, introduces one of Catholicity. Again, the argument is a standoff. To the extent that the Catholic, by choosing Catholicity as his ground, tacitly admits the fact of some kind of historical change having occurred in Catholic doctrine, though, he must now explain how that change may be concordant with the church's claim to embody the original faith.

In his *Essay on Development*, Newman starts not merely by offering a defense of change but by mounting an argument through which change becomes evidence of the validity of the Catholic church's claim to constitute an absolute authority. In doing so, he introduces into the argument a very different view of history,[7] one that may act as a positive empirical defense of Catholicism but may also open religion generally to the attacks of skeptic, inductive historians. He takes the Protestant charge of innovation and redefines it into its own justification:

> It is indeed sometimes said that the stream is clearest near the spring. Whatever use may fairly be made of this image, it does not apply to the history of a philosophy or belief, which on the contrary is more equable, and purer, and stronger, when its bed has become deep, and broad, and full. It necessarily rises out of an existing state of things, and for a time savours of the soil. . . . In a higher world it is otherwise, but here below to live is to change, and to be perfect is to have changed often. (*DCD*, 40)

To accept that perfection in religious doctrine must result from historical change rather than seeing such change as a process whereby the original revelation may become deformed or degraded, we must begin with the assumption that revelation is like any other historical occurrence, a natural event subject to natural laws. If revelation emanated directly from God, it would have, by definition, to be perfect, and, of course any change from perfection would have to be a change for the worse. For revelation, then, to be like other ideas, at the beginning marred by earthly taint, savouring of the soil, it must—at least in its articulation as material text—be a natural event like those ideas. In this case, the historical process of change can be seen as a process of purification, and change itself can be seen as a possible indication of perfection.

Newman does not strictly maintain that if an idea has a history of change, it is therefore a true or perfect one. Still, one can at least say that, while an idea may not be true simply because it has a traceable history, it will certainly be to some extent false if it does not have one since new ideas have not had time or opportunity to be purified by the articulations of the historical process. But historical development is here merely a negative test. It does not prove an idea's truthfulness but only shows that we cannot know that that idea is not false. Because Newman often holds a purely organic view of corruption, however, the continued existence of a body of thought that has also undergone change through history does become a presumptive argument in favor of its truth:

> Now it is plain, first of all, that a corruption is a word attaching to organized matters only; a stone may be crushed to powder, but it cannot be corrupted. Corruption, on the contrary, is the breaking up of life, preparatory to its termination. (*DCD*, 170)

By this organic analogy, an idea that becomes corrupt will either cease to exist or at least cease to be even remotely recognizable, in its new form, as an outgrowth of an older idea. Clearly the Catholic church has neither ceased to exist nor become unrecognizable in a new form. Since Catholicism had both maintained and developed Catholic doctrine through a long historical process and had not ceased to exist, that mere existence, in Newman's theory of history, provides a strong positive indication that the body of Catholic teaching is objectively true. Newman's historical theory seems to form an argument for Catholicism that has the support of more than simply subjective intuition, an argument that offers a historical case for Catholicism as the authority that properly teaches objective religious truths.

There was some question, though, whether Catholics would accept this view of history, and consequently this argument, any more than Protestants did. It looked, after all, suspiciously like the kind of historical theory that Mill, influenced by the distinctly un-Catholic Comte, was trying to spread in England. Materialists more normally argue growth as a positive good and process as a sign of progress toward a better state than do Catholic theologians, and that argument is used more frequently against Catholicism and religion in general than in favor of either. But Newman's argument was not in fact quite purely inductive or based all that firmly on an analogy with organic growth.[8] Because with the theory of history and development based on an analogy with growth, he combines a far more traditionally Catholic view of the problem of development, the positive argument for Catholicism just described will not hold up. Thus the persistent conflict in Newman's thinking—the conflict between an objective justification of authority and faith on the one hand and an intuitively based assertion of them on the other—recurs.

Newman's basic image for doctrinal development, first articulated explicitly in his final *Oxford University Sermon*, has no necessary organic element. In the sermon "The Theory of Development in Religious Doctrine" (written in 1843) and in the *Essay on Development* (1846), Newman depicts the activity of development as an act of furthering one's understanding:

> St. Mary is our pattern of Faith, both in the reception and in the study of Divine Truth. She does not think it enough to accept, she dwells upon it; not enough to possess, she uses it; not enough to assent, she develupes it, not enough to submit to the Reason, she reasons upon it. . . . And thus she symbolizes to us, not only the faith of the unlearned, but of the doctors of the Church also, who have to investigate, and weigh, and define, as well as to profess the Gospel.[9]

This theory is Newman's nearest approach to an organic concept of development (as opposed to the organic idea of corruption discussed above). The historical development of church doctrine is likened to the activity of the mind in thinking and reflecting; and the mind's activity—since the Romantics, at least—has often been thought of as an organic process. This epistemological analogy also creates considerable space for allowable doctrinal change. It does not, however, really assume that any change that is not corruption must therefore be growth, nor is the biological identity between the mind at one point and the mind at another the protection of doctrinal integrity as it would be in a thoroughgoing organic model. The quoted explanation stresses an essential identity between the formulation that a church doctor's or Mary's reflection results in and the aspect of revelation that sets that reflection in motion. For all the leeway it allows for development, this concept rests on a notion of a stable truth whose changing forms are necessitated by the limitations of human understanding.

If Newman's theory does present a workable hypothesis for explaining doctrinal development, it still does not really offer the kind of positive defense of Catholicism and its specific doctrinal changes that the organic discussion of corruption seemed to suggest. The claim that the developed doctrine has interpretive or logical unity with original revelation explains change as really a matter of surface appearance and argues for an essential unity between revelation and its developments. This formulation of the working of doctrinal development justifies the appearance of historical change within the church, but it cannot use the fact of change as an indication of truth in the manner that the metaphor of corruption suggested because it does not really admit the fact of change. Even if one granted that, provided the church's developed doctrine were of the type Newman claimed, it would not then represent a change of original revelation, one could still question whether in fact its specific changes in dogma represented advances in the interpretation of revelation or simple misinterpretations.

To deal with this problem, Newman gives to his argument, at the outset, a deductive turn:

> It is not a violent assumption, then, but rather mere abstinence from the wanton admission of a principle which would necessarily lead to the most vexatious and preposterous scepticism, to take it for granted, before proof to the contrary, that the Christianity of the second, fourth, seventh, twelfth, sixteenth, and intermediate centuries is in its substance the very religion which Christ and His Apostles taught in the first. (*DCD*, 5)[10]

This statement does not absolutely deny the possibility that there has been corruption and change away from revelation; but it thrusts the *onus* of proof on the accuser: "Of no doctrine whatever, which does not actually contradict what has been delivered, can it be peremptorily asserted that it is not in Scripture" (*DCD*, 71). Short of such an exhibition of inconsistency, Newman's theory remains tenable. If one takes the theory of development as a simple hypothesis in response to a difficulty, an attempt to explain an apparent inconsistency within a theory one already holds, then there is nothing illogical about giving it this deductive structure. If one believes in Catholicism but finds apparent changes in doctrinal positions a stumbling block, Newman's theory does indeed offer a workable hypothesis to explain the apparent changes. At the outset of this chapter, however, we saw Newman claiming that history explains itself to the observer, that "bold outlines . . . rise out of the records of the past." If Newman intends the implication here that the historical record is evidence of Catholic truth, then the assumption we are asked to allow becomes a monumental example of question-begging. If history, in its own bold outlines, provides an argument for the consistency and validity of Catholicism, then we should not have to assume that consistency and validity in order to see the outlines.

Newman seems to be trapped, then, in a series of equally disastrous alternatives. If he maintains that history is at least an objective indication, if not a proof, of the validity and consistency of Catholic authority, he will be found to beg the major question when he refers certain historical difficulties to an assumption of the validity of that authority. If, however, he argues that he is only removing a difficulty in a theory already held by presenting a historical hypothesis, we return to the question with which we began this section: What is the basis for maintaining Catholic truth to be objective? How can we get from a subjective faith to an objective knowledge? Newman's response to this dilemma is twofold. First, he defines a form of development that contains within the historical process the deductive assumption that protects it. He does this, however, through various extensions of his epistemological model, and so, since he no longer has a strictly historical argument on his hands, he redefines the nature of his discourse, moving toward the epistemological argument that the *Grammar of Assent* will accomplish.

In the original theory of development, despite the epistemological turn of the analogy between development and the reflective process of Mary or a church doctor, that process did not take place in the mind of any single believer or thinker. The unifying, original content of revelation was given from the outside, and specific theologians further articulated it by reflecting on that content and interpreting its meaning. This formulation clearly led to the possibility that a separated thinker or even tradition could arrive at an interpretation not contained in the original revelation.[11] And if Newman argued that the church's infallibility protected against such a misinterpretation becoming part of church dogma, he would be begging the question of the status of doctrinal change. He avoided this trap in later texts by resituating both the unifying idea of Christianity and the mind in which development took place.

Those texts see the church as relating to the revelation it articulates as doctrine in the way a mind relates to its own intuitions when it articulates them as conscious knowledge. Thus rather than being always there but not always known, revelation is always known but not always known consciously. The church's declaration is thus compared to one's first attending to something one has always believed in:

> This is sure to befall a man when he directs the attention of a friend to a truth which hitherto he has thought little of. At first, he seems to be hazarding a paradox, and at length to be committing a truism. The hearer is first of all startled, and then disappointed; he ends by asking "Is this all?" It is a curious phenomenon in the philosophy of the human mind, that we often do not know whether we hold a point or not, thought we hold it [sic]; but when our attention is once drawn to it, then forthwith we find it so much a part of ourselves, that we cannot recollect when we began to hold it, and we conclude (with truth), and we declare, that it has always been our belief.[12]

This formulation does indeed skirt the whole issue of defending new doctrines. If the church is always aware instinctively of the whole body of Christian truth, then historical development becomes simply a matter of an act of self-consciousness extended through a large period of time. Newman places the instinctive knowledge of revelation—he calls it a "phronema"—within the body of the laity. Authoritative decisions are a reflection of this phronema: "The people are a mirror in which the Bishops see themselves."[13] Thus, together, the laity and the church hierarchy operate as a single mind.

As an argument for how newly declared Catholic doctrine may be really identical with original revelation, this epistemological model may be quite satisfactory. As an argument for how we may know that the declarations of the church in fact have this status, the model has two problems. First, as with the original formulation, this model may tell us how we may see developed doctrine as part of original revelation, but it is not an argument for that identity since it already assumes it and then explains how it occurs.[14] Second, even if we assumed that development worked this way, it would still not guarantee the validity of church doctrine since the coming to consciousness of an intuition does not say anything about the truth of that intuition, and we do not know that the intuition itself is true unless we return to an Evangelical defense of intuition.

The answer to the second objection, in fact, makes the first nugatory. The act of self-consciousness to which historical development is compared is not simple reflection but is explicitly connected with the activity of reason. Thus, whether or not this thought process will lead inescapably to true statements, it at least does not claim validity on the basis of its own internal emotional state. In a paper, unpublished in his lifetime, in which he responded to questions about his theory of development, Newman compared the activity of church development to the activity of interpreting Aristotle:

> What do we mean by a man's being *master* of any subject, say science? What is meant by knowing the Aristotelic philosophy? Does it mean that he has before his mind always every doctrinal statement, every sentiment, opinion, intellectual & moral tendency of Aristotle? This is impossible. Not Aristotle himself, no human mind, can have a host of thoughts present to it at once. . . . A learned Aristotelian is one who can answer any whatever philosophical questions in the way that Aristotle would have answered them. If they are questions which could not occur in Aristotle's age, he still answers them; and by two means, by the instinct which a thorough Aristotelic intellect, the habit set up in his mind possesses; next by the never-swerving processes of ratiocination.[15]

An Aristotelian, then, first knows Aristotle instinctively and afterward complements that instinct with ratiocination. Each one protects the other. In the case of the Apostles, clearly no one theologian can claim this kind of knowledge. The church, however, is the perfect theologian. What an Apostle was in his person, the church is in its history.[16] It has the fullness of revealed knowledge in the phronema of its faithful, which it clarifies, protects, and makes conscious doctrine in its historical actions. It is evident at this point that Newman's theory of development is no longer a historical justification at all. All of these formulations assume the church's historical identity and tell us how that identity operates epistemologically. History is no longer the basis for a defense of Catholicism as truth but the evidence for the propriety of an analogy between the church's de-velopment and the process whereby an individual reaches a knowledge of truth. Newman must now justify that process.

We are now returned, however, to the problem with which we started, only in redoubled intensity. Newman has found an epistemological basis for arguing that the church is consistent. But since the consistency is a psychological phenomenon, we can no longer take the church's historical endurance as an argument for its validity. A person can be wrong and remain wrong. Further, since history as an objective basis for accepting Catholic authority no longer exists, why should we accept as that basis Catholic authority's having convinced someone else? In short, how can the arguments of an individual or an authority, based on the subjective factors of antecedent presumptions, instincts, and phronemas, become an objective validation, even if they are worked out by "never-swerving pro-cesses of ratiocination"? We can reasonably expound upon an instinct as long as we like and yet, one would think, it would remain an instinct. To the extent that it was an instinct shared by everyone, its validity would not need to be argued for. To the extent that it was not so shared, an argu-ment for its validity could not really depend upon its instinctiveness.

History has moved in Newman's thought from an external phenome-non to the record of a psychological one. At first, history was to be the external discourse that validated the claims of Catholic authority to ar-ticulate objective knowledge. But when it became an example of a certain kind of thought process, Newman was returned to the problem with which he began: the problem of claiming that religious doctrine has the same objective status as the statements of science or philosophy but with-out opening it to the demands we make of those discourses to demon-strate the validity of their statements either empirically or logically. To resolve that problem, he needs a theory of epistemology that will allow an individual and an authority to reach an objective truth with an essen-tially subjective method. But the historical theory was not simply a false step for Newman. That theory's combination of temporal distance and the appearance of difference in various doctrinal statements with essential unity recurs at crucial moments in his epistemology, and so the resulting structure of the *Apologia* is based on an epistemological theory that con-tains within it a historical theory that makes the meditative recounting of one's own history take on polemical value.

A Grammar of Certitude

For convenience, I have structured this chapter as if Newman, in the course of the 1850s, turned from a historical to a psychological defense of faith. To a certain extent, this structuring is deceptive. Newman intermittently recognized that his historical theories were tied to certain epistemological presumptions. After he had finished *Grammar of Assent*, he dated his first attempt at its composition as 17 June, 1846 (*AW*, 269), less than a year after his conversion. Conversely, he never completely dropped the use of historical argument. The last sections of *Grammar of Assent* are permeated with history, and his two late pamphlets, *The Letter to Pusey* and *The Letter to the Duke of Norfolk*, both use arguments based on historical development. A more accurate way of describing the movement of this chapter's first section would be to call it a change of emphasis. Newman's psychology of faith became increasingly more important until, finally, historical development became simply a large version of the psychological process of reaching certitude. That process, I now argue, came to rest on a paradoxical definition of consciousness.

To see how the *Grammar of Assent* acts as a buttress for Newman's historical theories and how it attempts to make a certain way of perceiving the objective truth of Catholicism a proof of that truth, we must first see the book as in fact concerned with finding a way to show how the beliefs of faith may be taken to be objectively true. Such a reading of the book is hardly uncontentious. Indeed, critics usually argue that in the *Grammar* Newman was concerned only with justifying the subjective state of faith as a proper response to the unknown and not necessarily with proving that faith provides objectively correct information about that unknown.[17] As recurrent as this interpretation of the work is, though, I think Newman's own statements about his intents lead to a view closer to the one I am presenting here.

The traditional reading of the work is perhaps based on the focus implied by its title, *Grammar of Assent*. Newman does not argue for the objective validity of all assents, only for the naturalness of assent as a mental state and, therefore, its justifiability. If the *Grammar* were mainly about assent, therefore, it would concern merely the justification for believing on objectively insufficient evidence rather than the justification of religion as objective knowledge. But if this were his sole concern, Newman need never have gone on to define that form of assent he labels "certitude." He offers that second definition, though, to reaffirm in this work his statement in *Idea of a University* that religious doctrines embody knowledge in the same way that other propositions do. Like the earlier work, the *Grammar* insists:

> In this day, it is too often taken for granted that religion is one of those subjects on which truth cannot be discovered, and on which one conclusion is pretty much on a level with another. But on the contrary, the initial truths of divine knowledge ought to be viewed as parallel to the initial truths of secular: as the latter are certain, so too are the former.[18]

Again, to assert that religious knowledge is knowledge in the same way as secular, that we may be rightfully as certain of the one as of the other, Newman must indicate that our belief in religious knowledge has either the same foundation as do our beliefs in secular knowledge or a foundation of equal strength and reliability. Now one's holding an unconditional assent can never, for Newman, imply that one is therefore undeniably correct or that one necessarily assents only to certain knowledge. Assents are arrived at in too many questionable ways and are too often mistaken for Newman to argue that because we assent to it, a proposition is therefore true. Nor can he argue that only assents based on irreproachable reasoning should be held as certainly true, for clearly, religious assents do not fit that description.

Newman wants in the *Grammar*, then, to define a subjective state of holding a belief, a state that, by the nature of the way we hold the belief, rather than as a result of the reasons for our holding it, we know to be a belief in a true proposition. This state he labels "certitude," and his definition of it makes clear that he defines it not only by the way the belief is held but by the belief's objective correctness. Thus he distinguishes between conviction and certitude:

> I have one step further to make—let the proposition to which the assent is given be as absolutely true as the reflex act pronounces it to be, that is, objectively true as well as subjectively: —then the assent may be called a *perception*, the conviction a *certitude*, the proposition or truth a *certainty*, or thing known, or a matter of knowledge, and to assent to it is to know. (*GA*, 195–196)[19]

Convictions, then, are *all* consciously held or reflex assents. Certitudes are held in the same way but are a subcategory of convictions. They are reflex assents in true propositions. Newman never gives external objective methods of making this distinction, but that is the very point of his theory. He argues that objective measurements do not exist but that there are subjective procedures for reaching an objective truth and knowing it to be such. If Newman can in fact describe a way of attaining and holding a proposition such that the subjective acts of attaining and holding indicate an objective validity, then he will have provided a reliable way to defend the infallibility of Catholic authority. Then, by stating the reasons behind his own belief in that authority, he will have put the pieces of his historical defense back together.

To create this form of subjective knowledge, Newman begins by denying inferential certainty to any form of reasoning that is not, like mathematics, based on self-contained abstractions:

> While we talk logic, we are unanswerable; but then, on the other hand, this universal living scene of things is after all as little a logical world as it is a poetical; and, as it cannot without violence be exalted into poetical perfection, neither can it be attenuated into a logical formula. Abstract can only conduct to abstract; but we need to attain by our reasonings to what is concrete. (*GA*, 268)

The purpose of this argument becomes clear when Newman considers the difference between an inferential conclusion and an assent. According to Locke, the strength of our assents ought only to equal the strength of the reasons that lead to them. It follows that, for Newman, except in the realm of mathematics, Locke's theory will never allow us unconditional assent because we can never have indefeasible reasons. But we are subjectively certain of the truth of some propositions, such as that we shall die or that England is an island. It therefore follows that as a matter purely of accurate psychological description, we ought to differentiate between an inferential conclusion (which, on Lockean grounds, can never be sure) and assents (which hold propositions to be true and not simply highly probable, regardless of the strength of the inferential evidence on which they rest). Unlike inferential conclusions, assents are unconditional. Here we come to the central stone in Newman's argument for the necessity of defining a mode of belief that believes what is true but that can be recognized as such a belief in terms of its subjective characteristics alone.

Newman has shown that our beliefs about the empirical world, our experiential conclusions, are as radically uncertain as any other of our apprehensions or beliefs, even our religious beliefs. He has also argued that, regardless of this logical cause for complete uncertainty, we do in fact come to certain conclusions that dissociate themselves from their inferential bases and become unconditional assents. Now a strict empiricist could argue that our making such assents does not prove that we ever have the logical right to make them. Newman would respond, though, that such a position is obviously unreal. It may be that, in terms of strict logic, we ought not to be certain of the proposition "we shall die," but we are certain, and common sense tells us that we are right to be. Despite the absence of logical or evidential demonstrability for any proposition, not only are we sure of some propositions but we allow that some of the propositions we are sure of, such as that we shall die, are objectively and certainly true. In other words, unconditional assent not only does exist but is assent to objective knowledge in some cases. Sometimes we can be certain. If we could only know when we are right to give unconditional assent, we would then know when we can be certain. We cannot know that on the basis of external evidence since no evidence is ever absolutely conclusive, but perhaps we can know it by how we hold the assent, by attempting to differentiate between assents and certitudes.

Newman does not argue, however, in the way some of his critics claim, that in a world where no knowledge is certain, we have as much right to believe one thing as another. He does not offer complete credulity as the alternative to complete skepticism. Defining *one* form of belief as belief of certain knowledge entails defining other forms of belief as not certain, thus refusing to argue that the act of belief is its own justification. To distinguish between modes of belief, then, Newman establishes a distinction between a simple and a complex assent. A simple assent, which is an unconditional holding of a proposition based only on probable evidence, is also unreflective, not necessarily even conscious of itself as assenting to the proposition. One may, however, choose to investigate the reasons behind a simple assent since "Acts of Inference are both the antecedents of assent before assenting, and its usual concomitants after assenting" (*GA*, 189). In such a case, if the original assent is reconfirmed, one has reached a complex assent.

This reconfirmed complex assent is now given greater validity than the simple assent had:

The new assent differs from the old in this, that it has the strength of explicitness and deliberation, that it is not a mere prejudice, and its strength the strength of prejudice. It is an assent, not only to a given proposition, but to the claim of that proposition on our assent as true; it is an assent to an assent, or what is commonly called a conviction. (*GA*, 195)

It would seem that Newman has made a definite turn here toward objective criteria, the turn implied in his discussion of how the Aristotelian scholar and the church achieve certain knowledge. The distinction between prejudice and conviction is that prejudice is simple, willful assertion whereas conviction involves a deliberate, rigorous, reasoned investigation of one's grounds before the reconfirmation of the assent.

But the new criteria are by no means completely objective. The activity of reflection does not, and obviously cannot, discover objectively certain proofs behind its assent. It simply makes the more or less probable inferences explicit and then consciously recreates the leap across the gap between probable inference and unconditional assent by renewing the decision to hold the assent. We should not, it would then seem, depend absolutely on the new assent's validity; and Newman's previously cited distinction between convictions and certitudes indicates that he recognized the remaining subjective element in his epistemological construct and, therefore, the residual possibility of error. The question, then, remains: is there any possible route from a conviction to a certitude that, by definition, would be a perception of a truth?

Before I discuss the problem of distinguishing between conviction and certitude, though, I must backtrack a moment in order to show the importance the distinction and the epistemological theories in general have for the earlier historical theories and how the historical theories shaped the epistemological ones. Whereas a certitude involves a deliberate, self-conscious investigation, a simple assent verges on being unconscious. It is an assent that people "barely recognize, or bring home to their consciousness or reflect upon as being assent" (*GA*, 211). The result of this description of simple assent is the possibility—indeed in religion the likelihood—of believing what we do not know we believe:

Thus, as regards the Catholic Creed, if we really believe that our Lord is God, we believe all that is meant by such a belief; or, else, we are not in earnest, when we profess to believe the proposition. In the act of believing it at all, we forthwith commit ourselves by anticipation to believe truths which at present we do not believe, because they never come before us. (*GA*, 151)

This may seem like an extreme formulation. We do not normally consider that by committing ourself to one proposition, we commit ourselves to all corollary propositions, much less that to actually believe the first proposition, we must already believe the others without even knowing them. Yet the theory follows necessarily from the hypothesis of unconscious simple assents,[20] and if all a simple assent entails is unconditional belief, it does seem an accurate description to say that we do assent unaware to numberless propositions.

The value of this theory to Newman's historical construct should be obvious. The instincts and phronema, the simple faiths and unpremeditated holdings of partial aspects of the inexpressible, full idea of Christianity— all these states—are states of simple assents. The acts of self-conscious development, of reasoning out and then affirming doctrinally, are the processes that lead to and then declare certitude. If a psychological theory demands that when we assent to a belief, we also assent to all beliefs corollary to it, then any belief that developing doctrine declared true would already have been implicitly believed by the phronema of the faithful. The problem of new revelation is thus eliminated. Certitude does not substantively change its assents, cannot if it is to be certitude. Rather, it reaffirms the assents with a new strength by bringing their content to consciousness. New theological formulations, in the same way, do not change original revelation but rather confirm it by increasing our consciousness of it. Further, in the same way that certitude implies the objective truth of the proposition it concerns, so development along these lines implies, rather than becomes an object in the way of, the infallibility of the Catholic church, which undergoes this process.

Moreover, as certitude writ large becomes a model for the working of church history, so church history may become a method of achieving certitude. Newman's final explanation of the status of his historical argument was not that it was objectively unanswerable but that it was persuasive to him. That argument now becomes its own kind of unanswerability. The historical explanations Newman offers are not arguments per se but self-conscious workings out and affirmations of arguments to which he has already given assent. As such, if they can be differentiated from convictions, they constitute certitudes, perceptions of that which is objectively true. Newman's theory of history is, then, buttressed by his theory of certitude even as his own act of certitude is given substance by his theory of history. This mutual interdependence, however, will only hold up if Newman can indeed create a firm distinction between the two kinds of complex assent, convictions and certitudes, can show us a way to determine when a conviction is a conviction of something that is true.

Newman's theory, of course, will not allow any objective methods of distinguishing. There are, however, subjective indications of whether we have properly arrived at a certitude—primarily the feeling that accompanies it:

> [Certitude] is accompanied, as a state of mind, by a specific feeling, proper to it, and discriminating it from other states, intellectual and moral, I do not say, as its practical test or as its *differentia*, but as its token, and in a certain sense its form. When a man says he is certain, he means he is conscious to himself of having this specific feeling. It is a feeling of satisfaction and self-congratulation, of intellectual security, arising out of a sense of success, attainment, possession, finality, as regards the matter which has been in question. (*GA*, 203–204)

Certitude is, in short, accompanied by a feeling of "self-repose." Newman explicitly denies that this is an objective test. Rather, he locates a subjective state, a sense of serenity, of knowing one has resolved a problem, and marks that state as evidence of holding a certitude. Stated so baldly, this criterion may not seem very strong, but in fact Newman does not think the feeling of repose comes easily. He insists that certitudes are rare, that people who say they are certain of a proposition usually have only a conviction of its probability and that when they are brought to book, they suddenly discover they are less sure than they thought (*GA*, 200). If one could identify when one had this sense of repose, a sense strong enough so that one experiences it rarely and can identify its uniqueness, then one could reliably distinguish between convictions and certitudes.

The essential problem with this method of distinguishing between convictions and certitudes is that the activity that distinguishes is also the activity distinguished. Complex assents, convictions, and certitudes are all acts of self-consciousness in Newman's theory. They involve bringing to one's awareness both the content of a simple assent and the content of the inferences that support the proposition to which one has assented. Distinguishing between conviction and certitude, however, or between certitude and false certitude, are all also acts of self-consciousness. Instead of becoming aware of the content of belief, we become aware of the manner in which we hold it, aware of whether or not we are secure, reposeful, and sure in our belief. But this is simply an extension of self-consciousness, not a qualitatively different kind of self-consciousness. In effect, then, in the act of distinguishing between types of convictions, between certitudes and false certitudes, we do not really end the problem but push it one step further back. In using consciousness to distinguish between types of consciousness, we have only created the need for a further judgment about the consciousness that distinguishes, a judgment that can only be carried out by a consciousness that will need to be further judged. Newman often presents certitude as a kind of infinite progress of self-affirmation: I know, I know that I know, I know that I know that I know (see, for instance, *GA*, 197). But his theory implicitly sets in motion the reverse process, an infinite regress of self-inquisition: I think I know, I think I know I know, and so on.

To snap this chain as thoroughly as Mill in Chapter II snapped the causal chain entrapping the will, Newman starts by blending together our perceptions of phenomenal and noumenal reality. In addition to arguing that empirical discourse does not offer any more objectively demonstrable knowledge than does any other kind of discourse, Newman also argues, effectively, that our apprehensions of and assents to propositions about the empirical world are not qualitatively different from our apprehensions of and assent to propositions of any other discourse about any other level of reality. He does distinguish between what he terms real and what he terms notional apprehensions and assents. This distinction, however, applies solely to the mode in which we apprehend and assent, not to the content of what we apprehend and to what we assent. A notional apprehension or assent is an apprehension of or an assent to pure abstractions; it perceives a relationship between terms without understanding or experiencing the referential content of the terms. Thus, I may apprehend the mathematical formula, if $a = b$ and $b = c$, then $a = c$, without knowing or caring what a, b, or c stand for. A real apprehension or assent is, at the first level, simply one concerning concrete propositions such as "the sun shines" or "the tree is in front of me." So far, there is nothing revolutionary about this distinction. Newman continues, however, to say that we may have a real apprehension of or assent to abstract formulas if we invest an abstract proposition's terms with experiential meaning. Thus I may apprehend the proposition "John is evil" notionally if the term *evil* is only a moral abstraction for me, but I will apprehend it really if I invest the term *evil* with some experiential significance such as "causing pain to others." It follows that even highly abstract propositions, those concerned with philosophy or theology, such as "God exists" or even "God is unity in trinity" may be apprehended really, in the same way as we apprehend the proposition "the sun shines."[21]

If we assent in the same way to propositions about our empirical experience and to propositions concerning abstract, generalized conclusions, then effectively there is no difference between perceptions of sense data and judgmental conclusions. If our apprehension of and assent to the proposition "the sun shines" is not different in kind from our apprehension of and assent to the proposition "God exists as unity in trinity," then the basis for the trustworthiness of the first will also be the basis for the trustworthiness of the second, and Newman can thereby present trust in one's own judgment, one's own consciousness, in the seductive light of the sole alternative to the complete skepticism involved in mistrusting our senses:

> If I do not use myself, I have no other self to use. My only business is to ascertain what I am, in order to put it to use. It is enough for the proof of the value and authority of any function which I possess, to be able to pronounce that it is natural. What I have to ascertain is the laws under which I live. (*GA*, 347).[22]

This passage again sets up a situation in which consciousness investigates self, "ascertain[s] what I am," in order to protect the use of the self's faculties. The faculties themselves are tested, though only to see that they accord with natural usage, not to see that they accord with any real situation. This situation breaks the original regress because the consciousness that identifies certitude does so merely by establishing it as a natural faculty without necessarily investigating its own activity within that certitude. Once that faculty has been identified as a natural part of the mind, we can no more question its informations than we can question the informations of sense data. As we must accept, barring the unusual danger of hallucination, that what we perceive in fact exists, we must assume that the apprehensions of our other faculties are also accurate. The alternative to either would be the end of thought and discourse.

The problem with this argument is that it proves too much. Any assent—since assents, like certitudes, are natural faculties—can be given the priority of a perception. Newman explicitly does not want to argue that all assents are accurate, that we should trust all our assents, for that argument would offer credulity as the sole alternative to skepticism. Rather than establishing certain formulations of religion as objectively accurate, that theory would justify any individual in the entertainment of his own prejudices. But if we must trust all our faculties, assent is, after all, as much a natural faculty as certitude. Thus once our consciousness has determined that we have assented, that assent would have the trustworthy status of any empirical perception, of certitude itself.

The solution to this problem, the reason Newman was never really aware of it as a problem at all, involves a definition of self-consciousness that Newman never emphasizes but that he implies in *Grammar of Assent* and delineates in the *Philosophical Notebook*. He never emphasizes the definition because a clear articulation of it, I think, makes its equivocal nature all too obvious. Yet it is precisely that equivocal nature that both holds together Newman's attempt to extract objective knowledge from subjective intuition and finally drives Newman from philosophy to the empirical demonstrations and narrative transformations of autobiography.

The first half of this equivocal definition of consciousness involves Newman's identification of it with the reasoning process. We have seen that he differentiates certitudes, as complex assents, from simple assents by their added awareness of the reasoning process that led to the original assent. Certitude, then, assents both to the original assent and to its evidential basis. But elsewhere Newman identifies certitude with the simple act of being aware of one's own assents:

> Certitude, as I have said, is the perception of a truth with the perception that it is a truth, or the consciousness of knowing, as expressed in the phrase, "I know that I know," or "I know that I know that I know,"—or simply "I know;" for one reflex assertion of the mind about self sums up the series of self-consciousness without the need of any actual evolution of them. (*GA*, 197)

This passage discusses no act of reason, inquiry, deliberation, at all. Certitude involves simply knowing that one knows. Yet surely, if as the passage suggests, certitude refers to self-consciousness without deliberation, then the objectifying criteria Newman gives certitude in order to differentiate it from such assents as prejudice would not necessarily be contained in all acts of certitude. Certitude would not necessitate the full and rigorous use of all the intellectual faculties of the subject, and it would not be, consequently, a rare occurrence. To make this passage correspond to the *Grammar's* general definition that certitude involves an awareness of its evidential basis, we are forced to infer that self-consciousness automatically entails reasoning, that as soon as we are conscious that we know, we are also conscious of why we know, that one act is identical with the other.

This identification is more probably Newman's implication than my inference since he argues for it explicitly in a passage in the *Philosophical Notebook* that confronts the associational theory of knowledge:

> My point is, not to deny that our knowledge comes from experience, not to advocate inner forms, but to say that our experience is not so much of external things, but of our own minds.[23]

This passage is perhaps not quite as conciliatory as Newman thinks. If we can have an experience of our own minds that is separate from our experience of the external world, then the mind must be an entity separable from the external sensation it receives, a contention that a consistently held belief that all knowledge is experience cannot really uphold. Newman confirms his separation from associationism in a statement immediately following that contends that, while the soul does not think in the complete absence of external stimuli, nevertheless, "as soon as it *is* roused, it reflects on itself, and thereby gains a number of ideas, quite independently of the external world."[24] Whether Newman realizes it or not, this statement depends upon "inner forms," a mind with a preexisting formation. If the statement is not quite as uncontentious as he would like to suggest, it is nevertheless a clear attempt at compromising between the claims of intuition and experience. And the compromising agent is self-consciousness. The mind may contain ideas independent of the external world, but those ideas can only be obtained through the mind's reflection upon itself, and that reflection is set off by external experience. Self-consciousness here, in opposition to the mind or soul, is clearly a reasoning entity. It experiences, reflects, learns.

This identification of consciousness with reasoning and deliberation tells us why certitude, by being an act of consciousness, automatically involves such reasoning and deliberation, but more, it removes the problem that Newman's claim that we must trust all our natural faculties, once we identify them as such, seems to entail, removes the problem of presuming that all assents are assents to truth. When consciousness identifies a belief in a proposition as an assent, a natural faculty, and reconfirms the assent, at the same moment, it also automatically transforms the assent into a certitude. In becoming aware of the assent, consciousness must reason upon it, know why it knows as well as that it knows. And in that act, it has created the complex assent of certitude.

But certitude was originally placed at the same level as a sensation and an assent in order to remove the problem of differentiating it from conviction. That act of differentiation, being like certitude, an act of consciousness, threatened an infinite regress of consciousness judging consciousness. Accordingly, certitude, and therefore its consequent acts of self-consciousness, were made unquestioned natural faculties, thus transforming the regress into a self-contained whole. Such an argument implies, however, that in addition to being a divorced act of reasoning, consciousness is also a primary, unquestionable epistemological act. And Newman makes this implication, as well as the other one regarding consciousness, quite clear:

> Our consciousness of self is prior to all questions of trust or assent. We act according to our nature, by means of ourselves, when we remember or reason. We are as little able to accept or reject our mental constitution, as our being. We have not the option; we can but misuse or mar its function. (*GA*, 61)

The passage sounds much like the previously quoted one that claims for acts of judgment the status of acts of sensation. The key phrase, here, however, is "our consciousness of self is prior to all questions of trust or assent." In the passage just cited in the *Philosophical Notebook*, consciousness is the reasoning, experiencing faculty, and not consciousness but the unconscious mind has ontological priority. This passage suggests, however, that consciousness has the same priority.

To accept both these tenets of consciousness will solve Newman's problematic alternatives. The first alternative opened certitude to demands of rigorous investigation without opening it to them enough to differentiate it reliably from conviction and thus left it unable to know when subjective belief constitutes objective knowledge. The second alternative solved that problem by claiming all natural faculties as inherently trustworthy once we are aware of them as faculties but was thus unable to distinguish certitude from assent and so suggested that all unconditional belief is equally trustworthy and each individual has a right to his own. To the extent that consciousness entails reasoning, it always transforms any assent it both becomes aware of and confirms into reasoned, deliberate certitude. But it remains an ontologically prior act, one whose informations are unquestionable. To accept both these tenets, however, involves accepting an equivocal definition of the content of consciousness: on the one hand it must be divorced enough from the mind, the self, to reason upon it in reflection; on the other hand it must be integral enough to the self to be an unquestionable primary faculty.

We can see how this ambiguity in Newman's definition of self-consciousness leads to the breakdown of philosophic discourse in a passage in the *Grammar* that offers an analogical explanation for the reliability of certitude. It is here that philosophy starts to be replaced by metaphor. Here too we can see the place for Newman's *Apologia* in his philosophy:

> We do not dispense with clocks, because from time to time they go wrong and tell untruly. A clock, organically considered, may be perfect, yet it may require regulating. Till that needful work is done, the moment-hand pehaps marks the half-minute, when the minute-hand is at the quarter-past, and the hour hand is just at noon, and the quarter-bell strikes the three-quarters, and the hour-bell strikes four, while the sun-dial precisely tells two o'clock. The sense of certitude may be called the bell of the intellect; and that it strikes when it should not is a proof that the clock is out of order, no proof that the bell will be untrustworthy and useless, when it comes to us adjusted and regulated from the hands of the clockmaker. (*GA*, 233)

The evasions of this passage lie in the phrases "organically considered" and "hands of the clockmaker." If we consider the normal—normal at least since Burke and Coleridge—opposition between an organic and a mechanistic system, it is odd to hear a clock being spoken of as "organically considered." The whole point about mechanisms, for those who reject them as fit analogies in certain cases, is that they are not organic; and therefore to compare them with things organic, to compare a clock with the universe or the mind, is a profound mistake, the mistake in fact of eighteenth-century rationalists. If we take the phrase in an older sense as meaning simply "considered as a system," or "considered as something organized," then it makes more sense, but the comparison of the mind to a clock runs directly contrary to everything Newman says in the *Grammar* about the mysterious, unmechanical, organic methods of the mind's reasoning process, about the intuitive qualities of the illative sense. Consciously or not, Newman wants the phrase to work both ways, I suspect. The intended meaning of the phrase would seem to be "a clock considered as an organized system," but the force of the phrase is the suggestion that a clock can be considered as like an organism and therefore can be compared to the mind. Thus the mind has the organized, reliable, comprehensible quality of a machine and yet that mysterious integrity, superseding reason, with which we endow organic wholes.

The next and most obvious problem is the identity, in this analogy, of the clockmaker. If the bell of the clock is certitude, Newman cannot mean the regulator to be ourselves since the process of arriving at a certitude is precisely the process by which we regulate our assents. Surely the clock cannot be its own clockmaker, regulating itself. But if the clockmaker, as in the frequent use of the simile, is God, then the passage becomes a monumental case of question begging. Certitude allows us to know certainly of God's existence despite the absence of logical proof or conclusive evidence. But how can we assume as the regulator of our certitudes the object of one of them? If we are wrong in our certitude of God's existence, who is to do the regulating?

As the word *organic* has to be taken in contradictory senses for the passage to make complete sense, the term *clockmaker* must be taken both to mean God and to mean ourselves. The regulator is God to the extent that clocks need clockmakers if they are to be regulated, to the extent that despite the attempt of the *Grammar* to make the process of acquiring sure knowledge an entirely internal one, an external object is needed to assure the validity of our certitude. Yet the regulator must be ourselves because the starting point of the *Grammar* is that demonstrative proof exists only in closed systems, that we can never have a definitive external measurement of the accuracy of our thought. The images of clockmaker and organic clock in effect contain in their metaphoricity the equivocal role consciousness plays in the philosophy as a whole. The clock, as organic, is both a reliable machine and a living entity. The clockmaker is the thing outside ourselves that is still of ourselves.

The *Apologia* can offer the experiential evidence of Newman's own consciousness as a demonstration that, equivocal or not, the philosophic definition of consciousness is empirically valid. In offering this demonstration, more than merely arguing for an isolated definition, the *Apologia* attempts to bind together the history of Newman's religious opinions as well as to recount them. We must remember that the dual definition of consciousness does not nerely solve some local problems of the *Grammar*. The *Grammar* addressed the central problem of Newman's intellectual career as a Catholic: the search for a definition of religion that made its teaching objective truth, protected by authority and discovered, at least to some extent, by reason. This definition could not, however, open religious arguments to the demands of objective verifiability we usually make upon an argument that claims to convey objective knowledge. Like Mill's theory of consciousness, though seemingly a subsidiary issue, Newman's definition becomes a central one through its importance to the rest of his theoretical constructs. Even more than Mill's definition, though, it holds within it the central response to the contradictory nature of Newman's religious theory. Consciousness is both objective, an act of reasoning, and subjective, a mental act of unquestionable ontological priority. That form of consciousness would make religion both an objective entity and a mental act that cannot be analyzed provided the *Apologia* could only make of the definition an empirical fact.

The amenability of the definition to embodiment in autobiographical narrative should not surprise us, moreover. Newman's theory of epistemology has moved constantly toward the kind of self-containment we often find in fictional narrative. If we ignore for a moment the definitional problems I have been discussing, the *Grammar* offers indeed the perfect self-confirming theory. By consciously articulating a certain belief in the theories he states, Newman can enact a certitude about the theory of certitude he posits. The definition of consciousness gives some logical support to the theory, upholding the validity of such self-confirmation, but it does so only if one will hold contradictory tenets within one definition. Of course, consciousness is the area where logical discourse breaks down for a Victorian, for an agnostic empiricist like Mill as well as for a Catholic ontological theorist like Newman. If a definition of consciousness can be empirically verified, then it will have all the support it can have. Thus the path from Newman's definition of consciousness to the exemplary narrative demonstrating that definition in autobiography is prepared. After all, what better document than an autobiography to verify a self-confirming theory of consciousness? In effect, the *Grammar* outlines a situation in which a meditative decision becomes an argument for the objective validity of that which the meditation decided was correct. It is a model for autobiography as argument by example, and the *Apologia* enacts that model.

Chapter VII
Belief as Example:
The Polemic of Self-defense

Arguing for the relevance of Newman's epistemological theories to the *Apologia*'s account of his conversion demands some biographical defense. After all, Newman did not write *Grammar of Assent* until 1869, five years after he completed the *Apologia*. In addition, there is a more obvious cause for the *Apologia*'s existence: the controversy with Kingsley. The chronological difficulty at least can be dealt with rather easily. Although Newman did not settle down to write the *Grammar of Assent* until the late 1860s, he had first projected a major philosophic work in 1859. At that time, his writing was delated to Rome on suspicion of heresy as a result of the *Rambler* article, *On Consulting the Faithful in Matters of Doctrine*. Although this affair was not cleared up, or Newman even made fully aware of the gravity of official suspicion, until 1867, he knew that Catholic authority was distrustful of him. So the time was not right for further polemical writing, and he turned to the philosophic problems that had been at the back of his mind since his conversion. Between 1859 and 1864, he wrote the memoranda that make up the *Philosophical Notebooks* from which I have been quoting.[1] Thus, theories not published until after his autobiography were actually worked out in the years immediately before it.

The Catholic hierarchy's suspicion of his ideas and the height of the English Protestant public's hostility toward him led him to turn from public argument and occasional writing to the working out in private of philosophic theory. But, at the same time, both the antagonism of his Catholic and Protestant audiences and his own sense of the importance of the theories he was working out led him toward breaking his silence with a theoretically pertinent autobiography. Newman felt that as a result of the public's hostility, his potential contribution toward a philosophy of religion was going to waste. He thought there was, then, an explicit, practical connection between rehabilitating his reputation and publishing his ideas:

> I should wish to attempt to meet the great infidel &c. questions of the day, but both Propaganda & the Episcopate, doing nothing themselves, look with extreme jealousy on anyone who attempts it. (*AW*, 259)

Only by establishing himself as trustworthy could he possibly argue in favor of ideas that were suspect in the eyes of a fearful and conservative Catholic hierarchy on the one hand and a hostile Protestant public on the other. The situation was obviously as ripe in its own way for the composition of an autobiography to explain and justify a philosophy through the empirical evidence of a life as had been Mill's plans in the 1850s to produce a philosophic pemican headed by his *Autobiography*.

The connections among Newman's philosophy, the time period in which the *Apologia* was written, and the kind of autobiography it is can be specified in far greater detail, though. To show in its concrete particularity the way in which the *Apologia* enacts an ostensibly empirical demonstration of Newman's epistemology, this chapter approaches the linkage from three directions. First, I argue that a close examination of the Kingsley controversy does not undercut a case for the philosophic motivation of the *Apologia* but instead shows how Newman's actions within that controversy move it in directions that would give an autobiographical response certain kinds of philosophic and theological relevance. Second, I discuss how Newman's historical and epistemological theories allowed self-explication to act as polemic—but only if that self-explication had a certain shape. Thus, as a result of the exigencies of his later theories, Newman is forced to reinterpret and reconstruct his conversion and the theories leading up to it through the narrative of the *Apologia*. Third, I show that, as in the philosophy proper, the theoretical twists of the *Apologia* are justified by a particular kind of self-conscious act, a moment that ostensibly embodies empirically the paradoxical structure of self-consciousness Newman outlined in the *Grammar* but that is, in the last analysis, entirely a creation of the narrative.

The Kingsley Controversy

The *Apologia* is one of the few autobiographies of which the situation of composition is fairly familiar—indeed virtually part of the text itself in that the book is often published in company with the pamphlets that led to its writing, as if to say they are necessary for understanding it. Looking at those pamphlets in the context of letters Newman wrote to friends as the controversy with Kingsley mounted, we begin to see the philosophical context that that controversy would construct for the writing of an autobiography. Those letters indicate that Newman wanted the battle with Kingsley to be on very specific issues and that if the war of pamphlets did not go in the proper direction, he was willing to drop it. Before he had even issued his first pamphlet, though after many of the letters it contained had been written, Newman was considering his options. Here was his first:

> To write a pamphlet—Well, I could make a short but telling one, out of the correspondence which has passed, consisting principally of *my* letters to MacMillan. But Cui bono? If they would have gone on, speaking of "Roman duplicity," "St. Alfonso," or my own delinquences in *act*, such as Number 90, Whately's charge against me of remaining a crypto-papist in the Anglican Church etc., etc. then, I could have written what would have been *worth* writing, both as regards the doctrine of Truth, and my own history. But this apparently is not on the cards.[2]

He was not interested in yet another controversy over a particular Protestant slander of Catholics, nor even over yet another accusation that he was a puzzle-headed skeptic. He wanted a particular mixture of charges that would connect a defense of his Catholicism with a defense of his personal history. And a close reading of the pamphlet he issued shows, in fact, that if such a charge was not on the cards, he was perfectly willing to shuffle and redeal.[3]

As the controversy proceeded, Newman became even more explicit about his intentions. Again writing to Badeley, this time after Kingsley's pamphlet had been advertised but before he had read it, he was no longer in doubt about what he expected:

> Now I am expecting Kingsley's Pamphlet on "What does Dr Newman teach?" [sic] for which of course I have prepared myself from the

first. I mean, I never had an opening to defend myself as to various
passages in my life and writings, and I have always looked forward to
the possibility of that opening being presented to me. I have for a
long time been attempting to arrange my letters and papers with a
view to it.[4]

It must be remembered that he had not seen Kingsley's pamphlet at this
point. Without reading it, he clearly felt that the cards had been adequately redealt. It is hardly surprising, then, that when he read the pamphlet, he did not long deliberate on the proper response. His "perplexity
had not lasted half an hour" (*Apologia*, 12) for the simple reason that he
had determined his response before the pamphlet ever appeared in print.

We can see how Newman directed his pamphlet at realigning the original controversy by looking at Kingsley's original charge:

Truth, for its own sake, had never been a virtue with the Roman
clergy. Father Newman informs us that it need not, and on the whole
ought not to be; that cunning is the weapon which Heaven has given
to the saints wherewith to withstand the brute male force of the
wicked world which marries and is given in marriage.[5]

There are two parts to the accusation. First, Kingsley states that priests
were morally lax with regard to the practice, not the teaching, of truth.
The second charge is that Newman teaches that truth for its own sake
"need not, and on the whole ought not to be," considered a virtue. The
distinction is an important one. Kingsley does not charge Newman, at
this point, either with lying or with holding an overly broad or skeptical
definition of what constitutes truth. Kingsley's first charge was, as
Newman said in the letter to MacMillan, not of real interest to him. The
second was not remotely defensible, a fact that caused the exchange of
letters that form the body of Newman's pamphlet. He was on firm ground
in these letters since Kingsley was unwilling to admit and unable to defend the palpable libel of his charge.

Nor was Newman really interested, I think, in either the libel or the
indefensibility of the second charge. While the letters themselves address
the question of Kingsley's unwillingness either to lay distinct passages before Newman in substantiation of his characterization of Newman's writing or to admit that he could not, the appended "Reflections on the
Above" nudges Kingsley in the direction of the charges Newman wanted

to answer. In the "Reflections," the imaginary dialogue has Kingsley agree to take Newman's word that he had never taught truth not to be a virtue, and the following exchange ensues:

> My *word*! I am dumb. Somehow I thought that it was my *word* that happened to be on trial. The *word* of a Professor of lying, that he does not lie!
>
> But Mr. Kingsley re-assures me: "We are both gentlemen," he says: "I have done as much as one English gentleman can expect from another."
>
> I begin to see: he thought me a gentleman at the very time that he said I taught lying on system. After all, it is not I, but it is Mr. Kingsley who did not mean what he said. "Habemus confitentem reum." (*Apologia*, 352)

If Kingsley could have kept his wits about him, he would have seen that Newman's irony rests on misrepresentation. Kingsley had never charged Newman with being a liar but with being a faulty teacher of morality. He could, therefore, quite consistently take his word for not having taught a thing since it was *not* his word that was in question.

Nor is there any chance that Newman would have missed such a distinction. Indeed, he reinstates it in the text of the *Apologia* when he argues that the fact that St. Alfonso Ligouri taught that lying was in some cases allowable did not indicate anything about Ligouri's own standard of morality (*Apologia*, 247–248). He had good reason to suspect, however, that Kingsley would miss the distinction, at least in the case of Catholics. After all, the tone of the original passage, if not the content, indicated a blurring of that line: the Roman clergy did not practice truth; Newman taught that they need not; it would seem that the one follows from the other. Newman was only pushing Kingsley to make explicit the implied charge of lying lurking beneath the indefensible but actual charge of having taught lax morality.

He was also encouraging a specific version of the charge of dishonesty. In the letter to Badeley, he had hoped that the charge that he was a "crypto-papist" as an Anglican would be brought up in the controversy, and his pamphlet makes one clear attempt to move the dispute in this direction. Twice he refers to the sermon "Wisdom and Innocence" as a Protestant sermon, once in the letters and once, putting the words in Kingsley's mouth, in the "Reflections." Kingsley charges him in his own pamphlet with obfuscation here. Kingsley would certainly not have called that sermon Protestant, and Newman himself had always been known to scorn the term and never apply it to himself (*Apologia*, 380). Newman had two responses to the charge. The first is unanswerable. Kingsley's case would not have been any better had Newman used the label "Anglican sermon" (*Apologia*, 400), for either way, the sermon was strictly irrelevant to Newman's teachings as a Catholic. The second response, however, is rather less convincing. Newman argues that as a Catholic he calls things Protestant that as an Anglican he would not because his points of reference had changed (*Apologia*, 401). In fact, with the exception of that pamphlet, Newman never did refer to himself as a Protestant. The distinctions between Protestant, Anglo-Catholic, and Catholic were always active ones for him. Moreover, he must have known that, almost as a direct result of the Oxford movement, the term *Protestant* had distinct resonances in the English ecclesiastical vocabulary and that it was not a term likely to be used, either by friends or enemies, as a description of a Tractarian sermon.[6]

Why, then, if the term *Anglican* would not have lessened the magnitude of Kingsley's blunder in citing, as a gloss upon Newman's Catholic tenets, a sermon written previous to his conversion, did Newman use the obviously more inflammatory term *Protestant*? The answer is, I think, simple. By for a moment emphasizing the division in his thought (not a normal procedure for him), he hoped to maneuver Kingsley into raising the old charge that Newman had been a covert Romanist. This might seem an overly subtle ploy to achieve such a specific end, but the letter to Badeley before his pamphlet indicates that he was hoping for such a charge, and the letter after it, before Kingsley's reply had appeared, indicates that he was expecting it. Moreover, Newman had good reason to suspect that Kingsley would react on cue. In the first place, the charge had been a common one, and in the second, Kingsley's use of the title "Father" rather than "Dr." to describe Newman as author of an Anglican sermon suggested that he placed some credence in the charge.[7]

Finally, I have been giving a picture here of Newman slyly manipulating Kingsley into a desired position, baiting two hooks, both of which Kingsley obligingly devoured. As a corrective to the standard picture of Newman innocently responding to an outbreak of pure bigotry, or even the more moderate one of Kingsley luckily fulfilling all the demands in an opponent for which Newman could have hoped, I think such attention to

Newman's rhetorical strategies in his pamphlet is useful. Still, he did no more than put Kingsley in a position in which Kingsley already felt comfortable. Newman's effort was not really to occupy the firmest ground he could, but simply the most pertinent. Kingsley's original accusation was the most easily refutable but also the least resonant. To make his defense polemical, his autobiography an expression of his philosophy, Newman needed to confront the issues of consistency and honesty. To bring these issues to the forefront, he did no more than nudge Kingsley in the direction of making clear what he had already implied in the original libel.

If we place the Kingsley controversy back into the context of the philosophy discussed in the last chapter, the reasons Newman wanted to face the specific charges of covert Romanism and dishonesty become clear. The charge of covert Romanism carries with it issues of the status of Newman's conversion and the reasons he once did not believe and later did believe that the Roman Catholic church represents an infallible authority in matters of religious dogma. These issues in turn revolve around the central philosophic problem of his career, how one can know that religious beliefs are objectively true without subjecting them to the canons of logical inquisition and external calibration that guarantee the status of scientific propositions. Thus to answer the charge of covert Romanism, Newman must explain the development of his beliefs and why they can now be said to have attained certitude; and his own life can be constructed into an example of his theories. The only way to answer the charge of dishonesty, of course, is to explain the content of and reasons for holding his beliefs and the reasons behind the changes he made in them. By doing this, of course, he also makes explicit, through conscious awareness, his inward assents, thus enacting that mode of holding beliefs which he claims is certitude. Consequently, defending the honesty of his beliefs against Kingsley makes of his autobiography an act of certitude and thus an argument in favor of those beliefs and the philosophy behind them. The extraordinarily felicitous title of Kingsley's pamphlet, "What, Then, Does Dr. Newman Mean?" stressing through its ambiguity a connection between the meaning of Newman's teaching and his life, only enhanced the philosophic and autobiographical relevance of the accusation of dishonesty.

Kingsley's charges, which Newman wanted so much to confront, give the *Apologia* its point and philosophic purpose. But they also result in its reconstructive fictiveness. Using his Catholic theories as the grid through which to see his Anglican life was both necessary to his structuring of that life and the purpose behind writing the life at all. The structure those theories gave was both the necessary condition of writing the autobiography (how was Newman to depict the validity of his conversion if he did not have a theory about how one knows when one has reached truth?) and the purpose of writing the autobiography. It was also, however, the structure that forced Newman to redefine his conversion and his past Anglican theories.

Rewriting a Theory

At the most general level, the necessity of either writing or rewriting early theories is I think endemic to Victorian autobiographies of conversion:[8] To the extent that one mounts a definition of consciousness to solve a problem that had led to a conversion and then structures one's autobiography in accord with that definition, one must describe the conversion in terms of theories that one could not have held at the time of the conversion. One must describe the activities of one's consciousness according to presumptions about self and perception that would not have influenced the way one perceived at the time of conversion or before. Nor is the problem simply one of disengaging narrative structure from the events narrated. Both the primary event and the narrative structure of an autobiography are consciousness. One does not shape the other; both shape each other.

One aspect in particular of his epistemological and historical theories led Newman to a particular formulation about his earlier theories, his conversion, and his later theories. That formulation is I believe demonstrably inadequate, but it is so theoretically and narratively satisfying that it has warped Newman scholarship ever since. It is that Newman's conversion involved no central change in any of his earlier beliefs, that his Catholicism was simply the working out of what he had always believed as an Anglican. The most obvious response to Kingsley's charge of being a dishonest, secret Romanist would of course have been to argue that while he at one time held certain religious beliefs, he had in all honesty changed them. Such an argument would not let him model his life on his historical theory of development, however, because that theory requires, for a development to be proper, that it involve no central change in the beliefs developed. More important, the *Grammar of Assent*'s definition of certitude and when it can occur does not allow a certitude ever to arise from a precise change of mind.

The reason for this limit upon certitude is quite simple: in the terms of Newman's theory, one cannot *reliably* change one's mind. This is so for Newman even though on one level the statement appears simply not true of the theory owing to the many mechanisms for changing assents, both deliberate and below the level of thought. For example, one may simply grow into and out of some assents, as one may grow into and out of habits (*GA*, 185). Here, however, the new assent has no more validity than the old, as neither is self-consciously investigated; both are essentially unconscious. One can also change an assent as a result of an investigation that turns into an inquiry, but here again, one does not actually change one's thoughts but consciously uncovers what it is that one thinks. When Newman describes a shift of thinking in which "at first no language could be too bold," but it is then found that "second thoughts are best, and their giving way shows that the belief did not come up to the mark of certitude" (*GA*, 200), it is not a change of certitude that occurs in the second thoughts. Rather, one discovers that actually the assent was to a probability that one's reflexive deliberation mistook for an assent to a truth. All of these changes adjust the mechanisms of subjective apprehension without discovering anything about the external world. One cannot reliably change in the sense of simply discovering a new truth about that world. One can, of course, attain to a new assent or discover a new truth, but the new assent or the new discovery is not very trustworthy because the evidences of the external world are always doubtful. Only repose and indefectibility, measures of subjective stability, mark certitude.

In terms of his views of historical development, this gap in the theory obviously poses no problems. Stability—the reflective development of one's views in the face of the world's constant innovations, novelties, heresies—is the mark of a pure and living doctrine. Indeed, by fashioning his life according to his model for certitude, Newman could use historical arguments both as reasons for his conversion and as validations of that conversion's accord with the proper mode of development. What he could not do was indicate that he had made any radical change in his earlier beliefs, not at any rate if he were to characterize his conversion as that conscious working out of prior assents that leads to certitude. Thus he had to deny the differences between his Anglican and his Catholic theories and replace them with his *narrative* reinterpretation of his conversion and the events leading up to it.

Indeed, one of the clearest indications of the *Apologia's* revision of Newman's life is in the details of those theories he describes as having changed and those he states remained stable. The only revision in his theories that he admits is an abandonment of his early anti-Catholicism, and he describes that conviction so as to differentiate it clearly from his other beliefs:

> The thought remained upon me as a sort of false conscience. Hence came that conflict of mind, which so many have felt besides myself;— leading some men to make a compromise between two ideas, so inconsistent with each other,—driving others to beat out one idea or the other from their minds,—and ending in my own case, after many years of intellectual unrest, in the gradual decay and extinction of one of them. (*Apologia*, 20)

Now a certitude is marked not only by a deliberate, self-conscious assent but by a repose that accompanies it, indicating that the mind, on that issue, is at rest. By describing his conviction of Catholic heresy as entailing "intellectual unrest," Newman thus shows it to be a false certitude, open to be safely changed in accordance with the demands of his philosophy.

On the more central issue of justifying the acceptance of faith on only probable grounds, Newman's account of his earlier theories and that account's implicit claim of consistency with his later Catholic beliefs come perilously close to simple misrepresentation. He ascribes to John Keble the Evangelical doctrine that makes love the safeguard of faith:

> I considered that Mr. Keble met this difficulty by ascribing the firmness of assent which we give to religious doctrine, not to the probabilities which introduced it, but to the living power of faith and love which accepted it. In matters of religion, he seemed to say, it is not mere probability which makes us intellectually certain, but probability as it is put to account by faith and love. (*Apologia*, 30)

Newman does not state directly that he disagreed with this formulation, but he does suggest that he went much further:

> I did not at all dispute this view of the matter, for I made use of it myself; but I was dissatisfied, because it did not go to the root of the

difficulty. It was beautiful and religious, but it did not even profess to be logical; and accordingly I tried to complete it by considerations of my own, which are to be found in my University Sermons, Essay on Ecclesiastical Miracles, and Essay on Development of Doctrine. My argument is in outline as follows: . . . that certitude was a habit of mind, that certainty was a quality of propositions; that probabilities which did not reach to logical certainty might suffice for a mental certitude; that the certitude thus brought about might equal in measure and strength the certitude which was created by strictest scientific demonstration. (*Apologia*, 31)

It is well that Newman admitted he used Keble's argument, because he used it centrally in the *University Sermons*;[9] and the theory he attributes to himself here as an Anglican is far more a description of his later theories than of the *University Sermons*. The dead giveaway is the use of the term "certitude" and its distinction from "certainty," a distinction that exists nowhere in the works Newman lists. At best, we might read it into certain of their passages. He is clearly placing a later theory into an earlier context, and the reason is not hard to find. By giving himself the later theory, he gives himself the ability to describe his conversion along its lines as an act of self-conscious reasoning.

Constructing a Conversion

We can see Newman describing his own consciousness in the third chapter of the *Apologia* along precisely the lines laid out by his theory. The third chapter is vital to Newman's description of his conversion because it describes the one aspect of that conversion that had never been generally known and that has since been the cause of critical dispute: the theological reasons, apart from his problems over Tract 90, for his decision that Catholicism was the one true faith. Those reasons are important to Newman's account, not only because they make the conversion seem the act of an incisive intelligence rather than that of a fanatic, but also because they constitute the inquiry and investigation into the bases of one's assents that the *Grammar* makes a condition of certitude. Those same reasons enable Newman to use the kinds of historical arguments that both show Catholic theology to be a development, rather than a departure, from primitive religion and show his conversion to be a development, rather than a departure, from his own original theology.[10] Thus the conversion, in Newman's account, enacts a certitude in its affirmation of the assents it comes to understand; and the description within the narrative enacts a further, definitive certitude in its conscious delineation as certitudes of the reflex assents of his conversion. Since the *Apologia* first appeared, however, many critics have thought the reasons outlined in the third chapter—particularly Newman's discovery of the historical significance of certain heresies and the theological significance of Augustine's statement about the value of Catholicity—were afterthoughts, the real reason for his conversion being his reaction to his treatment by the Anglican authorities.[11]

This interpretation faces one serious problem, however. Newman documents profusely his responses between 1839 and 1841, the period covered in Chapter III; and sources outside the *Apologia* seem to substantiate the central incident of his troubled reaction to Cardinal Wiseman's article on early church heresies and its citation of Augustine. Newman tells us in the *Apologia* that he read the article in the middle of September 1839, after his troublesome reading into the Monophysite heresy (*Apologia*, 109). And a letter of 22 September, 1839, refers to his reading of Wiseman:

> Since I wrote to you, I have had the first real hit from Romanism which has happened to me. R.W., who has been passing through, directed my attention to Dr. Wiseman's article in the new "Dublin." I must confess it has given me a stomach-ache. You see the whole history of the Monophysites has been sort of an alterative. And now comes this dose at the end of it. . . . I seriously think this a most uncomfortable article on every account. . . . I think I shall get Keble to answer it . . . but you don't suppose I am a madcap to take up notions suddenly—only there is an uncomfortable vista opened which was closed before. I am writing upon my first feelings.[12]

The letter seems to indicate a reaction very much along the lines described in the *Apologia*. Newman is troubled but willing to wait upon further thought. Still, although there is a seriousness about the magnitude of the problem, there is also a clear playfulness about the letter, especially in its extended medicinal analogy. Moreover, Newman seems genuinely confident that the problem will be answerable; he even attempts to relegate it to Keble, who was not, it should be remembered, the foremost theorist of the movement.

Newman had good reason not to be very concerned. The arguments from his reading of the Monophysite heresy and from Wiseman's article were simply not that new to him. In the 1836 article "How to Accomplish It," he had already confronted the issue of Catholicity, both with regard to Augustine's commentary on the Donatists and with regard to the Monophysite heresy.[13] Moreover, even if we assume that problem was suddenly brought home to him by the article, we find that he has returned, by 1841, to his standard response:

> People shrink from Catholicity and think it implies want of affection for our National Church. Well, then, merely remind them that you *take* the National Church, but only you do not date it from the Reformation. In order to kindle love of the National Church, and *yet* to inculcate a Catholic tone, nothing else is necessary but to take our Church in the Middle Ages.[14]

Catholicity is indeed a desideratum. But there is no reason to assume that at the points of divergence, it is the Roman Catholic church that has remained stable. The Anglican church may also be given roots in the Middle Ages.

The *Apologia* is on even flimsier ground in asserting that it was Augustine's phrase "*securus judicat orbis terrarum*" that really struck Newman as vital. Ultimately, of course, we cannot be sure that he did not react to the phrase. The fact remains, however, that while he mentions Wiseman's article frequently and his concern with the various heresies even more constantly, in letters both before and after the conversion, he never mentions the importance of the phrase itself or even quotes it. And there is a suspicious aspect to the description of its import in the *Apologia*. Augustine was supposed to be telling him in 1839

> that the deliberate judgment, in which the whole Church at length rests and acquiesces, is an infallible prescription and a final sentence against such portions of it as protest and secede. (*Apologia*, 110)

But deliberation, rest, and acquiescence are the marks of certitude only in Newman's later theories, not in the earlier justification of infallible authority. Again, it seems that Newman is restructuring the earlier experience to accord with the later philosophy.

One final indication remains that the importance Newman placed on the theoretical justification of authority was very much an afterthought.

He realized when he was writing Tract 90, he tells us in Chapter II, that he was responding to a crucial question: "The question of the Articles came before me. It was thrown in our teeth; 'How can you manage to sign the Articles? they are directly against Rome'" (*Apologia*, 78–79). Yet he states of the public reaction, "I was quite unprepared for the outbreak, and was startled at its violence" (*Apologia*, 87–88). Now, ostensibly, between 1839 and 1841, Newman had been undergoing serious doubts about the Catholicity of Anglican authority. In Tract 90, he consciously tested whether he would be allowed to take Anglican tenets in a Catholic fashion. Why then was he surprised at the outspoken denial of such an interpretation? Would not his studies have led him to expect such a reaction? The attitude he ascribes to himself at the end of the third chapter seems much more in accordance with his supposed doubts:

> I was indeed in prudence taking steps towards eventual withdrawing from St. Mary's, and I was not confident about my permanent adhesion to the Anglican creed; but I was in no actual perplexity or trouble of mind. Nor did the immense commotion consequent upon the publication of the Tract unsettle me again. (*Apologia*, 128)

This seems a more likely reaction: an expectation of trouble coupled with resignation to it. We can explain the contradiction inherent in these passages. The second chapter of the *Apologia*, though the dates of its title are 1833 to 1839, actually carries Newman through to 1841. The third chapter, covering the years from 1839 through 1841, is thus a chronological interpolation and not a simple linear extension of the narrative. It seems at least possible that the narrative technique of doubling back and reinterpreting reflects less the complexity of the period than an actual reinterpretation, that the theoretical knots of that period are only seen to be important after 1845.

Newman had to emphasize theoretical explanations for one simple but important reason. If he had converted because he felt betrayed by Anglican authorities, that conversion could not, by itself, have the status of leading to a certitude. It is not simply a matter of not being able bluntly to say, "I left the English Church from resentment at the way I was treated after Tract 90."[15] He could have given a similar explanation by saying that "the English Church proved by its actions toward me that it was not a Catholic authority and so I converted." But in the absence of a theory of what does constitute a proper authority, such an explanation would be meaningless. Nor could he explain that the actions of the Anglican church had forced him to change his mind about precisely that theory, given a philosophy of assent that does not allow a reliable discovery of new theories. Instead Newman was forced to find reasons that showed he really believed in Catholicism all along, that his mistake was simply in the interpretation of his original assents, that his beliefs in dogma and antiquity were actually supports and not refutations of the Catholic church. In this way, his conversion becomes not a change, but a development, not a novel way of thinking, but a self-conscious ratification, a certitude.

Newman's theory of certitude also allows him to explain the activity of reinterpreting through hindsight. The highly wrought proem to Chapter III offers this explanation, containing an implicit recognition and an implicit response to the charge of reinterpretive hindsight:

> For who can know himself, and the multitude of subtle influences which act upon him? And who can recollect, at the distance of twenty-five years, all that he once knew about his thoughts and his deeds, and that, during a portion of his life, when, even at the time, his observation, whether of himself or of the external world, was less than before or after, by very reason of the perplexity and dismay which weighed upon him,—when, in spite of the light given to him according to his need amid his darkness, yet a darkness it emphatically was? . . . yet again, granting that calm contemplation of the past, in itself so desirable, who could afford to be leisurely and deliberate, while he practices on himself a cruel operation, the ripping up of old griefs, and the venturing again upon the "infandum dolorem" of years, in which the stars of this lower heaven were one by one going out? I could not in cool blood, nor except upon the imperious call of duty, attempt what I have set myself to do. It is both to head and heart an extreme trial, thus to analyze what has so long gone by and to bring out the results of that examination. (*Apologia*, 90–91)

This passage tacitly admits that the reasons Newman is about to give are later discoveries, that at the time of the conversion he was "amid darkness." Yet the reasons are guaranteed as accurate because they are discovered by a self-consciousness that relives, as well as reflects, the original events, thus enacting Newman's equivocal theory of consciousness.

The experiment in self-consciousness starts calmly enough as the kind of investigation that leads to or reconfirms certitude. Newman will "analyze what has so long gone by" and from that distance "bring out the results of the examination." A cool and unimpassioned act, seemingly, but this examination involves a conscious reliving of an old event, "the ripping up of old griefs, and the venturing again upon the 'infandum dolorem' of years." Newman's consciousness reasons upon the old event, but the separation of time creates the effect of a doubling of, rather than a severance from, the self. Thus, as described in the *Apologia*, consciousness has both the attributes given to it by the theory outlined in the last chapter: it reasons, but in its reduplication of the self, it also has the quality of unquestioned priority with which Newman endows the self. Even the citation of the *Aeneid* adds to this binding of equivocal qualities: within the passage, the *infandum dolorem* is part of the years of the conversion, but in the *Aeneid*, that grief refers to the pain of *reliving* the fall of Troy, in having to tell of it. Newman here occupies precisely Aeneas's position of having to relive through telling. By having the pain of the original event compared with the pain of retelling, Newman almost suggests that the pain of reliving, of consciousness, is the primary sensation.

By describing his experience of self-consciousness, Newman seems to give a basis to the reasons he is about to describe and an empirical defense of his theory of self-consciousness. The content of the passage, however, coils relentlessly back upon itself. It is frustratingly self-referential, describing no moment in Newman's life so much as the moment of writing. It records the discovery of reasons not really originally there. Even when it describes a pain, it describes it in terms of a poem, thus supporting an equivocal theory with an equivocal citation. It is even more an interpolation than the chronological interpolation of the chapter it is about to introduce. Newman's defense of a theory of consciousness turns out to be quite literally a fiction of consciousness, almost purely a narrative construct. In a sense, that which makes the passage moving and persuasive is precisely that which makes it fictional. In the theory of assent that stands behind the passage, the emotions and intuitions of assent are guaranteed by the reasons of consciousness. Here, though, the reasons the writing records are guaranteed by the affectiveness, the emotional validity of the writing.

Newman's reconstruction of his conversion into an empirical example of his theory of consciousness embodies his version of an exemplary narrative, the first way philosophy may connect with narrative. The next chapter's formal analysis of the *Apologia*'s narrative structure shows how Newman's philosophy can be completely embodied in literary form. Before we enter into the realm of literary analysis, let me summarize, as I did with Mill, the philosophic path that took us here, the path that led us to the threshold of narrative form. The philosophic portion of this part explicated the contradictory demands Newman made of religious propositions, that they be seen as objectively true statements about the external world even though they are not externally provable. His argument that theology is one intellectual discourse among others implied that he should either be able to indicate the truth of Catholicism within the terms of logical or empirical demonstration or be able to articulate philosophically some reliable way of knowing when beliefs are true. He attempted to mount an empirical case in his historical argument for Catholicism, but that argument finally collapsed into the epistemological alternative of describing what kinds of perceptions are perceptions of truth. Newman's epistemological theory, now containing within it his historical theory, came to rest upon his equivocal theory of consciousness as both a separated, reasoning reflection upon the self and an ontologically prior aspect of that self. To defend the unquestionable priority of that equivocal reflection, Newman constructed empirical evidence in terms of the history of his own religious consciousness, a defense that embodied equivocal reflections and reconstructions of its own.

Philosophically ambiguous, Newman's religious writing and in particular the *Apologia* and its account of his conversion, are of course literary influences of the first order of importance. David DeLaura has shown that Newman's tone of "inwardness," a concomitant of the affectiveness of passages like the one I have just been discussing, "could be directly exploited in the new submetaphysical and emotionalist world of refined spiritual and aesthetic apprehension."[16] As a result, that tone significantly influenced literary figures such as Arnold and Walter Pater. Yet Newman would almost certainly have disapproved of such a use of his thought. He had no sympathy for the religion of sentiment:

> The prevailing use of unbelief just now goes on the principle that what a man's heart tells him is truer than any revelation, and that there can be no truth, no external revelation of truth which in its nature can possibly be received as that which his own self, his reason & heart, tells him, is received.[17]

A comprehension of both the philosophic status Newman claimed for his writing and the literary effect it in fact had can thus be a matter neither for a solely philosophic nor a solely literary analysis. The articulation of both the philosophy imbedded in Newman's narrative and the narrative structure of that philosophy, of the merging of the two discourses, is the aim of the next chapter's formal reading of Newman's *Apologia*.

Chapter VIII

Consciousness as a Narrative of Reflection in the *Apologia*

The relationship between turning a philosophic position into an exemplary tale and embodying it in a narrative structure reflects the inextricable connection between form and content in literary works. In exemplary narratives, a philosophic position serves as the theme emplotting a narrative sequence. By recounting the experience of his mental crisis, Mill narrates his theory of consciousness as a link in the chain of experience that is yet radically separate from that chain because of its status as a completing moment. By recounting the experience of his conversion, Newman narrates his theory of consciousness as a reflection of an innate self, a reflection that is both a separated act of reasoning on the intuitions of the self and still an intrinsic part of that self. Once a philosophic position has become part of the narrated content of an autobiography as the emplotting theme, it may then present itself as a model that gives narrative form to content and gives contentual significance to narrated form.

In the reading of Mill's *Autobiography*, it was the first process that I had to stress, the giving of form to the content of the life. Mill's *Autobiography* has so frequently been seen as undigested intellectual history that it seemed most important to understand how Mill's philosophy determined a set of interlocking themes to his life—those of education, growth, the assertion of will—and then, through the connection between Mill's theory of the structure of consciousness and his narrative structure, how that philosophy was also worked out in a narrative form that contained those themes. In other words, I questioned the standard opposition of philosophic significance and esthetic form in Mill's *Autobiography*, not by finding that the work had form as well as content, but by showing the way in which philosophic theory is esthetic form. There has been considerably more acceptance of both the esthetic form and power of Newman's *Apologia*,[1] but the bipolar opposition between form and content has been maintained by a persistent critical refusal to see the polemical and philosophic implications of the esthetic structures and rhetorical skills the critics elucidate. Thus in addition to showing how Newman's philosophy gives form to the content of his life, this chapter also addresses how that philosophy gives the public status of a polemical stance to the meditative form of autobiography.

It is a little surprising that none of the analysts of Newman's rhetoric and form has considered the relationship between his artistic skill and the status of his philosophy since the question was so intrinsic to the controversy out of which the *Apologia* arose in the first place. Part of Kingsley's suspicion of Newman's teaching involved his sense that Newman's skill at writing was deeply connected to his duplicity: "No man knows the use of words better than Dr. Newman," Kingsley stated in a sentence that even he later admitted implied that, consequently, Newman was skilled at twisting words so as to deceive his audience (*Apologia*, 347). And Newman made Kingsley's charge of a rhetorical skill that is also duplicity into one of the thematic centers of the *Apologia* by playing on the title of Kingsley's pamphlet "What, Then, Does Dr. Newman Mean."[2] In the context of this connection between rhetorical skill and dishonest teaching, one would think that critics who praise Newman's rhetoric or esthetic form in isolation from any consideration of their effect upon the logic of his thought and the subject of his narrative would wonder about the implications of that praise. My analysis of the way Newman's philosophy of consciousness shapes his narrative structure shows, I think, that Newman wondered seriously about those implications. And he articulated a connection between rhetoric and meaning, philosophy and form, far more deliberate and careful than the independence his critics imply whereby one can use rhetorical skill and still say what one means.

This relationship between esthetic form and philosophic content, an independence that may well be an opposition when it takes the form of a relationship between rhetoric and straightforward meaning, is an issue that involves more than the status of just Newman's *Apologia*, however. The polemical intents of Victorian prose do not coexist that comfortably with the formal analysis of it that has been part of its definition as a literary form. The situation of the *Apologia* shows us that this problem has not been created by modern criticism's retrospective definition of Victorian prose as a literary genre but was intrinsic to those works from the beginning. If, as I have said, the Victorian sage's intents were heavily polemical, the reception of those prose-prophets was notoriously literary. The *Apologia*'s context, suggesting an opposition between rhetoric and straightforwardness, hence between literary form and philosophic meaning, may have been an exaggeratedly controversial one. But Carlyle's persistent frustration with his inability to translate the universal appreciation he received as a writer into a reception of his teaching suggests that a relationship of independence between literary form and philosophic content could be as corrosive as that of opposition between rhetoric and straightforwardness, if less flagrantly controversial.

The *Apologia*'s thematization of its response to the charge of rhetorical duplicity in its self-presentation as a comprehensive answer to the question of what Newman meant challenges the relationships of either opposition or independence between philosophic meaning and literary or rhetorical form, as I go on to show. Consequently, a literary reading that sections off Newman's philosophic and polemical intents cannot even be comprehensive as a literary reading, just as a philosophic analysis of Newman's epistemology that does not broach the merger of that epistemology with narrative form cannot be comprehensive as a philosophic analysis. This chapter, like the one analyzing Mill's narrative structure, offers a literary analysis, a formal reading, that delineates the philosophic significance of narrative structure. To the extent that that reading is successful in its aims and to the extent that the *Apologia*'s formal and philosophic situation reflects the situation of Victorian prose in general, the method behind the reading offered here may be generalized into a method for reading Victorian prose that comprehends both its philosophic and its formal aspects. The delineation of such a method and its demonstration is the task of Part Three.

Newman's theory of consciousness (both as a separated, reasoning reflector of the self and as coincident with and sharing in that innate self's ontological priority) operates as a model for the narrative sequence and the narrative structure of the *Apologia*. That model is essentially one of simultaneous concentricity. His sense of the shape of the self and its development, of his conversion and the narrative that contains it, and his definition of the *Apologia*'s dual role as both meditation and polemic are not logical, developmental sequences from one to the other but homologous redefinitions of each other. In such a structure, explaining the status of one's consciousness, explaining the reasons behind conversion and the consequent defense of a religious philosophy, and finally explaining the formal status of the *Apologia* as a rhetoric that is a meditation that is a philosophy are not separable. Each aspect of the *Apologia* both redefines and partakes of the other aspects in a relationship comparable to that of concentric circles in which each wider circle enlarges the breadth but does not in any essential way change the shape of the circle within it. This concentricity is, of course, the relationship we have seen between the reflecting, reasoning consciousness and the self, which it ratifies by simply reproducing.

The first of these circles shaped by Newman's definition of consciousness is, fittingly enough, his discussion of his own self and its development. In distinct contrast to Mill, Newman posits, not merely an innate self, but an innate self that contains, implicitly if not explicitly, the essential configurations of Newman's whole, developed self and thinking. More pointedly, Newman outlines this self in clearly theological terms. Critics have noted the narrowness of the *Apologia*: it concerns, of an entire life, only the religious aspect and really only one facet of that.[3] But Newman's talent for music, his role as an educator, his love of the classics, all of these are beside the point because those traits were really not very important, certainly not that "true key to my whole life" (*Apologia*, 12) that he set out to present. That true key can be seen in theological terms—terms fairly distant from those normally used to describe or define the psyche—because the psychic shape of the self and the theological shape of his conversion and his consequent philosophy are aspects of each other, each one explaining the other. For the same reason, Newman's innate self, complete as it is *in posse*, is not truly complete until it goes beyond itself, working toward the theological definition of its world and its place in that world.

Finding one's place in one's world is a distinctly idiosyncratic act for a self that is essentially complete in both its nature and its knowledge. That activity of discovering is largely one of finding what it is that one has always known, what has always been the case, and who one has always been. In the place of Mill's education as a constant accretion of new experiences that lead to new knowledge and beliefs, Newman's progress involves more a decoding of what he has always been and what has always been there, a decoding of the true content of his beliefs. The narrative structure coincident with the theme of education in Mill is the common one that comprehends a sequence as a directed process of change. The narrative structure coincident with Newman's theme of decoding instead comprehends sequence as a progressive unfolding to Newman and the reader of a situation that is the same from the beginning. Critics commonly use this distinction between ways of structuring sequence to distinguish between types of fiction and character development.[4] But both the theme of decoding and the structure of unfolding present specific questions that lead to the further definition of the workings of consciousness and narration. In particular, the act of decoding goes through precisely the same stages and performs precisely the same acts as the acts of deceptive coding that made the decoding necessary. How then can we tell whether Newman is discovering reality or truth or further disfiguring it? Further, although the narrative sequence of unfolding is a common one in fiction, the separations we make between author, narrator, and reader and our willingness to be deceived by an author for purposes of suspense or complexity of esthetic effect—all aspects of reader response necessary to the workings of narrative as unfolding—do not extend naturally to our reading of autobiography. Mill may withhold from us his final position until his narrative reaches it on the principle that part of that position involves the process of discovering it, the process of the education itself. But if one merely discovers more clearly a truth one has always known, what value has the process of discovery and why bother to narrate it? If all elements of a life are given at the outset and the world has no effect on one, in other words, what experiences are worth narrating and why write an autobiographical narrative at all?

The second of Newman's concentric circles explicitly connects his theology to his narrative stance. In discussing how his study of history led to his conversion, Newman stresses the way his theory of development insists on the necessity for an identity of essence between the primitive position and its modern formulation while it places the entire activity of development in the realm of the studying historian rather than in any historical process. The proper study of history is to discover and articulate what has always been the case, and the content of history itself allows us to distinguish between disfigurement and the decoding of development. But the acts of discovering and distinguishing, which are the real acts of development, become constitutive of our knowledge of truth, and we must thus recount the experiences of that discovery if we are to understand that truth. As in the theology of the prior chapters, this study of history is a process of consciousness writ large (as Newman's image of the historical mirror stresses), and so the discussion of the conversion moves on to the *Grammar*'s formulation of certitude as an act of consciousness that reflects and yet changes the status of what it reflects by reaffirming it. The role of the narrative as a reflection of the events it narrates, a reflection that reaffirms the effect of those events, follows naturally. Indeed the narrative becomes primary in the same way that the study of the historian became primary, as a reflection that virtually constitutes the truth it reflects. This definition of theology and narrative stance is in structure identical to the earlier delineation of an innate self that still must discover what it knows. The second concentric circle gives that structure wider relevance by moving from the connection between psychology and theology to a connection between theology and narrative.

Further, these answers to the thematic question of how one is to differentiate between a decoding and a disfigurement and the structural question of the role of narrative when it merely reproduces what is already there are expandable into a response to the final question about the reliability of narrative's rhetoricity and literariness. We can see how Newman recuperates rhetoric as neither opposed to nor independent from referential content by further articulating the relationship between the structure of consciousness and the narrative structure in the *Apologia*. That articulation shows a homology between the process of reflection and the process of rhetoric that makes rhetoric intrinsic to an accurately meditative form, consequently establishing the literary meditativeness of autobiography as a polemical discourse. As the second concentric circle moved from a connection between self and theology to a connection between theology and narrative, the third circle moves from that connection to one between narrative and the discursive role of literary form, the polemical role of meditative form.

Thus Newman's theory of consciousness as an undifferentiated replication of the self's innateness and priority and yet also a replication that reaffirms and validates, works to structure the various discussions of self, theology, and narrative within the *Apologia* and to structure the relationship of concentricity between these discussions that expands and validates without changing the nature of what is expanded. And through my discussion of the three issues outlined above, I show how philosophy is narrativized in the *Apologia* and how narrative assumes philosophic significance. The final discussion of the reliability and content of rhetorical and literary form may consequently also be taken as the entry point to my wider claims for the relationship between philosophy and narrative in Victorian prose.

The Theological Self

Like Mill's *Autobiography*, indeed like many if not most autobiographies, Newman's *Apologia* begins with a sifting of childhood memories, a search for definitive or exemplary moments. Since, unlike Mill, Newman defines consciousness in a way that demands the existence of an innate self prior to experience, his search is far more successful. He finds, however, not a single, originating moment, but an achronological series of moments that cohere to establish both the extensiveness and the definitive qualities of that innate self. Two qualities in particular are important. First, not only certain traits, but a consciousness of those traits, are part of those earliest memories; so self-consciousness is part of the prior self. Second, in fairly short order, even before Newman has any extensive religious or theological experience, the early memories establish theological terms as the ones with which the self will be defined. These two qualities taken together determine the structure of the *Apologia*'s narrative sequence. The theological terms that describe the innate self also introduce within that self elements outside it, God and his outward manifestations. This introduction necessitates an analysis of aspects of the external world if one is fully to understand the terms that construct and place the self. Self-consciousness then not only becomes part of an innate self but demands an external factor, an element of analysis. Because this analysis of the external world remains an attempt to discover more about the configurations of the self and its beliefs, however, the narrative sequence must be one of unfolding rather than one of directed change or growth as it was in Mill's narrative.

Newman's innate self, from its earliest moments, contains within it virtually all that is necessary for its own satisfactory existence. From the outset, we encounter a self far more aware of its own existence and nature than it is aware of anything else. In that action of self testifying to itself, which he repeats constantly in the *Apologia*, Newman quotes an earlier statement by himself about a yet earlier aspect of his own existence:

> "I used to wish the Arabian Tales were true: my imagination ran on unknown influences, on magical powers and talismans. . . . I thought life might be a dream, or I an Angel, and all this world a deception. . . ." (*Apologia*, 15–16)

In discovering that the imagination so important to Newman was his from the beginning, we find also the explanation of his acute self-consciousness. Newman wishes the world might be a fantasy, even thinks it might be a dream. Only his sense of self is stable and acute—he is the Angel at the center of the deception. Since he is most immediately aware of himself, he must become conscious of himself before he can become fully conscious of a surrounding world. Here we see Newman describing his first moments precisely in terms of his formulations in the *Philosophical Notebooks*, in which one's first experiences were not experiences as an empiricist would define them, but experiences of one's own mind.

The philosophic formulation that glimmers uncertainly behind this dreamy incident, transformed more and more explicitly into religious terms, quickly becomes a primary aspect of self-definition. It has been argued that the *Apologia* and, for all intents and purposes, Newman's life do not really begin until 1816, the date of his first conversion at the age of fifteen.[5] It is true that Newman tends to refer to 1816 as an originating date, stating of his most important religious tenets, "What I held in 1816, I held in 1833, and I hold in 1864" (*Apologia*, 54). In fact, though, the *Apologia* has two pages before the first conversion, and the earliest experience it relates occurs when Newman is ten years old. Nor are these incidents preparatory to a first grand moment, for the conversion itself is handled as cursorily as what went before it, described and dispensed with in a page. The conversion seems so important, however, because it establishes for the first time explicitly the theological terms of the autobiography: the life will be a history of religious beliefs and an adventure in theological investigation.

But the theological terms seem adequate to comprehend Newman's life and the *Apologia* does not seem an account of simply one particular aspect of that life because that early conversion occurs as part of an achronological series of early memories, a kaleidoscope of images that sketch the contours of Newman's innate self even as they become progressively more religious in tenor. The desire that one's world might be that of the *Arabian Nights* merely indicates an exotic, perhaps an unworldly imagination. In the moment of Berkeleyean idealism, though, Newman markedly images himself as an angel rather than merely a dreamer. Psychology becomes theology far more explicitly, however, when Newman notes finding in his first Latin verse book an insignia he drew before the age of ten "which almost took my breath away with surprise":

> I have drawn a figure of a solid cross upright, and next to it is, what may indeed be meant for a necklace, but what I cannot make out to be anything else than a set of beads suspended, with a little cross attached. (*Apologia*, 16–17)

This passage and the one describing Newman's habit of crossing himself in the dark have been seen as intending to stress the absence of Catholic influence behind these actions in order to emphasize Newman's early loyalty to the Anglican church.[6] But surely no one, not even Kingsley, has ever thought that Newman was a secret Catholic from the age of ten, and if Newman wanted to stress his early Anglicanism, he might better have omitted the two incidents. What takes his breath away and must at least mildly jar his reader is the implication that with no exposure to Catholicism at all, Newman had an inherent proclivity toward Catholic ritual. Even if one will not follow Newman this far in attributing such specificity to the beliefs of his innate self—and even Newman is reticent about making this argument explicitly—the incident does suggest the appropriateness of religious language in describing a self even prior to its entrance into any history of religious opinions, establishing, at least in Newman's case, a basic correspondence between theological and psychic terms.

In this context, the seeming originary significance of the 1816 conversion becomes clear. More than merely establishing the religious subject matter of the *Apologia*, it also describes it as another moment of early and intense consciousness. Though external sources are involved in that conversion, it is entirely an internal event:

> I received it [the doctrine of final perseverance] at once, and believed that the inward conversion of which I was conscious, (and of which I still am more certain than that I have hands and feet,) would last into the next life, and that I was elected to eternal glory. (*Apologia*, 17)

The conversion is a change only to this extent: although not irreligious before then, Newman became consciously a believer at the age of fifteen. Instead of acting upon thoughtless superstition, he fell "under the influence of a definite creed" (*Apologia*, 17). In contrast to Mill's discovery of Bentham's philosophy, in which he found what he had been made into, Newman here finds labels for what he has always been. He is conscious of the conversion as an aspect of himself, as inward, and that consciousness is stable and atemporal, linking him with the Newman who writes of his persistent certainty of that conversion and with an eternal glory he expects. Thus the linkage between self, self-consciousness, and theological viewpoint is definitively established.

We seem to have, at the beginning, then, virtually a completed self. The existence of the external world is rather shaky, but the self and its Creator are firmly and undeniably there. And, indeed, Newman goes to great lengths to convince us of how little he changes in the course of his life. For theoretical reasons established in the last chapters, lack of change is a central theme in the *Apologia*; it is also a clear corollary of the picture of self and consciousness Newman is outlining here. Further, Newman again thinks in theological terms about the lack of psychological change. The line cited above about his continuity of views from 1816 through to 1864 occurs at the end of the first principle in Newman's account of the three basic theological principles he held between 1833 and 1839. The phrase is recalled and reasserted after Newman's description of his second principle: "While I am now as clear in my acceptance of the principle of dogma, as I was in 1833 and 1816, so again I am now as firm in my belief of a visible Church, of the authority of Bishops, of the grace of the sacraments, of the religious worth of works of penance, as I was in 1833" (*Apologia*, 57).

The only change Newman admits between 1833 and 1864 is that he no longer thinks the Roman Catholic church anathema, a change the *Apologia* carefully defines as one that does not touch the roots of belief according to the terms of the *Grammar of Assent*'s epistemology. There is, however, an important change between 1816 and 1833, the entrance of a visible church. This change indicates how the 1816 conversion's ratification of the propriety of theological terms in describing the self necessitates change and movement even in a seemingly completed self. Although Newman speaks of that conversion in persistently internal terms—of being more sure of it than he is of having hands and feet, of there being only two luminously self-evident beings, himself and God (*Apologia*, 18)—what he is aware of in each case is something outside himself, God or his state of election. But if simple self-awareness may lead us to an awareness of a God, it does not make us aware of what kind of God he is.[7] It is the desire for that information that leads Newman to the assertion of a visible church, a body that can supply that information. In this sense, the *Apologia* becomes, as one critic says, the story of "a man not seeking faith in God but a source of information about God, a means of drawing nearer, a medium of communion."[8]

Still, Newman does not describe this change as a change, but as an unfolding. He knows who he is through acts of self-consciousness even as that intensity of self-consciousness is part of the self of which he is conscious. At a certain point, however, elements of the self and the self-conscious are given labels that connect him with elements outside himself. The centrality in the *Apologia* of the theme of discovering information about these elements has caused the work to be described as a movement "from individualism to institutionalism, from self-regarding emotionalism to self-abnegating authoritarianism."[9] But in an important sense he never moves away from being self-regarding. The necessity for the institutions he searches for arises directly from the terms with which he describes his internal state.

There is still a question about Newman's turn outward, though, and his responses to it shape the analysis that follows of the self's place in the world. Although the 1816 conversion ratified his use of theological terms to describe the self, those terms had brought with them elements outside the self. Newman integrated those elements into the act of self-consciousness sufficiently for there not to be any obvious need to question their external implications. If God and one's election are internally given, why would one need further information? What kind of self-analysis leads one to the perception of the need for further information, and how can the analysis that searches for that information remain self-analysis, that is, an unfolding, rather than become an intellectual development?

In answering this question, we see most clearly the effect of labeling the self in theological terms. Newman does not seek to refine his understanding of those terms out of simple intellectual curiosity but because the terms force him into a bewildering confrontation with the external world's contradiction of his self-consciousness and the knowledge it gives him. He may see God within himself, but the God he sees is by definition an external entity; and so, when his perception of the external world does not confirm the existence of that entity, that perception must be described as a crisis of self-perception:

> The world seems simply to give the lie to that great truth, of which my whole being is so full; and the effect upon me is, in consequence, as a matter of necessity, as confusing as if it denied that I am in existence myself. If I looked into a mirror, and did not see my face, I should have the sort of feeling which actually comes upon me, when I look into this living busy world, and see no reflexion of its Creator. (*Apologia*, 216)

Newman here places considerable importance on what he does and does not see in the visible world; it is not a matter of indifferent curiosity to him. Looking into the world and not seeing God is like looking into a mirror and not seeing his face. The absence seems unthinkable; but one's first impulse is not necessarily to doubt the mirror.[10] Thus Newman's perception of the world must be attended to because it creates a contradiction in self-consciousness that must be resolved. The response to this contradiction suggested by the image of looking into the empty mirror is not to change the self, however, but to understand more fully that self and its place in the world in order to recuperate or resolve the contradiction. After all, if Newman does not doubt the mirror or the world, neither can he doubt his consciousness of his own existence and the existence of God that that consciousness entails.

To confront this threatening mirror of the external world, Newman must construct a system of interpreting that world, a system enacted by his conversion and finally ratified by an act of consciousness that reconstitutes the original sense of self. This system involves identifying a series of erasures and additions to the texts of the world and the self, an identification that implies not changing, but decoding the world or the self. The absence of God in the world, Newman argues, allows the presence of evil, but we also know by evil's presence that God is absent rather than nonexistent. Newman compares the vision of a world implicated by original sin to the sight of a boy "of good make and mind, with the tokens on him of a refined nature, cast upon the world without provision, unable to say whence he came, his birthplace or his family connexions" and concludes that "he was one, of whom, from one cause or another, his parents were ashamed. Thus only should I be able to account for the contrast between the promise and the condition of his being" (*Apologia*, 217). Newman sees both the inherent promise and the added and conflicting contrast to the promise. Further, he knows that the promise was there first even though the contrast is so overwhelming that it makes the promise look like the addition, "the tokens of a refined nature." The absence of God, of an aspect of original truth, asserts itself as an absence felt as a presence, then, in the presence of evil, which shows itself an unnatural addition. But how can we know which addition is actually an erasure mark of a presence, which presence is actually an unnatural addition? Why is the absence of God finally a presence itself and not simply a nonexistence? How do we know to doubt the mirror and not the self that does not see itself there?

Newman's problem here is one of restoration rather than revision. He is engaged in an interpretation intended to restore original meaning, in explicitly textual terms, rather than to change the self in response to the world or the world in response to the self. We can see this in his account of one effect of his early prejudice against Catholicism:

> As a boy of fifteen, I had so fully imbibed [Protestant antipathy to Rome], that I had actually erased in my *Gradus ad Parnassum*, such titles, under the word "Papa," as "Christi Vicarious," "sacer interpres," and "sceptra gerens," and substituted epithets so vile that I cannot bring myself to write them down here. (*Apologia*, 113)

Newman's early erasure and addition to the original text constitute his original sin, in Newman's own words "a stain on my imagination." He has taken away part of the original word and added on a false one. This passage is a change that restores the original words of the text, just as a proper interpretation of the world will restore the self's original relationship to the world. The problem of separating erasure from addition is stressed rather than solved by this passage, though. Its cleansing process, after all, is a re-erasure and a re-addition. Those words he put in the *Gradus ad Parnassum* he finds too vile to repeat. He therefore withholds them, putting back in their place the ostensibly original titles. Here, of course, the process is not subject to too much questioning. Newman's memory tells him that the words he finds in his *Gradus ad Parnassum* are not in the original work, but his own additions at an earlier time; moreover, other copies of the book exist to confirm his knowledge of what the original words were. The world, however, exists only as we have it, and so this textual model of a restorative and stabilizing interpreting system still leaves us the problem of separating erasures from additions, of knowing when we are decoding rather than disfiguring.

This anecdote of textual tampering contains within it both the bridge that connects Newman's analysis of the external world with self-analysis and the model through which he sees this dual process of analysis working to make the conversions of 1833 and 1845 unfoldings and restorations of his original self rather than changes or revisions. I have shown that the crisis of self- perception set off by the perception of God's nonexistence in the external world is resolved by the concept of an original sin that acts to withdraw God's presence from the world and mask the signs of its having been there. This passage of textual disfigurement now shows both how this original sin works and Newman's own specific participation in it. It is not simply a matter of a world that has acted in such a way as to mesh no longer with the purity of Newman's consciousness. Newman's consciousness—fallen, just as the world is—does in fact mesh with the fallen world and so produces the frightening vision of the vacant mirror. The restoration of the text, then, is both an understanding of the original state of the world and of the original state of the self. Newman, however, knows that erasures and additions cannot be separated, that a restoration must reenact the process of disfigurement that created the need for restoration.[11] To guarantee that his restorative activities are in fact unfoldings of what was there in the first place and not further changes, then, Newman in 1833 adds the concept of a visible church. By establishing a dogma that locates those acts of the self and the world that are disfigurements, that visible church reconstructs the original perception of God within the self. It explains the contradictions that the world seemed to present to that perception and the extent to which these contradictions were attributable to problems within the self as well as problems within the world. Thus the church extends Newman's understanding of the full context of his theological consciousness without materially changing that consciousness.

Since the world and the self have fallen from their original states, we need the church to tell us what the original truth was. Newman's 1845 conversion does not retract any aspect of this formulation but responds to a new problem within it: a contradiction, not within the world that the church explains, but between the claims of various churches. The problem is that some churches must have fallen away from primitive Christianity if more than one church claims to teach it and their teachings are contradictory. Hugo M. Achaval summarizes Newman's belief about the value of the church: "the Church is one with our Lord, in time, by the Apostolical Succession; in space, by its Catholicity."[12] The true church, then, will reproduce the unity of Newman's theological consciousness. But both the Anglican church and the Roman Catholic church claim this unity. The Anglican church, arguing its fidelity to original doctrine, rests its claim on antiquity, claiming to have spatial validity by having temporal validity. The Roman church rests its claim on "its Catholicity," claiming temporal validity as a result of spatial validity (*Apologia*, 101). Thus Newman states that his conversion is simply a matter of working out the validity of two arguments: "there was a contrariety of claims between the Roman and Anglican religions, and the history of my conversion is simply the process of working it out to a solution" (*Apologia*, 106).

Although this may seem a fairly intellectualized form of conversion, more a matter of theology than of autobiographical narrative, in fact this theological determination is also deeply a determination about the self. The church is here imaged as claiming the same kind of integral unity with God as Newman experiences in that definitive act of innate self-consciousness. Accordingly, determining which church has that unity is also further defining his own self and self-consciousness. Within this system in which theological distinctions are also determinations about the self, it is hardly surprising to find Newman arguing that developments in Catholic doctrine are not declarations of new truths but only official ratifications of what he has already believed, which gives him "the satisfaction of having to believe, that I have only been holding all along what the Apostles held before me" (*Apologia*, 227).

Although this connection between theology and self ties theological determination into self-explication while it creates an external medium through which the innate self can be defined and articulated, Newman's need for an autobiographical narration still seems somewhat questionable. Because his movement through the external world created by the theological problems of his conversions always occurs as an unfolding of the self and its innate beliefs, one wonders why he does not just detail his final understanding of the theological problems whose solutions determine that self. Further, although the church protects Newman's erasures and additions from being disfigurements rather than decodings, the discovery of that church is itself one of those acts of decoding. So the final distinction between an unfolding interpretation and a changing disfigurement remains in question. In short, Newman's external self-unfoldings are at once not enough of a change to justify the activity of a narrative and yet threaten to be too much of a change to justify his own claim of being always the same. Here Newman's theories of history and of consciousness connect explicitly with the autobiography, justifying both the choices made within the narrative and the role of the narrative itself. Here, then, narrative and philosophy explicitly intersect.

History, Consciousness, and the Role of the Narrative

The second concentric circle within the the *Apologia*'s narrative structure responds to the problems raised in the first by connecting the depiction of a theological self and self-consciousness with theories of history and consciousness and with the explanation of Newman's conversion. Thus the role of narrative is contained within, rather than questioned by, the sequence of unfolding articulated in the last section. History is particularly important here because it introduces a second narrative event in which hallucinatory mirror gazing occurs, while the historical context for this second moment of vexed self-consciousness gives new ramifications to conscious reflection, which is so thematically central to the *Apologia*. Once Newman has defined for this historical self-consciousness a constitutive value in the development of the self it still only reflects, he can then extend this consciousness into his conversion and its narrative reflection, giving narrative reflection the same value as the reflections of consciousness have.

The importance of Newman's theory of development both to his conversion and to his account of it in the *Apologia* has hardly gone unnoticed.[13] As with his explanation of certitude and Mill's justification of free will, however, in the absence of a clear theory describing the narrative transformation of philosophic discourse, these claims of connection have not been quite precise. It is less a matter of Newman's seeing how his theory of development led to his conversion, or even of his seeing his conversion in terms of that theory, then it is a matter of that theory allowing him to see his self-consciousness as a historical act. Consequently, Newman's historical research in the *Apologia* is imaged in a cen-

tral thematic moment as an act of mirror gazing, and that act defines the
role of history and its redefinition of self-consciousness. But if in the mirror of the Godless world Newman could not see himself, in the historical
mirror he saw a self he did not want to see:

> My stronghold was Antiquity; now here, in the middle of the fifth
> century, I found, as it seemed to me, Christendom of the sixteenth
> and nineteenth centuries reflected. I saw my face in that mirror, and I
> was a Monophysite. (*Apologia*, 108)

Newman's act of seeing himself in that mirror begins history's reconstitu-
tion of self-conscious reflection as having a constructive value. The first
thing to notice is that the Newman who looks into the mirror is not quite
the Monophysite who looks back. A Monophysite is one who holds the
Monophysite heresy to be truth. For Newman, Monophysite is a synec-
doche for the larger term *heretic*, a label no heretic, of course, applies to
himself. Unaware of his heresy, Newman might be a Monophysite; but
the act of recognizing his heresy, of seeing that he *was* a Monophysite,
contains within it the desire to change, to *be* other than a Monophysite.
The actor here, then, is not the past heretic but the present perceiver of
heresy, and the motive we are interested in is precisely the desire of that
present perceiver to be other than a heretic. Thus reflection in a historical
context would seem to give oneself the possibility not merely of unfolding but of changing for the better, of learning one's heresy and, therefore,
by implication, being given the opportunity to correct it.

But this form of change seems to exist in a context that identifies it as
resulting from an unnatural addition. One may change one's heretical
views, but if they are changeable, then they are not part of the innate self
being unfolded but are one of those obstructive accretions described in
the last section. Newman's definitions of history and historical change in
the *Apologia* seem at first glance to confirm this conclusion. At times, he
seems almost like Bossuet, identifying historical change directly with
heresy, claiming historical identity as the distinctive quality of Roman
Catholicism. Thus the mirror in which Newman sees himself is as magical as that in any fairy tale, showing sameness to some and differences to
others. In large outlines, history seems constantly to repeat itself, reflect
itself: "The drama of religion, and the combat of truth and error, were
ever one and the same; . . . the shadow of the fifth century was on the
sixteenth. It was like a spirit rising from the troubled waters of the old

world, with the shape and lineaments of the new" (*Apologia*, 109). More-over, to the Catholic, who resides in original truth and primitive Christi-anity, the mirror shows always the same face. Newman in his theological studies found Rome always to be in the same position. He is more specific here: it is "difficult to find arguments against the Tridentine Fathers, which did not tell against the Fathers of Chalcedon; difficult to condemn the Popes of the sixteenth century, without condemning the Popes of the fifth" (*Apologia*, 109). Newman searches for the fissure that will separate the pure, primitive church from the corrupt Roman one, and he simply cannot find it. The historical mirror presents always the same image, Rome where she is.

To heretics, the mirror is more fickle. The Protestant looks into it and finds himself here a Eutychian, there an Arian. The Anglican looks into it and finds himself here a Monophysite, there a semi-Arian. The theologi-cal bases of these heresies are by no means the same, but that is the power of Newman's historical mirror: it shows only what is always there. Rome's truth sees always itself. Heresies change constantly, and therefore the heretic sees only that heresy that occupied his position in another time and thus sees himself as constantly changing, constantly different. Fur-ther, one can specify the cause of change. I have been speaking of the magical mirror as a historical one, but that is not strictly true. It is a tem-poral one, but history is not simply the passage of time. It is the record of change. The distinction is implicit in Newman's chapter headings, which refer to the history of his opinions until his conversion to Catholicism is complete. Then we have a final chapter titled "Position of my Mind since 1845." The distinction occurs again in the summary of the period from 1841 to 1845, when Newman sees himself on his deathbed as an Anglican:

A death-bed has scarcely a history; it is a tedious decline, with sea-sons of rallying and seasons of falling back; and since the end is fore-seen, or what is called a matter of time, it has little interest for the reader, especially if he has a kind heart. Moreover, it is a season when doors are closed and curtains drawn, and when the sick man neither cares nor is able to record the stages of his malady. I was in these circumstances, except so far as I was not allowed to die in peace,—except so far as friends, who had still a full right to come in upon me, and the public world, which had not, have given a sort of history to these last four years. (*Apologia*, 137)

A deathbed is a matter of time, not of history, because its process is always the same. One deathbed may reflect another deathbed as Rome superimposes itself over Rome. What gives Newman's deathbed a history is the intrusion of the outside world, just as what gives Christianity a history is the intrusion of external heresy. Thus history records the change caused by the intrusion of foreign bodies, like the original sin that marred the world, the gifted boy and the desecrated Latin text. History is a violation of truth.

This recurrence of the opposition between original truth and interrupting disfigurement is deceptively premature, however. In the largest perspective, history cannot be defined as only errant change, because it also becomes the medium through which original truth is understood. The Newman who discovers his own error, after all, does so precisely through historical research, the research into the heresies that make up church history. Moreover, the very act of seeing oneself as a heretic in that mirror of history defines oneself as Catholic (again, neither a Monophysite nor an Anglo-Catholic would define his views as heretical). Thus by seeing himself in the vexing reflection of historical change, Newman learns something he did not know before about his innate self and its beliefs, that those beliefs are Catholic even as the labels he thought described them are actually not applicable to him but to heretics. This lesson about himself is only learned through history and only makes sense in the historical context in which the linkage Monophysite/Anglo-Catholic can occur and the label heresy apply to both linked terms. The act of historical self-consciousness learns something about the self that was always there, but only through a vexed rather than a duplicating historical reflection, and that vexing becomes a necessary medium for the self-knowledge and self-unfolding to occur. One cannot even maintain a hard and fast distinction between the reflective act and the innate self it reflects. After all, it is the observing Newman looking into the mirror, rather than the reflection, who first sees himself as a Catholic, even if, consequently, the Catholicism is then defined as a label for the self that hovers behind the vexed reflection.

This historical self-consciousness, thematized in the image of historical research as a form of mirror gazing, embodies in narrative the dual form of consciousness that links Newman's actual historical theories to his epistemological theories. And that historical consciousness protects its definitions and decodings from becoming the additions, erasures, and disfigurements to which it responds with precisely the same double identity that consciousness has in the *Grammar*: the same separation between consciousness and self that allows conscious activity to clarify the self coexists with that activity's participation in that self's unquestionable innateness. The question of narration's role and necessity in this system is answered by the superimposition of this relationship between consciousness and self upon the relationship between narrator and events narrated. Newman gives the place of the writer unusual emphasis in the *Apologia* and gives the act of writing a distinctively intense form of attention, spotlighting writing's tendency to clarify and strengthen the status of the self it also claims to replicate and suggesting the primacy of a narration it also defines as reflective.

Every chapter in the *Apologia* but Chapter IV begins with a discussion of the task of writing, and those discussions become more and more intense. This concern at the opening of the first chapter is relatively low-key, but by the opening of the second chapter it has become distinctly more emphatic. Following the conclusion of the first chapter, the justly famous passage describing the voyage from Sicily and the beginning of the Oxford movement, a passage rich with foreboding and intentionally mysterious overtones, Newman begins his next section with the flat statement "In spite of the foregoing pages, I have no romantic story to tell" (*Apologia*, 44). Newman has been frequently praised for his ability to re-create the past dramatically so that we experience it as he did. The observation is true enough, but the process is not quite that simple. The Newman who writes is as constantly before us as the Newman who lives the events described; and he tells us any number of times that the story he has to tell us is essentially one of choosing alternative theologies, not, as he says, a romantic story. Is the emotional vividness, then, an artistic lie to catch the reader's interest? The above citation ends with a semicolon, not a period. Newman completes the sentence "but I have written them, because it is my duty to tell things as they took place." To replicate the experience, he must also replicate its emotional terms. But he is not in quite the same situation when writing as when he had the experience. By implication, he now recognizes that the emotions were not requisite to the nature of the external event and that the retrospective knowledge of his conversion allows him to define the event in a way both more accurate than and different from any definition the self within the event could offer. Narrative doubling, then, like consciousness, both unfolds the self and explicates it in a distinctive way.

Because this passage refers to the Tractarian conversion, not to Newman's final position, its narrative's retrospective delineations might be seen as arising from the particular situation of describing beliefs no longer held, experiences thought to have been deceptive. Newman's constant claim of never having changed anything essential in his beliefs would by itself make this claim problematic. But the opening of Chapter III, referring to the experience of the 1845 conversion, makes clear that a redefining reflection is characteristic of the act of writing itself and not a particular manifestation of it. That passage, which I first cited at the end of the previous chapter, lays before us all the problems writing involved for the autobiographer to whom self-consciousness means not merely recounting but both reliving and reinterpreting past events and past emotions. It begins by noting the magnitude of the event under consideration. It continues by noting the difficulty of properly describing what one was not fully aware of at the time. It ends, however, with difficulties of a far different order:

> Granting that calm contemplation of the past, in itself so desirable, who could afford to be leisurely and deliberate, while he practices on himself a cruel operation, the ripping up of old griefs, and the venturing again upon the "infandum dolorem" of years, in which the stars of this lower heaven were one by one going out? I could not in cool blood, nor except upon the imperious call of duty, attempt what I have set myself to do. It is both to head and heart an extreme trial, thus to analyze what has so long gone by, and to bring out the results of that examination. I have done various bold things in my life: this is the boldest: and, were I not sure I should after all succeed in my object, it would be madness to set about it. (*Apologia*, 90–91)

In the last chapter, I discussed this passage as it embodies empirically Newman's ambivalent definition of consciousness and responded to problems in the *Apologia*'s account of the conversion. Here I want to concentrate on that which the passage refers to directly: the mere act of writing the account. It may at first seem strange that writing about the conversion is for Newman a bolder undertaking than living it. Yet the undertaking is possible for the same reason it is bold—the end is known. Because he knows the end, Newman relives the experience with intensified consciousness, thus intensified emotion and pain. Much of what he originally experienced during the conversion, Newman was not fully aware of, not knowing where it would all end, and thus he did not feel it that completely. Now, in full awareness, he will re-experience with a greater vividness.

Yet despite the boldness of setting out on such a project of re-experiencing, Newman is sure he will "succeed in [his] object." He is not a Milton calling upon God to inspire his "advent'rous song." Though his project is also bold, he depends on himself for the success of which he feels assured. The reason for his confidence is not that difficult to determine. Newman is about to describe his conversion, and he is certain of its success and correctness. The writing of that event will be successful not necessarily because of any special esthetic prowess but because he need merely reproduce conclusions of which he is already sure. The narrative here, the act of writing, does not merely describe or embody Newman's definition of consciousness but quite literally enacts it, claiming of itself that it is a replication—and therefore guaranteed of success—and yet at the same time an intensification that lives out more clearly that which it replicates and that therefore enhances the status of the events narrated.

Newman shows the adequacy of conscious unfolding to the self it unfolds and shows the necessity of narrative sequence in describing a stable self and a stable truth by extending the structure of the self outlined in that definition. The structure thereby comprehends within it the concept of historical consciousness and the justification that concept offers for narration. Constantly expanding the same structure so that it claims to contain within itself more and more diverse issues even as it claims to treat those issues in their own integrity, Newman makes the organizing principle of his narrative his theory of consciousness as both differentiated reflection and integral aspect of the self. And the final expansion of that structure entails justifying and containing the very rhetoricity of the work, a rhetoricity that the work's discussion of the role of narration makes primary and that the controversy to which that narrative responds makes suspect.

Rhetoric and Reliability

The *Apologia* is so thoroughly linked to the controversy that preceded it that it is sometimes hard to remember how distinctly idiosyncratic is an autobiography as a response to a theological controversy. The previous chapter showed how Newman had to position himself and Kingsley through the war of pamphlets to make that response appropriate. Because the success of the *Apologia* is now assumed owing to the work's place in the literary canon, we can easily forget how many ways such a response could have gone awry. One could for instance be persuaded of Newman's sincerity and still consider his arguments specious or even ludicrous.[14] Equally, one could consider the arguments strong but Newman insincere in making them. In effect, the autobiographical issue of sincerity interrupts the logical modes of evaluating argumentative discourse. And in particular, because of Kingsley's suggestion that Newman was a master of the duplicitous use of language, the status of rhetoric and literary effectiveness is the medium through which this interruption takes place. I have explained the philosophic reasons that made Newman want to confront rather than evade Kingsley's implication. Here I turn to the form that confrontation took.

The role of rhetoric within the structures of consciousness and narrative in the *Apologia* may be indicated by breaking down in more detail the structural components in Newman's mirror-gazing images of consciousness and their cognates in the narrative. Newman's mirror-gazing images create distorted reflections that lead to greater self-knowledge. Consciousness, not the innate self, establishes that situation when, looking in the mirror, it delineates a problem about the reflection, either the absence of self in the mirror or its unacceptable shape. The innate self that looks toward the mirror is first apprehended in its absence in the mirror of the world (implied by the absence of God there) or in its presence as a heretic in the mirror of history. In other words, one never sees the innate self reflected directly. Newman can only recover it fully after the measuring and analyzing activities of his consciousness have occurred. Both consciousness and the innate self stand on the gazing side of the mirror. The analyzing activity of consciousness in the face of the mirror's distortion is the sequential unfolding by which consciousness learns and knows the self.

The cognates to this system within the passages in which Newman describes himself in the act of writing are fairly easy to identify. In the place of the consciousness that observes the reflecting mirror is the narrator describing and reasoning upon his past self. In the place of the innate self recovered only by an analysis of its distorted reflection is the original act of self being narrated, the hallucinatory return from Sicily or the dazed traumatic period leading up to the 1845 conversion. Because those acts cannot be fully understood until after they have been narratively reflected and analyzed, they are not completed until they are narrated. The final component of the mirror-gazing system is, of course, the distorting mirror itself. One might be tempted to identify the mirror with narration itself, but that would be based more on notions of narrative mimesis than on the workings of either of these systems in the *Apologia*, for narration does not simply reflect the self and self-consciousness but comprises the whole reflective act that constitutes them, and its final effect is hardly distortion. The cognate to narration can only be the whole mirror-gazing system and not any part within it.

The key feature of the mirror that allows us to mark its narrative cognate is its distorting quality, and it is this quality that leads us through these interlocking structures to the role of rhetoric. The cognate to that distorted reflection is not narration per se but rather the re-created experience within the act of writing, a re-creation Newman often dwells on. That re-created experience involved both an emotional intensity and a recognition that that intensity was created by the rhetorical skill of the re-creation. Rhetoric, then—in particular, a deliberately crafted literary affectiveness—fills the place of the distorting quality of the mirror's reflection. Although distortion is the common accusation aimed at rhetoric, we must remember that the distortion in the mirror's reflection serves a vital purpose, for it is the first manifestation through which consciousness sees the innate self. Only by working through that distortion does one reach the full understanding of that self. If the distortions of rhetoric play the same role, then the role of rhetoric and literary affectiveness within the structure will have the same justification and consequently so will the role of autobiography as an argumentative discourse.

To reveal the connection between the working of autobiographical form as polemic and Newman's handling of the issue of rhetoric and to get at the precise nature of that handling, I must first work through the contemporary rubrics through which critics address the problem of rhetoric and sincerity. Few of even those literary critics with reservations about the *Apologia* express those reservations in the language of Kingsley, since they take accusations of duplicity to be irrelevant to evaluations of literary form. This issue, however, often seems to hover behind a criticism that some readers of the *Apologia* are willing to make: that Newman's insistence on logic and reason in his account, despite the emotional vividness of much of it, disables him from achieving a full understanding or communication of his own psyche. Thus George Levine, who writes appreciatively of Newman's belief in human irrationalism, complains finally that Newman is not irrational enough, that in the *Apologia* he refuses consistently to "push further back into his own consciousness" for the causes of his belief.[15] Compared to the criticism of insincerity or duplicity, Levine's charge represents a movement analogous to the one traced by Lionel Trilling between sincerity and authenticity as terms measuring the adequacy of a work to an author's internal life.[16] Rather than questioning whether Newman means what he says, whether he is honest, Levine questions whether Newman communicates who he is below the level of rational meaning. I do not want to fault Levine here for his connection with early critics of the *Apologia*. Rather, I think, both those early critics and Levine have articulated a central difficulty with the *Apologia* in response to that work's linking of highly emotional re-creation with a reasoned inquiry into the rhetorical bases of that re-creation and the propriety of those bases. Critics evade this difficulty (the relations among the formal status of the work as autobiography, its polemic ends, and its rhetorical and literary techniques) only by assuming an independence between rhetoric and sincerity or authenticity and praising Newman's rhetorical or literary technique without addressing the implications of that praise.

But this contradiction between emotional re-creation and the rhetorical skill behind it results from Newman's insistence on analyzing the workings of both the self who lived and the self who writes. Thus it relates directly to the dual status of the *Apologia* as a meditative and a polemical work. Until now, I have discussed the book as if it were simply a meditative work, an exercise in self-inquiry that will further confirm and strengthen Newman's state of certitude. That is, I think, the place the book creates for its own existence once it is read beyond the immediate context of the dispute with Kingsley. But the audience of that controversy did exist, and the book was first aimed at them. Moreover, as I have shown, when Newman argues the intellectual and emotional honesty of his beliefs, when he reveals the workings of his mind in a public meditation, he also, according to his epistemological argument for certitude, makes the best kind of polemical argument for the validity of those beliefs.

As a result of this dual status of the work, passages in the *Apologia* can be read in two directions at once. We can see the process at work by comparing a rhetorical treatment of Newman's brief description of childhood with my earlier discussion of it. According to the meditative structure I have set up for Newman's narrative, the account of the early value the young Newman put on imagination confirms the value of that imagination by doubling it in the older Newman's narration. An analyst of Newman's rhetoric argues, however, that "in describing angels and the undeniable religious institutions of his childhood and youth, Newman provides an explanation of how in later life he could sincerely believe in a continuing supernatural influence on the physical world and on human affairs."[17] In one reading, the later life confirms the earlier one. In another, the earlier life makes plausible the later one. Neither interpretation is incorrect; but each considers the work as operating with different formal intentions.

Marking these readings indicates the connection between the *Apologia*'s dual formal status and the problem of rhetoric, but it hardly resolves that problem. If Newman, with the cool reason that any careful use of rhetoric demands, creates the impression of an emotion to persuade readers, how are we to know that the coolness and the care do not mask deceit? This is, as I have said, the implicit question of any rhetorical study of Newman, though most of the rhetorical critics do not care to make it explicit. Whether one appreciates its rhetoric or its literary affectiveness, questions its sincerity or its authenticity, one thereby questions the validity or the adequacy of the *Apologia*'s dual status as meditation and as polemic.

Newman does not refute the connection between rhetoric and duplicity by a simple denial or a claim that rhetorical skill is independent of emotional honesty, though. His first step, which we have seen, is to define a place for reasoned observation, for self-explanation, that makes it a necessary part of the life. Then, in the second expansion of his structure of consciousness, he makes a reader experience not only the emotion of the character Newman but the reason and techniques of the writer Newman. We have seen how this works in terms of justifying narrative analysis in the previous section. In a passage from the end of the *Apologia*'s first chapter, the account of the illness in Sicily, we can see how the third expansion, the structure's comprehension of rhetoric works:

> Especially when I was left by myself, the thought came upon me that deliverance is wrought not by the many but by the few, not by bodies but by persons. Now it was, I think, that I repeated to myself the words which had ever been dear to me from my school days, "Exoriare aliquis!"—now too, that Southey's beautiful poem of Thalaba, for which I had an immense liking, came forcibly to my mind. I began to think that I had a mission. There are sentences of my letters to my friends to this effect, if they are not destroyed. (*Apologia*, 42–43)

We have here that vivid presentation of the emotion that is so frequently praised in Newman. The last sentence carries us in a slightly different direction, however. The fact of the experience can be documented in letters, proven reasonably to exist. If, with that suddenly matter-of-fact last sentence, we move back to the reference to Virgil and Southey, the import of the references shifts from emotional support to acceptance that his description of his emotion was a literary one and subject to literary appreciation and analysis. By revealing to readers the springs of the rhetoric, Newman has moved them from experiencers of rhetoric to allies in its production and analysis, allies in the project of reasoned meditation combined with a rhetorical communication of its results.

Newman does not mean this unveiling of the working of rhetoric to exculpate it in any easy way, I think, but rather aims to reveal its distortion and make it part of the narrative process. The submission of the original responses during the illness to the distortions of a description through literary reference is analogous to the distortions of self reflected in the mirrors of the external world and history. As those distortions are the first manifestations through which consciousness becomes aware of the innate self, so the distortions of rhetoric are the first manifestations of the mind and beliefs Newman reveals to the reader. As consciousness must work through those distortions in order to recover the innate self in a newly understood and confirmed status, so the reader is not left in those distortions but must work through them with the narrator to recover a newly understood and confirmed past belief or position of the mind. The distortion of rhetoric cannot be short-circuited for the same reason that the narrative unfolding cannot be dispensed with: The process of working through that distortion, the process of that unfolding, is the only way the innate self and its beliefs can be understood and confirmed. Prior to that process, the self exists only as a series of unarticulated assents; the original event lies buried beneath the daze of illness or trauma. The ideal reader operates in relation to the literary form as the narrator operates in relation to the act of writing and consciousness operates in relation to the mirror distortion. The reader whose mind operates according to Newman's philosophy sees, through the springs of the rhetoric, the content of Newman's act of meditation, and by recovering that act through the work of literary analysis, the reader comprehends and thus, by definition, also accepts the workings of Newman's assents and certitudes. The *Apologia* thus moves, through the reader, from meditation to polemic, all within the configurations of its literary form.

My use of the term *ideal reader* and my return to the concept of literary form should indicate that my argument here is not in the modern sense rhetorical or a reader-response analysis. I want, rather, to analyze how the form of the *Apologia* engulfs the polemical ends that these modes of criticism are usually best at marking. This inclusion of polemical end within formal analysis is, of course, my goal in these literary readings of Mill's *Autobiography* and Newman's *Apologia*. I want to articulate a concept of narrative form and a method of analyzing that form that include a comprehension of the philosophic content that is the context and the motivation of that form. By working through Mill's and Newman's philosophy, then by noting the relevance of those philosophies to their autobiographies, and finally, by marking the philosophic significance of narrative form, these analyses of Mill and Newman both move toward and exemplify a reading of Victorian prose that accommodates both its intellectual content and polemical aims on the one hand and its literary status and narrative form on the other.

Part 3
Carlyle, Arnold, and
the Reading of Victorian Prose

Chapter IX
Reading Victorian Prose

In the two central sections of this study, I have been tracing a movement from philosophy through autobiography to narrative. My point has been to indicate the availability to literary analysis of what we errantly think of as the content of intellectual history, in effect to show the narrative quality of ostensibly nonliterary discourse. In addition to their structural oppositions and their intellectual importance to their age, Mill and Newman were particularly helpful to my analysis because, unlike most other writers of Victorian prose, they had a clear sense of the discursive categories to which their various works belonged (they wrote separately philosophy, political analysis, theology, sermon, autobiography) even as they both had central, integrating concerns that tied their various discourses together. Because of their clear sense of divisions, it has been easier for me to separate provisionally works thought of as philosophy from those thought of as autobiographical narrative, if only to show how provisional that separation is.

In this concluding part, I fulfill the promise of my introduction and show how the movement I have described can be generalized into a methodology for the reading of Victorian prose. To do this, through a reading of Carlyle and Arnold, I deal with texts that do not sharply define themselves along traditional generic lines but quite comfortably slide across those lines and, as part of their polemical process, question our formal expectations. Is *Sartor Resartus* philosophy, fiction, or autobiography? Is *Literature and Dogma* a literary theory, a theological theory, or a fiction about biblical history? Merely by asking these questions, we can begin to see the interpenetration of philosophy and narrative form in Victorian prose. I hope the answers I give make explicit that interpenetration, which begins in the Victorian use of the word *philosophy*. The definitions

Mill and Newman give the word already predict the transformations I have been explaining.

We can see the particular way they used the word *philosophy* by looking at meanings they give to the words *poetry*, *science*, and *philosophy*. Both followed Romantic, expressive definitions of poetry. Mill maintains that poetry communicates subjective and internal states, and Newman essentially agrees: "Literature expresses, not objective truth, as it is called, but subjective; not things but thoughts."[1] To this concept of poetry, both men opposed two disciplines: science and philosophy. Science described the facts of the external world. For Mill, it was the result of perfect inductions, along the lines described by *A System of Logic*. For Newman, it was simply accurate description, without any subjective response. Philosophy, however, had a much more shifting and tenuous significance in the thought of both men. In one sense, philosophy is obviously opposed to poetic subjectivity and allied with science; it, too, is an objective description of the external world. Mill connected philosophy with science when he opposed it to poetry in his discussion of Wordsworth (*Auto*, 153). Newman also made this connection: "Knowledge is called by the name of Science or Philosophy, when it is acted upon, informed, or if I may use a strong figure, impregnated by Reason."[2]

In this sense, however, philosophy has clear and debilitating limitations. It can describe the external world or provide accurate knowledge of the external cause of an external effect, but it cannot provide a moral basis for acting upon the world. As might be expected, Newman is most explicit about this weakness:

> What is more common at the present day than for philosophers to represent society as moving by a certain law through different periods; and then, not content with stating the fact (which is undeniable), to go on to speak as if what has been, and is, ought to be.[3]

Philosophy here is valuable in its delineation of what is, but it is unsuited to determine what ought to be; and when it makes moral judgments, it tends to take what is for what ought to be. To some extent, Mill would agree with this accusation. Philosophic analysis provides accurate information to aid us in our decisions. But, as the *Autobiography*'s account of the mental crisis argues, it also has a tendency to undercut the basis for action, decision, and emotional commitment. As a result, Mill saw the value of something that he called illusion (as opposed to delusion):

A delusion is an erroneous opinion—it is believing a thing which is not. An illusion, on the contrary, is solely an affair of feeling, and may exist completely severed from delusion. It consists in extracting, from a conception known not to be true, but which is better than the truth, the same benefit to the feelings which would be derived from it if it were a reality.[4]

This is a very delicate balance. The value of an illusion lies in the emotion it contains. But that value depends on a recognition that the illusion is false. To a certain extent, therefore, the emotion must be inauthentic. The desideratum, obviously, is a discipline that will combine the truth of philosophy with the moral or emotional strength of poetic expression.

Yet both men call this discipline philosophy, too. The idea of wholeness, of finding the value in both sides of a controversy, of binding together the reasoning and emotional aspects of the personality, permeates Mill's thought. And Newman frequently opposes to the religion of sentiment the claim that religion is a philosophy that accommodates not only emotional intuition but objective reason. Nor is this use of the term *philosophy* in two senses an accidental equivocation. By calling their integrating discipline philosophy, Mill and Newman claim for that discipline, which creates wholeness by forming a compromise between subjective intuition and objective reason, the objective status inherent in the meaning of philosophy in the first sense of the term. If the term *philosophy* holds within it both the notions of inwardness, with all the Romantic poetic extensions that term has, and the notion of objectivity, it follows that what Victorians think of as philosophic, they already think of as literary as well. That by itself should lead us to look for the literary underpinnings of Victorian philosophy and the philosophic underpinnings of Victorian literature. But more specifically, the problem of defining consciousness, and the connection between its possible definitions and the forms a narrative structure may take, link Victorian philosophy and Victorian narrative inextricably.

Thus the roles I have defined for consciousness and narrative, through my discussion of autobiography, have broad ramifications for the discussion of Victorian prose. The movement I have been tracing from philosophy to narrative occurs in nonautobiographical Victorian prose as well. Indeed, by analyzing directly the correspondence between epistemological definitions and narrative structure, I think, we can trace the movement within individual works as well as through a series of works by the same author. And this analysis provides a methodology that may solve various problems in the reading of Victorian prose. I cannot, of course, within the limits of a concluding part, demonstrate fully the applicability and relevance of the methodology I think this book implies for the reading of Victorian prose; but I do sketch what such a methodology might look like, what problems it solves, and what readings of the two central figures, Carlyle and Arnold, it leads to.

One of the enduring problems confronting the critic of Victorian prose has been to define what constitutes the literariness of works that label themselves history, philosophy, journalism, criticism—anything but fiction, poetry, drama. Although treating, say, *Past and Present* and *Culture and Anarchy* purely as historical documents—treating them as historians treat nineteenth-century newspapers, the Oxford *Tracts*, the text of a Chartist pamphlet—does not even approach an adequate handling of the richness of Carlyle's and Arnold's prose, it has at least the advantage of being able to explain and justify clearly its own procedure. Whatever else the works are, they are products of the time and therefore historical documents. Moreover, unlike much poetry and fiction, Victorian prose works present themselves as topical and pertinent; responsive to the issues that concern historians of the nineteenth century; and responsive in terms of the abstract, argumentative discourse that constitutes history and philosophy rather than in terms of imaginative literature.

There have been, either in theory or in practice, three methods that respond to this problem. The first essentially treats Victorian prose as if it were a body of documents in intellectual history even as one calls the prose "literature." Thus, in books describing intellectual backgrounds to Victorian literature, the ideas of Carlyle, Arnold, Newman, and such are summarized as context rather than analyzed as literature. Sensing, however, that this approach does not really explain why we persist in reading the texts rather than the conveniently terse summaries, an impressive body of critics in recent years has been engaged in the theory and practice of analyzing the prose as literature, producing the second and third methods.

The second method, one not often explicitly articulated, involves a rigid separation between what a critic takes to be a work's content and what he takes to be its style. This separation results, in practice, in a discussion of image patterns and rhetorical structures that seem to operate at a level parallel to and divorced from a text's ostensibly obvious explanation of its ideas and arguments. If such a theory is not openly defended much anymore, the number of articles that discuss symbolism in Mill's *Autobiography*, rhetoric and imagery in the *Apologia*, Arnold's *Essays in Criticism* as a quest novel, the use of novelistic concrete detail in *Past and Present*, indicate how common the practice remains.[5]

There is no question that the application of this methodology reveals instructive aspects of the works these critics discuss, and all of these articles offer helpful analyses. None of them, however, really explains the effect the works have on the reader, and all of their implicit assumptions about what the works self-evidently mean in fact persistently simplify the writers' ideas. The result is that the Mill given us by philosophers, the Newman explicated by theologians, the Ruskin of art theorists, and the Arnold of literary theorists and social critics often turn out to be far more complex and interesting than those same writers depicted by literary critics. It may be true that "when the outlooks of these sages appear in the bald epitomes of literary histories, they lose their last vestige of interest. They provoke only bored surprise that anyone could have insisted so eagerly on half-incomprehensible dogmas or trite commonplaces."[6] It seems also true, though, that when one turns from the literary critic explicating Mill to the philosopher, one is surprised at how much more complex, influential, intelligent, and engaging Mill's ideas have suddenly become. One result of this has been to reassert the first method of reading the prose, straightforwardly analyzing idea and argument.[7]

The third method has very nearly become the reigning orthodoxy in the approach to Victorian prose. As first formulated in John Holloway's still important *The Victorian Sage*, this theory holds that the Victorian prose writers spoke to us from a particular stance, that of the prophet or sage who intended more to make us see ideas differently than to express new ideas. The sage is interested in "seeing old things in a new way."[8] Thus both what a sage said and how he said it were important: since he wanted to make us see the idea in a new way, thus appreciate it more fully, how he stated an idea became part of the idea itself, an aspect of our re-seeing. In a reformulation of this idea that allows us to read with even more nuance the texts of Victorian prose, George Levine argues that "one of the best ways to begin [the study of nonfictional prose] . . . might well be to attempt to regard great essays of the past as one regards fiction—as creations of imaginative worlds in which the writer himself becomes a character."[9]

The value of this theory is self-evident in the acute readings Holloway gives in *The Victorian Sage* and Levine offers in *The Boundaries of Fiction*; and the influence of their approach on the separate readings in my study should be too obvious to need much acknowledgment. Yet if this approach avoids the intellectual and literary flattenings of the other two, it still tends to defuse and domesticate the works owing to its tendency to make them meditative and imaginative at the cost of their frequent polemicism. To explain how an atheist can read Newman's *Essay on Development* with pleasure, Levine argues that despite Newman's explicit demand that we take his argument as a challenge to convert, a reader of the argument as literature need merely appreciate the authenticity of Newman's belief without responding to its explicit challenge of his own belief.[10] And Levine and William Madden have quite explicitly located the literariness of Victorian prose within its meditativeness: "One of the criteria for identifying genuinely artistic prose . . . [is] . . . that it be produced by a disinterested mind, a consciousness that is both open and free, immanent and contemplative, one which, in Keats's phrase, does not have designs upon us."[11] Even with an author as clearly meditative as Newman, though, surely a reader who starts from this position will find a tamer and less exciting Newman than the Newman who thought he was challenging our beliefs, not to mention one unlike the Newman that Newman himself thought he was.

But we do not, I think, have to throw up our hands and admit that some literature is inextricably tied to extraliterary belief even for its effect as literature. Instead I attempt on the one hand to delineate the connection between consciousness and polemic to see how an expression and investigation of one's consciousness may become part of a philosophic or historical argument and, on the other hand, to show more precisely the connections between consciousness and formal narrative structure.[12] Again, my treatment of Mill's and Newman's autobiographies is an extended attempt to define and demonstrate how to make these connections between ideas and literariness, between consciousness and narrative form. The possibility for the same kinds of connections is there as well in nonautobiographical works.

The application of the reading process practiced here to authors as distinctive as Carlyle and Arnold cannot be mechanical, nor should it create the impression that each author merely enacts, with slight variation, a rigid structural process. In the first place, we must abandon the rigid divisions implicit in first isolating epistemological issues and then discussing separately types of narrative embodiment. That structure was designed to show, in a particularly clear and exemplary fashion, how the movement from philosophy to narrative works. Neither Carlyle nor Arnold, however, saw himself as writing within the standard philosophic tradition. And while they were concerned with systemic integrity (despite Arnold's disclaimers), they were not concerned with standard canons of logical consistency. Indeed Carlyle explicitly questioned the value of those canons. As a result, we do not find in either writer a movement from a preliminary concern with a non-epistemological philosophic issue whose handling raises the issue of consciousness, to separate empirical evidencing and narrative embodiment. Indeed Carlyle's and Arnold's linked concern with the problems of consciousness and of form exist at the outset and throughout. Thus if they do not enact the movement from philosophy to narrative with the rigid clarity of Mill and Newman, the intersection of those two discursive modes is nevertheless more thematically central in their texts. The methodology that connects epistemology with narrative allows us both to grasp the literariness of Carlyle and Arnold and moreover to comprehend their precise intellectual concerns in new ways because the works of both authors are about discovering how to make that connection for themselves. Carlyle does so as a way of virtually inventing the role of Victorian prose-prophet. Arnold does so as a way of at last defining Victorian prose as a discourse and then defining the special place he sees his definition as allowing him to occupy both philosophically and formally.

Chapter X

Experience Teaching by Philosophy:
The Epistemology of Carlyle's Histories

We can best delineate the way Thomas Carlyle's theory of consciousness embodies itself in narrative form by tracing his movement from his earlier literary and philosophic essays to his later nineteenth-century narrative histories. Indeed, in addition to showing how philosophic polemic finally embodies itself in narrative form in Carlyle, delineating the connection between epistemology and narrative in his works also gives new insight into the nature of Carlyle's discovery of history.

The chronology is familiar enough: after publishing *Sartor Resartus* unsuccessfully in *Fraser's* and having built only a modest reputation as a reviewer of German literature and a mystic author of such philosophic sports as "Signs of the Times" and "Characteristics," Carlyle finally made his name with the English reading public as a historian of the French Revolution. And after that first history, both of his extended projects, first *Oliver Cromwell* and then *Frederick the Great*, had history as their subject. The wonder is not that Carlyle took so long to find his métier, however, but that he found it at all. The essays he wrote in the late 1820s and early 1830s indicate not an inattention to history, as if it were a discipline whose value he had not yet discovered, but an active distrust of history's efficacy. Between *Sartor* and "Characteristics," on the one hand, and the essays Carlyle started to write in 1833 that led toward *The French Revolution*, on the other, we do not find the simple extension of old ideas into a new genre that many critics have depicted. Rather, as a result of reevaluating other significant aspects of his beliefs, Carlyle breaks with his first evaluation of history.[1]

And yet, the early essays and *Sartor* contain many of the ideas Carlyle was later to articulate in his histories: his belief that materiality was a deceptive veil, his doctrine of work, even his search for heroes and his demand for a society of hero-worshippers. Moreover, it is through the antihistorical perspective of the early essays that Carlyle developed his later historiography. The link between the earlier and the later theories is Carlyle's articulation of a properly philosophic consciousness. Through the reasons Carlyle gives in his early essays for his belief that history as it is written and understood is valueless, we can put together his definition of the structure and role of consciousness. His evaluations of consciousness are deeply contradictory. On the one hand, he stresses the importance of transcendental objects of consciousness, as if the truth perceived were the only importance and any concentration upon the mechanism of perception—consciousness itself—were detrimental and vitiating. On the other hand, he insists that the interpretive activity of consciousness constitutes human freedom. But one would think that the priority of a unified, transcendental object would constrain that activity (even if beneficently as a truth rather than oppressively as an authoritative body) rather than allow it. We can also see him searching in those early essays for a form to embody his evaluation of consciousness and its objects, a search that leads him, paradoxically, back to history. Thus, even as the contradictions inherent in Carlyle's response to the problems of consciousness and interpretation led him to turn to history, the antihistorical source of his thinking shaped an attitude toward his historical subject matter and a placement of his narrative that was ahistorical as history is normally understood. To understand the form Carlyle's later histories took, we must understand their antihistorical roots, the developing philosophy of the early review-essays, the initial attempts of *Sartor Resartus* and "Characteristics" at finding a discourse to embody his evaluations of consciousness, and the reasons these attempts led him to turn to the discourse of history he had earlier thought of no value.[2]

History and Philosophy

We can see the apparent theoretical distance Carlyle had to travel before he could begin to write history if we compare "On History Again," an essay written in 1833 only slightly before he began research on the French

Revolution, with the earlier piece "On History," written in 1830. "On History Again" states unequivocally that "only he who understands what has been, can know what should be and will be" (*Works*, XXVIII:169).[3] And although Carlyle is fairly forbidding in this essay about the requirements for truly understanding history, he is also oddly sanguine, arguing that history gets itself understood despite the weaknesses of historians. Historians may not always know what to look for, but "by natural tendency alone, and as it were without men's forethought, a certain fitness of selection, and this even to a high degree, becomes inevitable" (*Works*, XXVIII:174).

The earlier essay, "On History," is considerably less sanguine, even though Carlyle wrote it as part of a projected history of German literature.[4] He seems no less insistent on the importance of historical knowledge:

> As we do nothing but enact History, we say little but recite it, nay, rather, in that widest sense, our whole spiritual life is built thereon. For, strictly considered, what is all Knowledge too but recorded Experience, and a product of History. (*Works*, XXVII:84)

Our actions are nothing if not history, and history is the basis of our spiritual life. Yet Carlyle in "On History" does not think we can understand history. Referring to the classic formula that history is philosophy teaching by experience, a formula that would seem almost a necessary consequence of the passage cited above, Carlyle nevertheless has reservations:

> The truth is, two difficulties, never wholly surmountable, lie in the way. Before Philosophy can teach by Experience, the Philosophy has to be in readiness, the Experience must be gathered and intelligibly recorded. (*Works*, XXVII:85)

Here and throughout his explication of these sentences, Carlyle rather surprisingly predicts what has come to be a truism of twentieth-century historical relativism. History cannot teach through experience because before we can know what the experience teaches, in order to interpret the experience, we need already to have the knowledge it would teach us; "the Philosophy has to be in readiness."[5] Further, since there is an infinite amount of historical data, an intelligible selection process presumes the knowledge that that data is supposed to give us. Of course history's infinite expanse is also a problem for the historian in the later essay, but there, "natural tendency," the process of passive forgetfulness rather than active research, does the selecting. This earlier essay presupposes no such natural tendency.

As Carlyle continues to explain the impossibility of writing accurately meaningful history, though, he also effectively implies the insignificance of history as a discourse, forcing us to reinterpret his opening statements about history's importance. His criticism of narrative as a form that falsifies historical truth becomes an implicit questioning of history's connection to truth:

> For as all Action is, by its nature, to be figured as extended in breadth and in depth, as well as in length; that is to say, is based on Passion and Mystery, if we investigate its origin; and spreads abroad on all hands, modifying and modified; as well as advances toward completion,—so all Narrative is, by its nature, of only one dimension; only travels forward towards one, or towards successive points: Narrative is *linear*, Action is *solid*. Alas for our "chains," or chainlets, of "causes and effects," which we so assiduously track through certain handbreadths of years and square miles, when the whole is a broad, deep Immensity, and each atom is "chained" and completed with all! (*Works*, XXVII:88–89)

One has only to retemporalize the spatial metaphor here to see how devastating this statement is about history as a discourse. If the linearity of narrative corresponds to the linearity of at least our conception of time, then action, which moves solidly through that line, is essentially atemporal, transcendent, and eternal in its significance. The passage's second sentence, of course, immediately criticizes empiricism and that philosophy's insistence on the primacy of causal analysis, but more than that, it denies the significance of history as a system of time-bound events. Only an event's role as part of an organic whole, its being "completed with all," creates that event's significance, not its causal implications or its effects. To the extent, then, that history like narrative, as a discourse that concerns the temporal relatedness of things, is linear, it falsifies rather than communicates truth. Narrative merely reflects history's linearity and its consequent causal fallacy.

The implications of "On History" and their connection with Carlyle's epistemology are explicit in other essays whose concerns are wider than simply history. "Signs of the Times," for instance, criticizes Locke's philosophy precisely as historical rather than epistemological:

It is not a philosophy of the mind: it is a mere discussion concerning the origin of our consciousness, or ideas, or whatever else they are called; a genetic history of what we see *in* the mind. The grand secrets of Necessity and Freewill, of the Mind's vital or not-vital dependence on Matter, of our mysterious relations to Time and Space, to God, to the Universe, are not, in the faintest degree touched on in these inquiries. (*Works*, XXVII:64)

Carlyle here attacks not merely narrative linearity but any genetic considerations at all. Genetic explanation was, of course, the nineteenth-century response to the failure of ontological explanation. By turning to Kantian antinomies and formulations of the noumenal, Carlyle may give the impression of turning his back on antiquated English philosophy for the more creative German thought, but he also insists on the old religious notion that truth is, almost by definition, atemporal, a quality of eternal essence rather than of time-bound matter.[6]

The linkage of the terms *genetic* and *history*, moreover, tell us why Carlyle could claim both that history contains all truth and that, as a discourse, it is of only the most limited value. At first glance, the terms *genetic* and *history* seem redundant. What kind of history would be ungenetic, unconcerned, if not with first causes, at least with second or third causes? Carlyle's problem with the genetic is the essentially temporal nature of its causal analysis. His ungenetic, hence significant, history would therefore have to be a history not locked into time. Indeed, if the *Oxford English Dictionary* is correct in attributing the first use of the word *genetic* in this sense to Carlyle, he might well be inventing the term in order to create a distinction between types of history where no distinction was before, thus establishing the concept of atemporal history. Truth would exist in atemporal history in that, being eternal, it would of course exist at all times, past as much as present and future. Further, since each element of truth is related to all elements, it would indeed be true that "our spiritual life is built" on history, built on it in the sense that our spiritual life is part of the whole of spiritual life existing throughout as well as across history. But *not* built on it in the sense of arising from it. History, as that which spatially contains all time and thus all truth, is the basis of all knowledge; but that history cannot be understood by standard historical analysis.

Carlyle's contrast between genetic history and philosophy of mind directs us toward the discourse he hopes will embody truth more effectively than narrative history. Because his definition of that philosophy denies any place for that history, we can see in it the connection between its epistemology and its suspicion of history as a discourse that may embody that epistemology. That definition occurs in general terms in an essay on Novalis in which Carlyle compares Scottish Common Sense philosophy unfavorably with German philosophy, not because his countrymen were too skeptical, but because, in a sense, they were not skeptical enough:

> For as to the Argument which [Reid] and his followers insist on, under all possible variety of figures, it amounts only to this very plain consideration, that "men naturally, and without reasoning, *believe* in the existence of Matter"; and seems, philosophically speaking, not to have any value; nay, the introduction of it into Philosophy may be considered as an act of suicide on the part of that science, the life and business of which, that of "*interpreting* Appearances," is hereby at an end. (*Works*, XXVII:24)

Carlyle objects to Reid and his school not because they deny the existence of Matter as essence but because they identify the essence of Matter too easily with its appearance, its phenomena.[7] Carlyle does not share the empiricists' belief that phenomena and our sensation of them are the only reality. But he is no more convinced of the existence of Matter than the most radical empiricist. Rather, he believes that phenomena bear no connection with reality at all. Interestingly, he does not argue for this separation as a logical consequence of anything but insists that philosophy presumes the separation. Addressing that separation thus defines philosophy. If philosophy's reason for existing is to address that separation, to interpret appearance, its existence obviously presumes that materiality is merely appearance and that there is a content beneath that appearance that can be reached through interpretation. This presumption has three clear consequences. First, truth is once again separated from space and time, the preconditions of matter, and thus made an atemporal entity. Second, the discourse that treats of truth is metaphysical philosophy—and we have already seen Carlyle's skepticism about the relationship between history and philosophy. Third, truth can only be reached by the mind moving outward freely to work its will on the material world, actively interpreting that world rather than merely perceiving it.

To understand Carlyle's progress first through the highly convoluted texts of *Sartor* and "Characteristics" and finally back to a rethinking of the possibility of history, we must be very clear both about the evaluations and definitions of consciousness that are set up here and about their highly self-contradictory nature. The first consequence outlined above involves a univocal truth that is the aim and object of consciousness, its only proper goal. The third consequence, however, values process over goal, the workings of consciousness as it interprets nature rather than its goal. If the univocal truth creates value, one would think that process would be merely instrumental. If process itself is value, then one wonders why Carlyle insists on a univocal object of consciousness.

The path from these contradictory consequences to Carlyle's turn toward history is, fittingly, not a linear one, leading as it does through Carlyle's most deliberately nonsequential, interpretively playful works, *Sartor* and "Characteristics." These works, each from a different perspective, try to articulate forms of discourse that respond to the contradictory demands of Carlyle's epistemology. Both the epistemology and the discourse either ignore history—in *Sartor*—or explicitly undercut it—in "Characteristics"—and so working out the way philosophic thought determines the shape of discourse in these works may seem to lead away from history. But only by following Carlyle away from history can we see his path back. What we see in the discussion of *Sartor* and "Characteristics" is a definition of consciousness whose reflection in discourse leads to two forms of dead-ended discourse. Turning back from that dead end involves returning to history for antihistorical reasons. And thus the evaluations of consciousness and philosophy that lead away from history finally lead back to it.

Sartor and "Characteristics"

Despite the importance of philosophic context to *Sartor Resartus*, most of the work's critics have failed fully to grasp the elements of that context. Most commonly, seeing *Sartor* through the grid of Carlyle's later—and importantly revised—thinking, critics have tended to depict the work as an earlier, more flexible articulation of those ideas and have distorted our picture of its form accordingly.[8] More recently, paying less attention to context and more to the obvious formal density of the work, a formal density that earlier critics had either short-changed or insufficiently accommodated, some critics have depicted the work as hermeneutically enclosed in that reflexive and indeterminate manner of Romantic self-awareness and Romantic irony, accordingly short-changing the didactic or, at any rate, determinate aims of the text.[9]

Neither of these kinds of readings is sufficient, I think, precisely because Carlyle's formal and philosophic aims were contradictory: The third philosophic consequence outlined above implies that the primary value of thought and discourse is not the object of interpretation but the process of interpretation per se, the activity of the mind interpreting. And this implication does lead in *Sartor* to a text that is acutely self-conscious, acutely aware of its own processes. On the other hand, the first philosophic consequence discussed above implies the existence of a transcendental truth that, if not material, is still the object of thought rather than the thought process itself. And both Teufelsdröckh and the Editor have, as an important goal of their philosophies, the discovery of this truth. This contradiction constitutes both *Sartor's* form and the reason that form finally breaks down into a philosophic paralysis that demands the revisionary formulations of "Characteristics."

Sartor's focusing upon the activity of the mind interpreting, the activity of consciousness, relates to the work's explicit eschewing of that linear narrative dependent upon causal chains that "On History" earlier rejected. In a passage I cited in my introduction, the Editor notes approvingly Teufelsdröckh's rejection of this linear discourse:

> Our Professor's method is not, in any case, that of common school Logic, where the truths all stand in a row, each holding by the skirts of the other; but at best that of practical Reason, proceeding by large Intuition over whole systematic groups and kingdoms; whereby, we might say, a noble complexity, almost like that of Nature, reigns in his Philosophy, or spiritual Picture of Nature: a mighty maze, yet, as faith whispers, not without a plan. (*Sartor*, 52)

Critics have, of course, long discussed *Sartor's* lack of logical development. And they have offered alternative structures, the most helpful being those that involve concentricity: statement followed by repetition and analogy with developing difference.[10] Although these definitions may help a reading of *Sartor*, they structure the text too simply and too soon. These kinds of structures are not exactly unknown in logical discourse after all, and Carlyle pointedly does not define an alternative narrative structure. Rather, moving from the way Teufelsdröckh interprets to the problem of interpreting Teufelsdröckh, he compares that problem to the problem of interpreting nature properly. His purpose is not to tell us how we may interpret but to move our attention from type of interpretation (logic as opposed to something else) to the act of interpretation itself.

The merging of this concern for process of interpretation itself with a deliberate creation of a text that refers to itself, and consequently a deliberate intensification of consciousness, occurs when the Editor later returns to Teufelsdröckh's method and his own:

> Neither, in so capricious inexpressible a Work as this of the Professor's, can our course now more than formerly be straightforward, step by step, but at best leap by leap. Significant Indications stand out here and there; which for the critical eye, that looks widely and narrowly, shape themselves into some ground-scheme of a Whole: to select these with judgment, so that a leap from one to the other be possible, and (in our old figure) by chaining them together, a passable Bridge be effected: this, as heretofore, continues our only method. (*Sartor*, 208)

Again, the Editor here does not refer directly to Teufelsdröckh's text but to his own method of making sense of that text. This referential turn has two results. First, it once again calls our attention to the act of interpretation, to how we must interpret Teufelsdröckh, rather than how he interprets the world. Second, it re-creates, in its interpretation of Teufelsdröckh, Teufelsdröckh's method of interpreting the world: just as Teufelsdröckh does not operate by a Logic in which truths are attached to each other's skirts, neither can the Editor move through Teufelsdröckh's text step by step. Both must leap nonsequentially in order to reproduce the transcendental meaning, either of the world or of Teufelsdröckh's text. Teufelsdröckh's method of interpretation, which focuses on the primacy of interpretation, evidently forces the text that interprets him to re-create, rather than simply explain, both that method and that primacy. Thus in explicating Teufelsdröckh, the Editor also explicates himself, and in explicating himself, he also explicates Teufelsdröckh. Interpretation does not reach a goal but becomes more and more self-aware.

Not surprisingly, *Sartor* constantly calls into question the precise status of both the Editor's text and Teufelsdröckh's. The observation that the work is in the form of a marginal commentary on a text that we never actually see is one of G. B. Tennyson's most helpful correctives to earlier Carlyle criticism.[11] But it is also true that *Die Kleider* itself is a marginal commentary on a hypothetical volume Teufelsdröckh could have written but did not. Having claimed that "'as Montesquieu wrote a *Spirit of Laws* . . . so could I write a *Spirit of Clothes*'" (*Sartor*, 35), Teufelsdröckh goes on to explain why he did not write that and what he has written:

> Nay, what is your Montesquieu himself but a clever infant spelling Letters from a hieroglyphical prophetic Book. . . . Much, therefore, if not the whole, of that same *Spirit of Clothes* I shall suppress, as hypothetical, ineffectual, and even impertinent: naked Facts and Deductions drawn therefrom in quite another than that omniscient style, are my humbler and proper province. (*Sartor*, 36)

Note, Teufelsdröckh does not claim that he chose not to write the *Spirit of Clothes*, but rather that he suppressed it, having drawn from it aspects of the text of *Die Kleider*, which he now presents. In other words, *Die Kleider* like *Sartor* depends upon a prior text. But the process is also reversed. Despite the arguments of recent critics, there is some indication that the text of *Sartor*, at least in a sense, *is* also the text of *Die Kleider*: at one point the Editor speculates, "Or has the Professor his own intention; and laughs in his sleeve at our strictures and glosses, which are indeed but a part thereof?" (*Sartor*, 213). If the Professor has intended the glosses and strictures of the Editor, then the text of *Die Kleider* is not complete without them. Only the combination of text and gloss constitutes the text. This playfulness, of course, confuses the normal divisions between the act of interpretation and the object of interpretation. Every text is itself a gloss, every gloss also an integral text. One has only interpretations of interpretations, each interpretation reenacting rather than explicating the structure of the interpretation it interprets.

Despite the vigorous interest in the process of interpretation as valuable in itself, however, and the consequent intensifications of consciousness, the first consequence of Carlyle's definition of philosophy—the existence and importance of transcendental truths—still plays a vital role in *Sartor*'s metaphysic. Although Carlyle never defines what specifically is or are the transcendental truth or truths that lie behind the appearance of materiality, only the existence of those truths gives meaning to the central metaphors of the work. Clothes have value, after all, because they reflect the inner truth they clothe. And the vital doctrine of symbols only makes sense if not merely dispersing the material appearance of a symbol is possible but recognizing that symbol's specific eternal significance as well:

> In the Symbol proper, what we can call a Symbol, there is ever, more or less distinctly and directly, some embodiment and revelation of the Infinite; the Infinite is made to blend itself with the Finite, to stand visible, and as it were, attainable there. (*Sartor*, 220)

A symbol is only separable from the rest of materiality by its peculiar relationship with the Infinite, which it embodies. This means of course that the Infinite has definable features, capable of an embodiment that makes it visible—if only metaphorically.

Although this stress on the object of interpretation diverges in tendency from a valuing of the process of interpretation for its own sake, Carlyle in fact avoids contradictoriness at this stage through an identification of process with object.[12] He makes the identification between process and object an explicit part of Teufelsdröckh's philosophy at least:

> To look through the Shows of things into Things themselves he is led and compelled. . . . The whole energy of his existence is directed, through long years, on one task: that of enduring a pain, if he cannot cure it. Thus everywhere do the Shows of things oppress him, withstand him, threaten him with fearfullest destruction: only by victoriously penetrating into Things themselves can he find peace and a stronghold. (*Sartor*, 205–206)

To decipher the logical conclusion here, we must read this passage backward. Teufelsdröckh is tormented by appearances. He can cure the pain of that torment only by dissipating appearances and penetrating into essence. But Teufelsdröckh does not achieve cure: his existence is directed at learning to endure what he cannot cure. Since he is also compelled to look through Show, the suggestion is that the process of looking through is the equivalent of endurance, for the end of penetration would be cure. But that process of looking through achieves the same end as penetration since it looks through things into Things. And indeed, if we remember the often discussed doctrine of *Entsagen*, so endurance brings the same peace as does cure. The process does not arrive at, but effects, its objects.

Although process can be reified into object, reflexiveness and consciousness re-create a contradiction between the first and third consequences outlined at the end of the last section, a contradiction that leads to the alternative, almost mirror-reversal metaphysic of "Characteristics," the breakdown of which finally leads back to history. Focusing on the primacy of interpretation and its process entailed the creation of a spiral of interpretations of interpretations, texts that were always marginal, even as marginality was the only originality. As long as each interpretation confirms the next, there is no problem in reifying process. But such a perpetual confirmation is impossible if we are to be able to maintain a distance between Editor and Teufelsdröckh. That distance is necessary for interpretation, which depends for its purpose upon a difference between the object interpreted and the significance interpretation finds, but it implies the possibility of divergence between one interpretation and another. As soon as an interpretation diverges from the interpretation it interprets, however, the process of looking through, which became the Thing penetrated, breaks up into a series of deliberations that lead backward constantly away from the object so that instead of dissipating materiality, interpretation is paralyzed in a paroxysm of self-deliberation that never reaches materiality.

We see precisely this paroxysm in the late chapter "The Dandaical Body." The bulk of that chapter is Teufelsdröckh's analysis of dandyism and poor-slavery as religions that will soon divide England between them and turn the nation into two warring camps. The problems with Teufelsdröckh's conceit are, first, that we do not know whether we are to take it as the result of ignorance or irony and, second, if we give him the benefit of the doubt, we do not see what knowledge the irony adds. Identifying rich idleness and desperate poverty as religions does not seem to reveal any particular new insight into the heavily analyzed problem of the condition of England (heavily analyzed even by 1830–1831). We get the impression that Teufelsdröckh's insistence on ontological analysis has here obfuscated rather than penetrated the material surface. But this view of the chapter might be merely a commonly held critical judgment of Carlyle's ending to *Sartor* were it not for the Editor's conclusion:

Never perhaps did these amaurosis-suffusions so cloud and distort [Teufelsdröckh's] otherwise most piercing vision, as in this of the

Dandaical Body! Or was there something of intended satire . . . . If
satire were actually intended, the case is little better. There are not
wanting men who will answer: Does your Professor take us for
simpletons? His irony has overshot itself; we see through it, and perhaps through him. (*Sartor*, 287)

Though this passage ends with a claim of insight, in fact the direction of
our perception is not into, but away from, the chapter's topic. This paragraph points us away, as our own deliberations perhaps already have, from
the social situation to Teufelsdröckh's analysis of that situation. Moreover,
the interpretation of Teufelsdröckh has within it the same problems as the
original interpretation. Are we to take it that the Editor is too English to
see Teufelsdröckh's real point or that Carlyle is here, through the Editor,
drawing back from the extremities of his own thought as represented by
Teufelsdröckh? Or is the Editor, in his complaint, himself being ironic (as
he more than occasionally is), heading off possible objections by making
them look flat-footed? In effect, every divergence of interpretation from
its object is magnified by the reflexiveness of the text until the original
object of interpretation disappears and the philosophic activity that was
meant to penetrate becomes itself impenetrable.[13]

The ontological discourse that was intended to penetrate matter, when
it actually confronted something concrete, a social situation, ended in a
paralyzing, backwardly moving vortex. If we look at "Characteristics" as
an attempt to overturn this vortex by replicating *Sartor*'s discourse in
mirror-image reversal, we can see precisely how that essay leads to the
final turn toward history. To regenerate the ability to act as well as to
interpret, in the place of *Sartor*'s making consciousness its own object,
Carlyle in "Characteristics" attacks consciousness directly, attempting to
mount his ontological discourse without it. But his attack is consciously
an acutely conscious one. By this attack, the essay becomes a history of
sorts, but a history that constantly attempts to circumvent its own chronologies. In both its form and its ideas, one of his most brilliant but also
most self-destructive early essays, "Characteristics" represents a kind of
impossible limit to the ontological discourse Carlyle was trying to construct in order to embody his contradictory evaluations of consciousness.[14]

To take the essay's argument first: Carlyle contends, almost as if he had
Sartor's concluding paralysis in mind, that consciousness is the root of all
contemporary problems because it vitiates man's freedom to act: "let the

free, reasonable Will, which dwells in us, as in our Holy of Holies, be indeed free, and obeyed like a Divinity, as is its right and its effort: the perfect obedience will be the silent one" (*Works*, XXVIII:8). The linking of freedom and silent obedience is not here simply an easy paradox. The silent obedience is not to an external master but to one's own impulses. Unconscious action is free to act upon thought and will. Consciousness, on the other hand, by taking the mind for its object, announces and investigates thought but does not simply act on it. It thus ends by calling the will, of which it is supposedly conscious, into question because it unlinks will, thought, and action. "In the perfect state," Carlyle argues, "all Thought were but the picture and inspiring symbol of Action" (*Works*, XXVIII:25). Consciousness interrupts this wholeness, making pure freedom impossible. Thus, of the moral realm of consciousness, conscience, Carlyle states, "To say that we have a clear conscience, is to utter a solecism; had we never sinned, we should have had no conscience" (*Works*, XXIII:8). Similarly, he would argue, to say that we are conscious of free will is a solecism. Had our will been completely free, we would not be conscious of it. One would almost think that this author could not be the same writer who in *Sartor* tried to create a discourse whose self-consciousness was intended to enact the mind's freedom through the activity of interpretation.

Almost, one would think, until one realized that we must be conscious of ourselves even in order to diagnose our problem as consciousness. Moreover, this paradox is not a problem with Carlyle's argument but an intrinsic part of it. He is, in fact, quite playful about it, at one point locating the prevalence of reviewers as a mark of diseased self-consciousness in literature even as he admits what a reader cannot help remarking for himself, that the essay presents itself as a review of two books on metaphysics. But even when it has diagnosed itself as the problem, consciousness cannot either turn itself off, as the essay seems to hope it might, or transcend itself as *Sartor* tries to make it do. It can only become ever more acute. Even if, as in Scottish Common Sense philosophy, the mind willfully turns away from metaphysics to faith in the existence of matter, this abdication does not re-create unconsciousness, in the sense of creative activity, but willfully creates the end of will and freedom: Carlyle called it an "act of suicide." Consciousness can only shut itself off, then, through death. But neither can it transcend itself, intensifying itself into a quality that breaks its own chains:

Consider it well, Metaphysics is the attempt of the mind to rise above the mind; to environ and shut in, or as we say, *comprehend* the mind. Hopeless struggle, for the wisest, as for the foolishest! What strength of sinew, or athletic skill, will enable the stoutest athlete to fold his own body in his arms, and, by lifting, lift up *himself*? (*Works*, XXVIII:27)

In a sense, the problem of consciousness is partly that it can never become acute enough. The separations it entails between the mind and itself, the separations that disrupt the connections between will and act, can never become acute enough for consciousness to act upon itself. The athlete can never lift himself up. In terms of the passage on Scottish and German metaphysics, neither alternative is satisfactory. Willful belief is both the abdication of and the death of thought, an act of suicide. An entry into the free play of interpretation, however, here as in *Sartor*, entraps the mind in the coils of philosophy and consciousness. One of the appearances we interpret will always be that of our own sensations, but we will never interpret that appearance enough to dissolve it into essence, enough to lift ourselves up.

In the fully witted way in which "Characteristics" raises the expectations of a historical essay and consciously frustrates those expectations, we can see the connection between the role of history in Carlyle's thought and this vortex of consciousness and interpretation, which first occurs in *Sartor*. At first glance, the essay seems to create a mythic but nevertheless genetic history of the fall into consciousness. Particularly when he talks about healthy, unconscious and unhealthy, conscious societies, Carlyle writes in terms of a historically located state of primitive health—"accordingly, it is not in the vigorous ages of a Roman republic that Treatises of the Commonwealth are written. . . . So long as the Commonwealth continues rightly athletic, it cares not to dabble in anatomy" (*Works*, XXVIII:14)—and implies a decline, marked by consciousness, and occurring in a time frame. Even when talking about philosophic development per se, Carlyle uses the language of chronology. If he does not explicitly identify a philosophically untainted state, he still establishes priority: "Religion was everywhere; Philosophy lay hid under it, peaceably included in it. . . . Only at a later era must Religion split itself into Philosophies" (*Works*, XXVIII:15). The reason for establishing this historical model is not that hard to figure out. Because Carlyle realizes that unconsciousness cannot occur once consciousness has set in, he must posit unconsciousness as an ontologically prior state. Priority, however, is an inevitably genetic concept and automatically entails the language of chronology. Even an organic metaphor such as the essay's insistent identification of unconsciousness with health, consciousness with disease, by figuring health as a prior state that ends, creates the image of chronological sequence.

Although this historical model is a conceptual necessity, Carlyle clearly lets us know that the model is merely a conceptual and a narrative convenience, not a narrative reflection of any actual sequence. In fact, both in its chronologies and its narrative, the essay carefully frustrates historical expectations. In the opening passages, the disease of modern man and modern society is clearly defined as consciousness: "let but any organ announce its separate existence, were it even boastfully, and for pleasure, not for pain, then already has one of those unfortunate 'false centres of sensibility' established itself, derangement is already there" (*Works*, XXVIII:1). The announcement itself is the disease here, and not anything announced. Later, however, the essay defines consciousness as a symptom of the prior problem—the loss of faith—even possibly a symptom that presages cure: "the Self-Consciousness is the symptom merely; nay, it is also the attempt toward cure" (*Works*, XXVIII:20). Still later, lest one think the opening did not label unbelief as the first cause of disease only because Carlyle was not ready to broach that topic, the modern era in which belief fails is again implicitly attributed to consciousness, which resumes causal priority. And yet later still, it is the Epoch that causes consciousness (*Works*, XXVIII:32). This constant reversal of chronology should not be taken as a flaw in Carlyle's myth or an aspect of it that he had not thought out. We have seen his view of genetic history and causal explanation already. He is here, I think, trying to put that view into play by showing us that if linear narrative creates a historical sequence, one must uncover the arbitrariness of that sequence to see the true, simultaneous, relationship of things. In the place, then, of the studiously nonsequential leaping that was the form of the various texts making up *Sartor*, "Characteristics" denies sequence by using it against itself.

The problem with this formal self-consumption is not that the text is ahistorical in its play with chronology but that it is not ahistorical enough. In the same way that consciousness cannot turn itself off, neither can history. Having raised the expectations implicit in the language of cause and chronology, Carlyle could offer contradictory sequences but he could not end the notion of sequentiality entirely. His mythic history thus offers two futures, not as alternative results of proper or improper decisions, but simply as mutually exclusive inevitable outcomes. In the first prediction, history becomes an endlessly repeating cycle:

> It is a chronic malady that of Metaphysics, as we said, and perpetually recurs on us. At the utmost, there is a better and a worse in it; a stage of convalescence, and a stage of relapse with new sickness: these forever succeed each other, as is the nature of all Life-movement here below. (*Works*, XXVIII:26)

In the second prediction, unbelief simply terminates, not through the will of man or the activity of thought, but of its own fever: "Metaphysical Speculation, if a necessary evil, is the forerunner of much good. The fever of Scepticism must needs burn itself out, and burn out thereby the Impurities that caused it" (*Works*, XXVIII:40). Although this second ending may sound better than the first, for Carlyle's desiderata of freedom and ability to act, each ending is disastrous and disastrous in a way analogous to the theoretical alternative of consciously willed unconsciousness or increasingly intense consciousness. The second end of history parallels the less desired alternative of willed unconsciousness and suicidal death. In the second end, termination is imposed by an inevitable external process. The fever burns itself out as a natural causal process over which man has no control. To wish for such an ending is to wish for things to be taken out of one's hands, to abdicate responsibility in the same way the Scottish philosophers did. The cyclical alternative, though, can offer consciousness only the possibility of recognizing its own cyclical entrapment; and that recognition is, of course, part of the cycle of entrapment, not a transcendence of it anymore than in *Sartor* consciousness could transcend itself.

Finally, what Carlyle discovered through his movement from *Sartor*'s metaphysic to that of "Characteristics" was not that his ethical, metaphysical, and epistemological theories were invalid but that he needed a new kind of discourse. In scorning genetic history for ontological analysis, he found that that analysis, imbedded in the sequentiality of language, either paralyzed itself with the analysis of that sequence or became tainted by narrative linearity. Either his discourse stressed the process of consciousness at the cost of losing sight of its univocal, transcendental object or, by trying to turn consciousness off, denied it the freedom that allowed it to see beyond material causality. Thus the structure of history caught up within itself the philosophic discussion of consciousness and stained that discussion with its own inevitable constraints of causality and chronology. In effect, Philosophy teaching transformed itself into philosophy teaching by Experience and thus was undercut by all the flaws in that process outlined in "On History." But perhaps the process could be reversed. Perhaps by concentrating directly on historical discourse, one could use that discourse to arrive at a coherent ontological content and thus create a truly ungenetic history, a history moreover that could contain the destructive contradictions of Carlyle's epistemology, could contain both his insistence on a transcendental object of consciousness and his valuing of the interpreting activity of consciousness. Perhaps one could create an Experience that teaches by Philosophy. Such was the discourse Carlyle started to theorize about in the essays immediately following "Characteristics," particularly in "Biography"; such was the discourse he enacted in the narrative stance of *Past and Present*.

The Narrative Voice of History

Sartor tried to integrate an interest in a univocal object of consciousness with a valuing of the interpretive activity of consciousness by creating a reflective discourse in which consciousness became its own object. When that reflectiveness ended in the paralysis of an ever-retreating interpretation of interpretation, "Characteristics" tried to re-create stability by using consciousness and history to shut themselves off, only to find that the vortices and chronological contradictions of conscious unconsciousness and ahistorical history could never become intense enough to cancel themselves out. Thus we can see how narrative discourse calls into question an epistemology it cannot successfully embody, forcing Carlyle either to rethink his epistemology or continue his discursive innovations. The former was unthinkable, but the latter led him, finally, back to history, though an oddly defined history.

For the history Carlyle created to be ungenetic and to be a realm in which the mind could both play freely and discover its own freedom, it had to have two qualities: First, it had to be an area in which the mind could discover itself and yet be an area alien enough for that discovery not to be a threatening act of self-consciousness. Second, despite an ostensibly fixed factual content, history had to be available for the same kind of interpretive activity that Carlyle wanted consciousness to apply to phenomena. After all, the historian trapped by facts would be no more free than the philosopher trapped by materiality.[15] These two qualities Carlyle created through his famous view of history as biography and through his doctrine of Fact.

"History is the essence of innumerable Biographies." It is perhaps the most famous line in the essays. Less well known is that, in its first incarnation in "On History" (*Works*, XXVII:86), the sentence begins an explanation of why history is impossible to write. Since we do not even understand fully the essence of our own life, Carlyle goes on to declare, we cannot hope to understand the essences of history's innumerable biographies. Only in its second incarnation, in "Biography" (*Works*, XXVIII:46), where Carlyle quotes himself without naming himself as his own source, does the aphorism become an explanation of the value of history. Neither from "old interminable Chronicles" nor in "modern Narrations, of the Philosophic kind" does Carlyle hope for much of value. Rather, he looks to history to learn about the lives of others, others who live versions of his own life: "what hope have we, except the for the most part fallacious one of gaining some acquaintance with our fellow-creatures . . . how, in short, the perennial Battle went, which men name Life, which we also in these new days, with indifferent fortune, have to fight" (*Works*, XXVIII:47). It is clear enough here that history has been made entirely into a mirror in which the historian and reader may see themselves.[16] When we add to this passage one a few pages earlier defining the perennial battle—and thus what constitutes our sole interest in other lives—the stable, ungenetic, ontological content of Carlyle's history becomes clear: "this same struggle of human Freewill against material Necessity, which every man's Life, by the mere circumstance that the man continues alive, will more or less victoriously exhibit,—is that which above all else, or rather inclusive of all else, calls the Sympathy of mortal hearts into action" (*Works*, XXVIII:44–45). The content of history, the struggle for the mind's freedom, is thus the same as the motivation for turning to history, the desire to break the constraints of philosophic discourse. Moreover, this content has no tainting causal or temporal element. "Every man's Life" expresses this "perennial Battle." Accordingly, the writer and reader of history can find in it the atemporal philosophy of mind that would not emerge from the ahistorical *Sartor* or the anti-historical "Characteristics." Two questions arise, however. First, what has occurred that allows history, as innumerable biographies, at first an unreadable and unwritable history, to become so comprehensible here? Second, why, if history is about ourselves and the perennial problems of mind, is it not open to the same criticism of consciousness that "Characteristics" leveled at metaphysics, the same paralysis of consciousness that gripped *Sartor*?

The answer to both questions lies, I think, in Carlyle's doctrine of facts, a vastly misunderstood aspect of his theory. Both Carlyle's biographer and his reading public valued his histories for the meticulous, factual accuracy they adhered to as well as for the vivid scene and character painting they managed to achieve within the constraints of that accuracy.[17] And contemporary critics have often agreed.[18] It would be odd, however, for a writer who consistently branded any attentiveness to material reality as entrapment by appearance and who labeled "Dryasdust" the historian who obsessively documents statements, to be particularly concerned with the empirical existence of what he recounted. The evidence is overwhelming that Carlyle was extremely careful, of course,[19] but a look at the reasons he gives in "Biography" for his interest in facts shows clearly that what he valued about facts was not precisely their factuality:

> Fiction, while the feigner of it knows that he is feigning, partakes, more than we suspect, of the nature of *lying*; and has ever an, in some degree, unsatisfactory character. All Mythologies were once Philosophies; were *believed*: the Epic Poems of old time, so long as they continued *epic*, and had any complete impressiveness; were Histories, and understood to be narratives of *facts*. (*Works*, XXVIII:49–50)

To see what Carlyle is saying about facts, we must first get beyond a common misreading of this passage. Normally, Carlyle is taken to mean here that even though fiction, unlike lying, lets its audience know that it is feigning, its feigning nevertheless connects it to lying. Actually, though, Carlyle says nothing about what the feigner tells his audience. He marks as a potential distinction only that "the feigner of it knows he is feigning." If we take "while" to mean "even though" and take the focal contrast to be between fiction and lying, the passage becomes incoherent because no one ever thought that a liar did *not* know he was lying (otherwise, what is the difference between lying and being in error?). If we take "while" to mean "when," however, and take the focal contrast to be between fiction and mythology, the passage will again make sense, if not the sense usually attributed to it. Mythologies differ from fiction in that they were once believed by both teller and told. Fiction is like mythology in that both are empirically inaccurate, but fiction is like lying rather than like mythology in that the teller recognizes that he is being inaccurate. Mythology is thus like history in that it is believed. Consequently, the passage goes on to explain, what makes epic poetry valuably different from fiction—what makes epics histories even—is not their empirical accuracy, for they have no more of that than does fiction, but the belief writers and readers place in their empirical accuracy.

Not empirical data as opposed to imagined detail but belief as opposed to open feigning constitutes the difference between history and fiction. Carlyle makes even clearer that not the accuracy of the text but the belief in that accuracy is the primary constituent of historicity by asserting that to the extent that Homer and his listeners did not believe his gods "were real agents," his work was not history but instead "hollow and false." It follows that facts are important not because they are factual but because they are believed to be factual. The quality of believing, though, belongs not to the historical text but to the reader and writer of it. History is now both readable and writable because what makes it history is not precisely its accuracy in recounting innumerable biographies but its writers' and readers' beliefs in that accuracy. And that belief becomes a further tie between the content of the history and the readers of it, making that discourse even more potentially a philosophy of mind. Since for history to be history, its audience must believe it to be history, and since belief is a subjective function of that audience, history can only become history through the addition of an element of its audience, and thus the audience must necessarily see itself in something that is partly a creation of itself.

If facts become facts by our belief in them, they are enticing to Carlyle not merely as believable but also as somehow alien, demanding an effort in order to be quite comprehended. And in this alienness lies both history's interpretability, its vital link to the free play with materiality that was important in philosophies of the mind, and history's protection against the debilitating self-consciousness of metaphysical discourse. One of the peculiarities of Carlyle's histories is that whenever the narrative mentions that something is a fact, two things are likely to happen. First, we can be pretty sure that this fact will be relatively unimportant, or at least what Carlyle calls our attention to about it will be unimportant, both to the events of the history at hand and to any received notion of what are the significant events of the historical period in which it appears. And second, the narrative will come to a stunning halt as we are called upon to consider and meditate upon the factuality that makes this event important. In *Past and Present* (*Works*, X:45–46), the meditation upon King John, not as the signer of the Magna Carta but as having given some money to Jocelyn's monastery, nicely exhibits this occurrence in a historical narrative. Perhaps even a more significant example is the fact Carlyle uses in "Biography" to explicate his theory of fact. He begins by calling upon us to consider

> how impressive the smallest historical *fact* may become, as contrasted with the grandest *fictitious event*; what an incalculable force lies for us in this consideration: The Thing which I here hold imaged did actually occur; was in very truth, an element in the system of the All whereof, I too form part. (*Works*, XXVIII:54)

He then unveils his fact, the existence of a peasant who had some contact with Charles I after one of the battles of the civil war. But Carlyle calls our attention, not to the role of the seemingly insignificant in large, political events, but merely to this peasant having showed up at all in the pages of history, merely to his existence: "Singular enough, if we will think of it! This, then, was a genuine flesh-and-blood Rustic of the year 1651" (*Works*, XXVIII:55). And he goes on to consider how strange it is that the rustic did all things one might guess rustics would do.

We should note two things here. First, what Carlyle fixes our attention on is not quite what we all share with the peasant, though we are reminded of that, but, rather, the peasant as a detail of history so alien from us that his existence might have slipped away unnoticed but for his fortuitous connection with Charles. Indeed, even when Carlyle discusses a famous figure, as in the passage about King John, he tends to stress the evanescence of the fact, the tenuousness of our hold upon it:

> How intermittent is our good Jocelyn; marking down without eye to *us*, what *he* finds interesting! How much in Jocelyn, as in all History, and indeed in all Nature, is at once inscrutable and certain, so dim, yet so indubitable; exciting us to endless considerations. For King Lackland *was* there. (*Works*, X:46).

Lackland was there, but Carlyle wants us to remember that less than he wants us to remember how flickering and strange is our image of him. Thus, although Carlyle's history is a method for considering truths about ourselves, and about such metaphysical issues as free will and necessity and what is eternal in human existence, one cannot quite brand this history as self-conscious because its surface at least, that which at the immediate level we perceive explicitly, differs from us.

The second thing to note is that, although one presumes Carlyle did not actually invent the appearance of the peasant or King John's visit to the monastery in the historical texts in which he found those "facts," that is about all he did not invent. His guesses about the shape of the peasant's life have no particular evidential sanction, and the energy he expends and the excitement he creates about our knowledge of the peasant's existence are purely a function of his own response to the fact and not any aspect of the fact itself. By the end of Carlyle's consideration of the fact, we still only know that the peasant existed and nothing more about him, but we know very much more about how Carlyle interprets that fact of existence. Similarly, most of the passage about King John expresses excitement over the mere presence of the fact as a thing to think about. Carlyle even admits that "with Jocelyn's eyes we discern almost nothing of John Lackland" (*Works*, X:45).[20] The empirical data of history do not constrain Carlyle at all. Facts are important neither for any information they offer in and of themselves nor for any information their cohering together might lead us to. They are simply the occasions for interpretation to turn itself outward, occasions for the interpreter to deflect his attention from himself while still allowing him to discover himself. Facts are not experience teaching philosophy because what is taught does not arise from the facts; they are experiences ripped from temporal context, used to teach a philosophy that was there but could not express itself directly; they are experience teaching by philosophy.

It could be shown, I think, through an analysis of Carlyle's great narrative histories, how deeply those histories were shaped by the historiography worked out here, how entirely the subject of those histories served not as the focus of attention but as an external vocabulary through which to express the metaphysical and epistemological concerns of the narrative. Obviously there is no space for such an analysis. To indicate what one might look like, though, I conclude by showing how the narrative stance of *Past and Present* embodies the historiography of these early essays. My text is the first paragraph of Chapter VI, Book II:

> Within doors, down at the hill-foot, in our Convent here, we are a peculiar people,—hardly conceivable in the Arkwright Corn-Law ages, of mere Spinning-Mills and Joe-Mantons! There is yet no Methodism among us, and we speak much of Secularities: no Methodism; our Religion is not yet a horrible restless Doubt, still less a far horribler composed Cant; but a great heaven high Unquestionability, encompassing, interpenetrating the whole of Life. (*Works*, X:66)

Now, the speaker here cannot be quite Carlyle's social prophet unless that prophet also lived in a medieval monastery since the "we" of the first line, referring as it does to "our Convent," places the speaker in such a monastery.[21] Carlyle, of course, often assumes the voice of Jocelyn, whose journal he uses in the "Ancient Monk" segment of the book. But this is a very peculiar thirteenth-century monk indeed who can refer knowledgeably to Corn Laws, spinning mills, and Methodism. Neither nineteenth-century prophet nor thirteenth-century monk, then, this voice can yet contain both of them in a single first-person pronoun. Perhaps the English nation through time, perhaps human consciousness itself through time, this "we" can only exist in a special narrative time that transcends chronological time. Moving across centuries, as it does, the "we" might even move across the text to encompass the reader.

Again, Carlyle speaks to his audience about themselves but through a figure outside themselves. More, this strange voice of history can achieve the one thing that was impossible in "Characteristics": an experience of unconscious faith can announce itself, even give us its experience, without becoming tainted by consciousness. "We" in the nineteenth century, perhaps, able to compare Methodism to Jocelyn's faith, can never know unconsciousness. And Jocelyn in the thirteenth century, with no knowledge that his faith was anything particularly unique or worth remarking on, unable to compare it to Methodism, can never perhaps articulate his vital experience. But the "we" who includes both of us, the "we" created by the voice of Carlyle's narrative history, can put us together to tell us what neither of us knew before. That which we never knew before is the transcendent, eternal object of consciousness at which our interpretation aims. It is the Jocelyn who is not ourselves. But also, he is ourselves, part of the "we," available only through the act of interpretive consciousness that the narrative creates and allows. Thus the text creates a time out of time, a consciousness that is both self-directed and other-directed, a special narrative time and space in which Carlyle's epistemology can occur. And it is this historical time out of time that I think Carlyle had in mind when he said in "On History Again," "Only he who understands what has been, can know what should be and will be." There is no presumption of causal analysis here, of philosophy teaching by experience. Rather, the presumption is of a special vocabulary and a special stance that history allows, enabling us to investigate the ontology of the mind without becoming caught up in the coils of consciousness with which metaphysics threatens us. Of this history that has no intrinsic interest in history it might indeed be said that what it teaches us, we can know in no other way. And both what it teaches and the way it teaches are the creation of Carlyle's strange and idiosyncratic narrative histories, histories that to be understood even as histories can only be read in terms of their narrative form, but also narrative forms that can only be comprehensively analyzed through an understanding of their embodiment and expression of an epistemology for which Carlyle can find no other embodiment, no other expression.

Chapter XI

The Gaze within the Text:

The Expansions of Arnold's Critical Discourse

The centrality of Matthew Arnold's position in the body of texts we demarcate as Victorian prose manifests itself clearly in the number of other Victorian prose writers that critics connect him to. As a start, he has been compared with all of the other three writers with which this study has dealt.[1] And, of course, his influence is properly seen as stretching through Walter Pater to Oscar Wilde and the late Victorian aesthetes. But what kind of discourse must it be that can send out filaments to figures as wildly diverse in style as Newman and Carlyle, in temperament as Carlyle and Pater?

One part of the answer to this question resides, I think, in Arnold's constant and primary concern with establishing literary criticism and literature as discourses with global relevance, engulfing social criticism, religion, and philosophy. Although Carlyle first blurred the lines between philosophic content and the formal embodiment of that content, making his philosophy inescapably a narrative, still his first concern was with the type of consciousness he saw as necessary, moving from there to the construction of a form that could embody his epistemology's antinomic shape. Arnold, on the other hand, cares first about the possibilities of his discourse. Moving from calling his discourse "literary criticism" through calling it "criticism" to calling it "culture," and often making the terms interchangeable, Arnold aims at establishing his own discourse as a normative one. Only in order to establish his essentially literary discourse does Arnold move toward constructing an epistemology. If Carlyle moves from epistemology to discourse, Arnold moves from discourse to epistemology, and by so doing, he makes his project definitive of and for Victorian prose. He assumes that philosophic discourse, despite its ambitions toward being transparently referential, has literary density, and he is thus able to ask key questions concerning the philosophic status of literary form.[2] Since these questions must also concern any writer of a prose that is both imaginative and polemical, philosophic and literary, Arnold's task does indeed draw from and affect the rest of Victorian prose.

The second answer to the question of how Arnold could both extrude and be ensnared in such diverse webs of influence and coincidence involves a central contradiction in the way his work presents itself. Arnold can be connected both to Carlyle's earnest propheticism and Wilde's aestheticism because he seems, to different critics, to be either earnest social prophet or deliberate aesthete.[3] More usually, and I think more accurately, critics mark the uniqueness of Arnold's writing in its application of a light, sophisticated, even dandyist tone to an entirely earnest social criticism.[4] Here, again, Arnold's ability to stand at the turning point of two types of Victorian prose, Carlyle's on the one hand and Pater's on the other, marks his centrality to the project of Victorian prose. By calling Victorian prose a project, I am of course assuming that it had a certain coherence of aims and intentions, even if only the coherence that a literary history gives the literary canon. If Carlyle can be said to have invented Victorian prose—and by constructing a writing that polemicized in favor of an epistemological stance through the shape of its narrative, he certainly determined the task and stance of subsequent prose writers— Arnold both reinvented it and gave it its literary history. In a set of passages in "Function of Criticism at the Present Time," which I discuss in detail below, he gives the prose its history and coherence by defining his own special place in it as that of discovering the necessary tone that must be taken if social criticism is to be effective. Both of these answers to the question of Arnold's diverse literary relationships are versions of the same answer, at least for my purposes, for the argument of this reading is precisely that Arnold's tone relates to his subject matter as an embodiment of the epistemology he creates to found his claims for the significance of literary criticism/criticism/culture.

Before I can make this argument, however, one misconception about Arnold's tone must be cleared away. Again and again, we read about its urbanity, its charm, its importance as a rhetorical device. In this vein, critics quote Arnold's letter to his mother of October 1863, in which he claims that "one at last has a chance of *getting at* the English public" and links that chance to "exercising the power of *persuasion*, of charm," as evidence of his consciously assuming his style as a polemical device.[5] If it was intended primarily as a rhetorical device, though, the tone should be marked not as part of Arnold's success as a writer but as a signal failure. To his own audience, at least, far from helping to persuade, the tone created an attitude toward Arnold that at times virtually precluded serious discussion of his ideas. If, for instance, we see *Culture and Anarchy* as dangerously authoritative at moments, its first audience saw it rather as effete, overly delicate, "trifling with aesthetics and poetical fancies."[6] In other words, as a result of his tone, Arnold had a hard time getting himself taken seriously, a hard time precisely in getting at the English public, and he was aware of that problem.[7] Yet he continued to use the tone, continued to use it even in his religious criticism when, often, far from persuading, it antagonized. We must account for the tone at a deeper level, then, as somehow more central to his discourse than a technique applied for rhetorical ends would be. And, I argue, we must account for it as part of an epistemology aimed at grounding that discourse.

From Poetry to Literary Criticism

Although I have said that Arnold looks to epistemology to justify discourse rather than vice versa, in a sense the problem that sets his project in motion is first an epistemological one. And yet it is an epistemological problem that runs through his poetry so thoroughly that to respond to it, Arnold essentially ends the poetry in the 1853 "Preface to the Poems," with its self-crippling theory of literary discourse. Although the "Preface" partly responds to Arnold's choice to repress "Empedocles on Etna," the earlier "Mycerinus," particularly its conclusion, poses the problematic situation of the poetry with pointed clarity. After a Browning-like dramatic monologue, in which Mycerinus rails against the injustice of the universe and, in response, dedicates himself to a life of hedonism, a third-person narrator breaks in to describe the perpetual feast that follows Mycerinus's decision. And then suddenly, the narrator breaks into his own interjection to hypothesize one reaction that Mycerinus might have to that feasting:

> It may be on that joyless feast his eye
> Dwelt with mere outward seeming; he, within
> Took measures of his soul, and knew its strength,

> And by that silent knowledge, day by day
> Was calm'd, ennobled, comforted, sustain'd.
> It may be; but not less his brow was smooth,
> And his clear laugh fled ringing through the gloom . . .
>
> (lines 107–113)

This is, of course, the Lucretian meditative resignation that critics commonly hold to be Arnold's response in the poetry to the pressures of the world.[8]

The Lucretian stance here is not Arnold's but Mycerinus's, though, at least in the first instance. And the problem with it is that it is so perfectly self-enclosed that the narrator's attempt to read it perforates his lines with tenuous reservations and finally ties their syntax into a formidable knot. For one thing, because this resignation neither is nor can be motivated psychologically, because it is an act of the will tearing itself out of the depressing experience of externality to gain strength through a self-consciousness that has no external ties, it cannot be indicated through the dramatic monologue. It shares none of the logical or psychological sequentiality by which dramatic monologues work. Indeed, it has no sequentiality and is thus yet another interjection inside an interjection. Because it comes out of nowhere, we cannot even know whether it has come at all. "It may be" that Mycerinus has experienced this strengthening, self-conscious resignation, as we are told twice. But because we are told twice, we cannot help noticing that it may not be.

And we cannot know which is the case, not because there are no outward signs but because the outward sign we have could mean either yes or no. "But not less" the line continues, as if it were going to tell us that, although Mycerinus might have experienced resignation, he did not act like it. In fact, though, the line continues "but not less his brow was smooth." Now one would have thought the obvious sign of Lucretian resignation's greater strength relative to hedonism would be the ennobling calm the prior line ascribes to it, as opposed to the slightly desperate hilarity the poem ascribes to hedonism. But here the line implies that the hedonism could cause a smooth brow—either as well as resignation or in contrast to it; we cannot be sure which. Lucretian resignation is so disconnected from the world, then, that it is entirely mysterious. Not only can we not know when it occurs, we cannot know what the effect of its occurrence might be. We get the feeling that this stance is finally unsatisfactory for Arnold, not because it is antisocial or refuses to deal with the world's problems, but because its nature is absolutely unknowable. It is a poetic assertion with no epistemic density.

In the explanation for suppressing "Empedocles on Etna" that Arnold offers in the 1853 "Preface," the hesitations of "Mycerinus" to accommodate its Lucretian resignation to a discourse become reasons for doubting the value of such poetry and for doubting the value of the stance of resignation. Poetry, Arnold's "Preface" argues, in Aristotelian mode, gives joy through representation. It may represent suffering and still give joy, but one thing it cannot do:

> What then are the situations, from the representation of which, though accurate, no poetical enjoyment can be derived? They are those in which the suffering finds vent in no action; in which a continuous state of mental distress is prolonged, unrelieved by incident, hope or resistance; in which there is everything to be endured, nothing to be done. In such situations there is inevitably something morbid, in the description of them something monotonous. When they occur in actual life, they are painful, not tragic; the representation of them in poetry is painful also. (*CPW*, I:2–3)

At first glance, this passage seems to foreshadow T. S. Eliot's later remarks about the need for an objective correlative. For a tragedy to be satisfying, the suffering it describes must be able to externalize itself in action. Eliot's comment, though, is more a technical one about the necessity for finding an external symbol that will appropriately convey a character's inward state. Arnold's comment, in contrast, is an esthetic judgment based on a psychological one. In life, if we cannot vent our suffering in action, we will be pained—frustrated, one guesses. And a text that has no external action appropriate to its character's suffering will—one assumes through the mechanisms by which Aristotelian mimesis causes identificatory responses in an audience—likewise be painful. Thus Arnold finds unsatisfactory the Lucretian stance advocated by his poetry for reasons simultaneously esthetic and psychological. Esthetically, a poem is bad if it does not offer actions to match its emotions, objects for consciousness to respond to. But the reason that that is bad further implies that Lucretian resignation itself, because of its enclosed nature, also frustrates and pains rather than ennobles and calms. In short, Lucretian resignation cannot be satisfactorily embodied esthetically because it is unsatisfactory as an emotional stance. Both discourse and consciousness, we find simultaneously, must have an external object.

To correspond to the problems Arnold found with Lucretian resignation and the poetic discourse that embodied it, he has two problems with the form of the "Preface" itself. One, he wrote about to Arthur Clough in connection with the "Preface": "how difficult it is to write prose: and why? because of the *articulations of the discourse*: one leaps these over in Poetry—places one thought cheek by jowl with another without introducing them and leaves them—but in prose this will not do" (*CPW*, I:217). This is essentially a restatement of the Lucretian problem in different mode. Just as the Lucretian stance was mysterious and disjunctive in its self-enclosed nature, poetry itself is disjunctive. But if prose is to exit from the Lucretian dead end, it must be more "articulated," more constructed into a sequential whole. In fact, though, Arnold's prose never works through this kind of articulation. The movement from topic to topic in "Function of Criticism at the Present Time" and in *Culture and Anarchy*, though it gives the impression of a flow without break, is as subject to odd vagaries and leaps as is the argument of the "Preface." The prose differs, though, from the poetry because while there is no more articulation between the objects of discourse than in "Mycerinus," there are in fact discrete objects. Consciousness is not enclosed and self-referential but directed at external topics, often one after the other. The coherence in Arnold's prose is not in logical sequence—or in patterns of imagery or some other standard poetic device—but in the transformatory effect that Arnold defines as the result of consciousness trained fixedly on external objects.

Arnold raises the second problem in an introduction to the first printing of his 1857 lecture "On the Modern Element in Literature." Speaking of that essay's manner, he writes, "The style too, which is that of the doctor rather than the explorer, is a style which I have long since learnt to abandon" (*CPW*, I:18). The remark seems to refer to the gravity of tone in this and earlier essays, as opposed to what became, in *On Translating Homer* and after, the standard one of light improvisation. Doctors speak from chairs of poetry, while explorers must make their way by their own wit. If Arnold changed his tone for this reason, that choice would have larger implications since it indicates a deliberate shift from the calm melancholy of Lucretian resignation to something more like the manner of the feasters in "Mycerinus." Just as consciousness was given an object, without making it any less meditative, it is now given a new manner, without essentially changing its intellectual stance.

With Arnold's two self-corrections here, I am now ready to put together a proleptic sketch of the definitions of consciousness and narrative that are to structure his critical discourse. First, these definitions are a revision of, but not a replacement for, the Lucretian resignation I have been discussing. Mind now fixes on an external object rather than the self, but it still does not move from object to object or thought to thought with any external logic. Rather, the fixed gaze creates a significance that derives from inwardness but has distinctive marks of external effect. As with Mycerinus's hypothetical withdrawal, one cannot explain the transformation from gaze to significance. It is perhaps an inexplicable, almost a magical occurrence. But it is no longer unknowable. Second, this gaze operates in the narrative through the tone of Arnold's light narrator, who does not give reasons but meditates on certain external details—a text, an event, a current law or public figure—then derives a rule directly from the meditation and moves on to the next object. Third, this narrative stance both explains and is embodied by Arnold's manner of *blague* and rule giving. The light tone constructs the unimpassioned distance from the object necessary if the gaze is to occur and still be primarily an act of willed consciousness and not random perception. It is not so much designed to convince an audience of unpalatable positions as to enable the particular perceptions Arnold looks for. The transformation from dandy to social prophet, occurring with the dandy's gaze on some object, enacts in the narrative the epistemology that enables the narrator's perceptions.

I said earlier that Arnold, in contrast to Carlyle, develops his epistemology in response to the demands of his discourse. Yet I have just been suggesting that his dissatisfaction with his poetic epistemology led to a search for a new discourse. That suggestion is deceptive precisely because the above sketch of Arnold's epistemology and discourse is very much proleptic. What we have in Arnold's retraction of the poetic stance and hesitation about his early prose is not a program for a new direction, in poetry or in prose, but indications of the form that program was to take when there was a reason for setting it in motion. The reason occurs with the suppressed and heavily reworked ideas about the value of literary criticism that Arnold developed in his articles about Bishop Colenso's commentary on the Pentateuch. In the two essays on Colenso, "The Bishop and the Philosopher" and "Dr. Stanley's Lectures on the Jewish

212 Carlyle, Arnold, and Victorian Prose

Church," Arnold for the first time hazards formulations about the applicability of literary theory to extraliterary fields. The formulations shift constantly and contradict themselves, but they are worth following closely. Although Arnold essentially suppressed the essays, he referred to the Colenso controversy and his final explanation of it again and again, indicating both a discomfort with its original shape and a deep concern with what he took to be its final significance. That final significance defined the expansive values of literary criticism that he needed in order to become the particular kind of social and religious critic he wanted to become.[9] This expansion involved the first formulation, in "Function of Criticism,"of the epistemology and narrative that I outlined above. Thus, in fact, the discursive claims we will see Arnold struggling toward in the Colenso essays lead to both his epistemological theories and narrative structurings.

The core of the problem Arnold has with Colenso's book is essentially that it is both vulgar and absurd.[10] Colenso sets out to prove the historical inaccuracy of the *Pentateuch* by demonstrating the various mathematical inaccuracies it contains. Arnold's response is a rather jaded sigh:

> Such are the Bishop of Natal's exploits in the field of biblical criticism. The theological critic will regard them from his own point of view; the literary critic asks only in what way can they be informing to the higher culture of England or Europe? This higher culture knew very well already that contradictions were pointed out in the Pentateuch narrative; it had heard already all that the Bishop of Natal tells us as to the "impossibility of regarding the Mosaic story as a true narrative of actual historical matter of fact." (*CPW*, III:49)

The tone here is unmistakable. Colenso has had the bad form to prove laboriously what everybody who was anybody knew already and to prove it in a particularly tiresome manner. Both Arnold's insistence on referring to Colenso as the "Bishop of Natal" to emphasize his provinciality and his quoting Colenso's flat-footed prose with its repetitions of "true," "actual," and "historical" indicate the basis of Arnold's criticism. The question is, what significance is this criticism to have? Since Arnold does not quite want to apply Wilde's notion that society really should live according to the dicta of bon ton, he must, therefore, discover the social and intellectual relevance of those dicta.

And, indeed, the first three pages of "The Bishop and the Philosopher" concern not Colenso but the purview of literary criticism. That discussion gets Arnold into immediate problems, but they are not the problems generally attributed to him. He begins by saying that, while all books must be criticized by the professionals within their particular disciplines, all books "have also a general literary criticism to undergo, and this tries them all, as I have said, by one standard—their effect upon general culture" (*CPW*, III:41). The effect upon general culture is not quite the standard we might think it, though. Dividing religious books into those that edify the many and those that instruct the few (he will not allow the value of instructing the many), Arnold explains that

> so far as by any book on religious matters the raw are humanised or the cultivated are advanced to a yet higher culture, so far that book is a subject for literary criticism. But, undoubtedly, the direct promotion of culture by intellectual power is the main interest of literary criticism, not the indirect promotion of this culture by edification. (*CPW*, III:41)

Readers frequently object to the elitism inherent in this statement and all too explicit throughout the essay. Why must Arnold always depict the general populace as not deserving of instruction, as in need of general humanization? Although Arnold's tone is indeed often condescending, nevertheless the charge of elitism misses the point. The few here are not the aristocrats but the educated, and his protest against the notion of instructing the many is really a protest against the degradations of popularization. The real problem is that one would have expected literary criticism's province to have been to measure edification, not instruction, instruction being, after all, the province of the particular fields in which a book claims to instruct. He does not want to make edification the province of literary criticism here because edification, as it is described on the essay's next page, seems the purview of a certain kind of sentimental literature we generally think of as below critical notice. Now literary criticism might serve the purpose of perceiving the absolutely ridiculous, the category in which Colenso falls, but one wonders why it should bother. The philosophers, theologians, and historians who try the works of their own field will more than take care of the task of dismissing the trivial and the ridiculous. Clearly, Arnold thinks that his literary perception of Colenso's absurdity has greater significance than this, or he would not insist that literary criticism's major task is to try a work's intellectual value, nor would he use sounding terms like "general culture."

Moreover, Arnold does not merely fault Colenso's inept biblical criticism but offers Spinoza as a counterexample of how free thought may be instructively applied to the Bible. In explicating Spinoza, Arnold offers, more than an alternative to Colenso; he offers an example of the analysis of an instructive discourse that literary criticism may have to offer that a specialist might not. Arnold labels Spinoza "the philosopher" and gives an extended and approving summary of his treatment of the Bible. But what function does literary criticism perform here? Arnold does not enter into a philosophic analysis or critique of Spinoza precisely; presumably that would be the purview of a philosopher. He merely explains Spinoza's ideas for those too ignorant to be aware of him and explains them as an example of how to treat the Bible creatively. In other words, he instructs the uninstructed many and does so through edifying exemplification. Effectively, then, the distinctions between edification and instruction blur in the task that literary criticism performs.

And they blur further when we find literary criticism's criterion of judgment:

> To be great, [a philosopher] must have something in him which can influence character, which is edifying; he must, in short, have a noble and lofty character himself, a character,—to recur to that much-criticized expression of mine,—*in the grand style.* This is what Spinoza had; and because he had it, he stands out from the multitude of philosophers, and has been able to inspire in powerful minds a feeling which the most remarkable philosophers, without this grandiose character, could not inspire. (*CPW*, III:181–2)

Here, edification has clearly become the peculiar province of literary criticism, not merely the value we can infer that its discourse has, but also the value it explicitly concerns. Arnold establishes the connection between edification and literariness, calling Spinoza's character edifyingly noble because it is "in the grand style." Arnold uses that label, of course, in his early essays, from the 1853 "Preface" through, most notably, *On Translating Homer*, to describe a certain poetic effect of straightforward, direct nobility. More, this literary quality, which provides edification, is also, in the case of philosophy as of poetry, a condition for transforming a merely noteworthy philosopher into a great one. In other words, edification is no longer a laudable but not very interesting way of handling the multitude. It is a mode of being, a character, that elevates. Although this new criterion obviously destroys the essay's opening, it is wholly productive in a movement toward creating a global discourse out of literary criticism. It gives literary criticism a definably literary object of discernment, edification as a manifestation of the grand style, even as that object operates to create the greatness of philosophy and, at least arguably, of all other discourses.

Colenso still creates problems, however, and to answer those problems, as they were raised by contemporary critics, Arnold wrote his second essay on the subject, "Dr. Stanley's Lectures." After all, even if the instructed already knew that the Pentateuch was not to be taken as history, the storm in England over Colenso's book indicated that his ideas were news, and unwelcome news, to large numbers of people. Now if Spinoza edified by instructing at certain high levels of culture, why could it not be argued that Colenso did the same to that not after all inconsiderable audience who found his book not absurd but upsetting? To answer this criticism, Arnold makes a distinction that, had he held it thoroughly, would have completed the task of defining a global role for literary criticism. He argues that "the speculative life of intellect, of pure thought," is different in kind from "the religious life"; thus, applying to religion an idea that is true in terms of the intellect can make that idea false. For instance, though Galileo was correct in arguing from mathematics that the earth moves, had he applied the idea to the Bible, which was not meant as mathematics or as intellectual speculation, "his '*the earth moves*' in spite of its absolute truth, would have become a falsehood" (*CPW*, III:67–68). And since Colenso does precisely this, while "theological criticism censures this language as unorthodox, irreverent: literary criticism censures it as *false*" (*CPW*, III:69).

Before I discuss the reservations Arnold builds into this distinction that vitiate its force and the coherence of the Colenso essays, I would like to jump forward to his reformulation of it in "Function of Criticism." That formulation, which is historically deceptive but philosophically more viable, shows us how Arnold will pose his expansive claims for the significance of literary criticism as a discourse and how those claims are epistemologically based. In the later essay, Arnold claims that he had been saying "*there is truth of science and truth of religion; truth of science does not*

become truth of religion till it is made religious." He defends himself against
the criticism that he had made it "'a crime against literary criticism and
the higher culture to inform the ignorant'" by asserting that "the ignorant are not informed by being confirmed in a confusion"(*CPW*, III:277).
By arguing that science and religion are ontologically separate discourses,
Arnold can claim that Colenso could not be edifying through informing
in any sense because, by confusing two discourses, he was, in the par-
lance of the earlier essays, writing what was false. In combination with
the eliding of the distinction between edification and instruction, this
discursive distinction makes of literary criticism an epistemological act
with impressive extension. We start with a judgment of the vulgarity of
Colenso's project and see that that vulgarity is infinitely distant from the
personality in the grand style requisite to philosophizing in an edifying
manner, and thus we see not merely a literary difference but the difference
between trivial and great philosophy. Through literary criticism's ability
to define the difference between objects, or discourses, we further see that
Colenso's vulgarity also derives from taking religion for a form of science
and thus constitutes a falsehood. This literary criticism, to operate, must
perceive character and define objects; clearly it is thus a form of consciousness as well as a form of discourse itself. And the definition of that
form of consciousness will confirm Arnold's claims for the discourse.

But he is not really ready to go this far in "Dr. Stanley's Lectures." We
see there, still, a nagging feeling that, after all, what Colenso says is true,
absolutely, like Galileo's statement, and that to call it false for religion is a
figure of speech. We see this reservation first in that he does not distinguish the two discourses purely as being different discourses—religion
and science—as he does later in "Function." Instead he divides them into
"the free, speculative life of intellect" and "religious life," "religious"
here clearly being in opposition to "intellect." The return later in the essay of Arnold's elitism, more radically articulated, confirms this suggestion of a hierarchy:

> Those on whose behalf I demand from a religious speaker edifica-
> tion are more than [the] multitude; and their cause and that of the
> multitude are one. They are all those who acknowledge the need of
> the religious life. The few whom literary criticism regards as exempt
> from all concern with edification, are far fewer than is commonly
> supposed. Those whose life is all in thought, and to whom, there-

fore, literary criticism concedes the right of treating religion with absolute freedom, as pure matter for thought, are not a great class, but a
few individuals. (*CPW*, III:79–80)

Clearly there is a hierarchy of truth here. Religion is a need of the vast
multitude. For a very select few only, pure thought is possible. Although
Arnold's few are so few that his elitism is no longer a matter of class distinction but of a distinction virtually between genius and the rest of the
world, still he has with a stroke destroyed all the foundation upon which
his argument has been building. If edification is now not needed, even if
only by the very few, then it is no longer quite the ultimate sign of greatness, of the grand style. And if even that fewest of the select few can do
without the religious life, then it is not quite an alternative form of discourse; it is also a less elevated form. To expand the possibilities of literary
criticism, Arnold has to give up his sense of it (and himself) as belonging
to an innately separated avant-garde. He has fully to accept the implications of making it an epistemology. In that form, it may be a rigorous discipline, but it can no longer be a form of inherent separation. The Colenso
essays start this process of reformulating criticism as epistemology.

Criticism and Culture; Mind and Text

Arnold kept returning to Colenso, in "Function of Criticism," in *Culture
and Anarchy*, in *God and the Bible*, but always in terms of the revised formulation of the thesis that "Function" offers.[11] The essays were clearly
important to Arnold in marking literary criticism's first incursion into extraliterary fields. They also indicated a need for various rethinkings in
order to solidify the newly found extensions for criticism, and those rethinkings are the central task of his major work in the 1860s and 1870s.
"Function of Criticism" establishes the major lines of the epistemological
and narrative structures that will support his extensions of literary criticism. It takes criticism as a form of perception and thus gives it its first
extensions. But certain social data still resist its operations, mostly because it refuses to make sufficiently global claims. *Culture and Anarchy*
extends the epistemological operations of criticism to a description of
how society works, making *mind* and *society* interchangeable terms.
When a certain resistance to this operation remains in the refusal of cer-

tain details of society to fit comfortably into this model, Arnold, in his theories on religion, makes his final extension: imposing the original account of the relationship between mind and object, which was expanded to become the relationship of culture to society, upon the relationship between a text and its external referent. Thus he finally arrives at a way of allowing literary criticism to operate globally, by defining a text that unilaterally transforms, rather than simply gestures toward, its referent.

In the first expansion "Function of Criticism" makes, Arnold shortens the term *literary criticism* into criticism. The essay's ostensible main contention—that despite creativity's higher place, criticism still has a vital function—makes clear that the concept's roots are still literary. But the language used to describe it is almost all perceptual and epistemological. The famous dicta, of course, that it is "the business of the critical power . . . 'to see the object as in itself it really is'" (*CPW*, III:261) and that "its business is . . . simply to know the best that is known and thought in the world" (*CPW*, III:270), make clear enough criticism's perceptual and epistemological aspects. But the passage leading up to the second dictum gives the critical act its real specificity as an act of the mind:

> It is of the last importance that English criticism should clearly discern what rule for its course, in order to avail itself of the field now opening to it, and to produce fruit for the future, it ought to take. The rule may be summed up in one word,—*disinterestedness*. And how is criticism to show disinterestedness? By keeping aloof from what is called "the practical view of things;" by resolutely following the law of its own nature, which is to be a free play of the mind on all subjects which it touches. (*CPW*, III:269–270)

We can begin by noting how easily Arnold holds together here those two demands of consciousness whose divergence so vexed Carlyle: the demand to see an object and the demand to engage in an activity, a free play. Criticism sees the object as it really is by fixing an extended, rapt gaze upon it; its seeing is a fixing of consciousness on an object, but that fixing is still enough of an activity to be describable as a free play. But it is not a movement from object to object. Its disinterestedness will allow it to resist drawing practical conclusions, or really any conclusions. Its aim is to know purely through gazing.

That gaze is the revision of Mycerinus' self-enclosure. Its importance to Arnold's project and the importance of Arnold's tone to the creation of that gaze can be seen in his careful construction, in "The Function of Criticism," of a canon of critical and socially engaged prose, of what we would call Victorian, imaginative prose. The line starts, not where we might normally start it, with Coleridge or Carlyle, but with a figure that the nineteenth-century writers frequently saw as both a man of letters and a profound social critic—Edmund Burke. Arnold's use of Burke, and the passage he chooses to discuss, are both strange and indicative. He quotes the last paragraph of *Thoughts on French Affairs*, a highly atypical moment in Burke's later writings in which, after one of his more furious attacks on the French Revolution, he suddenly entertains the possibility that the revolution really represents the forces of progress and that he will thus "appear rather to resist the decrees of Providence itself, than the mere designs of men. [He] will not be resolute and firm but perverse and obstinate." [12] And then he abruptly breaks off. Arnold writes of the passage:

> That return of Burke upon himself has always seemed to me one of the finest things in English literature, or indeed in any literature. That is what I call living by ideas: when one side of a question has long had your earnest support, when all your feelings are engaged, when you hear all around you no language but one, when your party talks this language like a steam-engine and can imagine no other,—still to be able to think, still to be irresistibly carried, if so it be, by the current of thought to the opposite side of the question. (*CPW*, III:267)

To grasp precisely what this passage does, we must first realize that Burke is an example more constructed than perceived here. The quotation from him is atypical and is hardly acted upon, is almost merely a concluding rhetoric (perhaps the abrupt breaking off may indicate a real psychic uneasiness, but it hardly indicates a return upon himself). Moreover Burke's opposition to the French Revolution in the early stages of 1790–1791 was hardly yet the language his party was talking. He was thrust into an increasing opposition for some years. Thus his return upon himself is more a yielding to the steam engine of party than a resistance (though not much of a yielding because not much of a return). [13]

The constructed Burke acts out that critical gaze that is a conscious meditation while it is still directed at an external object, still an activity of mind even as it fixes itself upon the object of its meditation. We begin with "a return of Burke upon himself," a moment of conscious deliberation. One would say that this is a moment of self-consciousness—Burke returns upon himself—except that both the passage Arnold quotes and the sequence of his consideration indicate that the self Burke returns upon is his consideration of the French Revolution. He turns from the activity of espousing an action to an entry into pure thought that carries him to the opposite side of the question. He looks at the question, and his looking constitutes the activity of mind, an activity that is called "one of the finest things in English literature." We should note that Arnold's criticism here is also acting out Burke's gaze. By fixing on Burke, a political figure of some significance, in a moment of high political crisis, he freezes that figure's political thought into a moment that can be described as literary; yet that same moment, with its clear allusions to the inability of Liberals around Burke to exit from the steam-engine language of party, has social and political, as well as literary, implications. The disinterested, meditative gaze, merely by subjecting itself to the discipline of gazing without trying to act, is transformed, through its discovery of significance, of the best that is known and thought, into an action with political resonance. The gaze—both Burke's and Arnold's upon Burke—is, thus, the activity that makes literary criticism so central.

If Burke were the only half-literary, half-political figure Arnold considered, one would not want to make much of it as a construction of a literary tradition for Arnold to define his own place within. But Burke begins a discussion of disinterested thought that leads to a consideration of Carlyle and John Ruskin, a discussion that clearly identifies the tone of the narrative as the proper enactment of the gaze within the text. Arnold has just proclaimed that the British constitution, seen from the speculative side, "sometimes looks,—forgive me, shade of Lord Somers!—a colossal machine for the manufacture of Philistines" (*CPW*, III:175). And he continues:

> How is Cobbett to say this and not be misunderstood, blackened as he is with the smoke of a lifelong conflict in the field of political practice? how is Mr. Carlyle to say it and not be misunderstood, after his furious raid into this field with his *Latter-day Pamphlets*? how is Mr. Ruskin, after his pugnacious political economy? (*CPW*, III:175)

William Cobbett is the example of a thinker who has tainted his thought by having engaged in actual political practice. The case of Carlyle and Ruskin, though, is more delicate. Arnold cites not actions, but political criticism—writing. And what taints them with practice is not action but tone, Carlyle's fury (which makes his writing a raid) and Ruskin's pugnacity.

Clearly, Arnold suggests here that proper tone is a necessity for effectively engaging in political criticism, that Victorian prose must learn to speak in a different voice. But his point is not simply rhetorical. Carlyle's and Ruskin's tones are misunderstood in parallel with Cobbett's political practice. A tone of fury or pugnacity, of emotional engagement, becomes an actual engagement with the object that disrupts the critical gaze. And we see, of course, in Arnold's broaching of his remarks upon the constitution, how he feels such criticism can be carried out. The light tone, the joke about Lord Somers, the metaphor of the machine, which calls attention to itself as wit, all enact an extended consideration of the constitution that contains the final conclusion rather than leads to it. Arnold's tone, then, constructs the distance and duration that allows critical consciousness to make its expansive claims, to define the problems of the constitution in a way only it can know. By fixing on Victorian prose as one of its objects, the critical gaze enacts its transformatory power in a way that defines the special effects and form of Arnold's discourse even as it places that discourse within a tradition, one Arnold calls "criticism" and we might call "Victorian prose." In justifying his writing, Arnold thus invents for himself the discursive form and tradition to which that writing belongs.

We now have a definition of a form of consciousness that constitutes the critical act and gives it extension, and we have as well as a narrative handling of the division between voice and topic that reflects and demonstrates the theory of consciousness. Thus Arnold defines the critical gaze as he acts it out in his considerations of Burke, Ruskin, and Carlyle, his considerations transforming the gaze into an implicit theory of Victorian prose rather than sequentially leading to that theory. Coincidentally, we have an explanation and a justification for the odd disjunctures I mentioned above in talking about the 1853 "Preface." Arnold's essays often seem to have points connected by only the haziest of transitional logic. The thread of argument in "Function of Criticism" often has far less significance than the points of consideration that occur on that thread. The real organizing principle of Arnold's narrative sequence is, rather, the theory of criticism one puts together from the effects of the various meditations, which constitute the general meditation of the essay. Consciousness meditates on single objects and leaps from object to object and as a result is transformed into considered conclusions.

This is Arnold's theory in a fairly complete form, and the model through which to read his prose. But it is successively and finally daringly expanded in various works to meet the deficiencies it encounters. We see the problem in "Function of Criticism" in a fairly trivial controversy over Arnold's consideration of the English Divorce Court.[14] Arnold used, as an example of the result of critical consciousness directed at objects of social reality, the conclusion—drawn from the hideousness of the Divorce Court—of the elevating character of the Catholic theory of marriage (*CPW*, III:281). FitzJames Stephens, in the *Saturday Review*, responded that Arnold had no right "to 'object to practical measures on theoretical grounds'" (*CPW*, III:533). Arnold responded, in a later footnote, that he had precisely not engaged in practical criticism but had considered the court speculatively, in the light of the Catholic theory of marriage; and in the light of that theory, it looked hideous. When speculation has taught the critic that, he concludes, he will find "lights and resources for making it better, of which he does not now dream" (*CPW*, III:534). Arnold has shifted the import of his critical meditation here and thus played into Stephens's hands. His original contention was that the Divorce Court's hideousness taught us the elevation of the Catholic theory of marriage. He now argues that the Catholic theory of marriage shows us the hideousness of the Divorce Court in such a way as to enable more intelligent action. To this, Stephens replied shortly that once one accepted that one was to have a Divorce Court, the question was whether it was "more hideous than it ought to be,"[15] and to answer that, we need a legislative theory, not high-sounding phrases. As Sidney Couling concludes, "Stephens was again clearly right, and the result was the withdrawal in 1869 of a second long footnote."[16]

The question remains: why did Arnold shift his original argument in such a way as to make it vulnerable? The answer, I think, is that Stephens's attack had implicitly challenged the significance of a conclusion that a critical meditation reaches. The elevating quality of the Catholic theory of marriage is all very well, but what has our meditation on the Divorce Court really led to? That Arnold's answer to this question must be withdrawn indicates a residual resistance of certain kinds of details to the meditative gaze of literary criticism. Though we may find various inaccuracies in the description of Burke, even perhaps a narrowness in the dismissal of Carlyle and Ruskin,[17] finally these objects of consciousness do yield a theory to the critical gaze. But the Divorce Court presents a kind of detail that cannot be accommodated within the text of Arnold's criticism as it stands. To accommodate that kind of detail, he must create the possibility of society turning that gaze upon itself in order to recuperate its own details, in effect making society as a whole a possible literary critic. This is the task of *Culture and Anarchy*.

In the same way that the first expansion of literary criticism, which "Function of Criticism" undertook, changed its main term to *criticism*, so *Culture and Anarchy* expands the claims for this process by, in the first instance, calling it "culture." Culture's basic identity with criticism is established clearly enough with its opening definition, which labels it "a pursuit of our total perfection by means of getting to know, on all the matters which most concern us, the best which has been thought and said in the world; and through this knowledge, turning a stream of fresh and free thought upon our stock notions and habits" (*CPW*, V:233). The extensions Arnold's first chapter will add upon the original concept are already implicit here too. That aspect of culture that is a continuing process rather than a fixed event already inheres in the notion of its being "a pursuit of our total perfection." Not only does such a concept now have duration without determinate end, but it also has more than one characteristic stage. The original critical awareness in search of knowledge is now a preliminary to fixing the critical gaze upon our actions in the world in order to transform them. "Sweetness and Light" further articulates these concepts but really does not change them, and indeed they do not yet constitute all that much of a change from the criticism of "Function of Criticism." Unsurprisingly, then, when that chapter was first published as the article "Culture and its Enemies," it received the same sorts of criticisms as did "Function." Culture could not really judge of details but was merely "a pouncet-box to spare [the] senses aught unpleasant, holding no form of creed."[18] This time, however, Arnold was prepared with a series of transformations that took him the balance of the book to elaborate.

In his second chapter, Arnold claims to make the great discovery of Culture, which gives the book its title. Culture discovers the need for an authority to regulate anarchy. In its first formulation, this discovery is rather unthreatening. Called upon to show what action Culture suggests, Arnold calls instead for a restraint from action: "if I can show [action] to be, at the present moment, a practical mischief and dangerous to us, then

I have found a practical use for light" (*CPW*, V:116). Either this statement is empty oratory, though, or it *is* threatening. If an authority literally squelches action, it could be an oppressive power. If it operates only
as a standard against which to measure action, one wonders why one
needs its embodiment. Arnold argues that the state can regulate eccentric
action without being oppressive because the state represents the best part
of all of us, what he calls our "best selves":

> By our *best self* we are united, impersonal, at harmony. We are in no
> peril from giving authority to this, because it is the truest friend we
> all of us can have; and when anarchy is a danger to us, to this au-
> thority we may turn with sure trust. . . . We find no basis for a firm
> State-power in our ordinary selves; culture suggests one to us in our
> *best self.* (*CPW*, V:134–135)

Lionel Trilling early on pointed out the potential circularity here. If the
state, as Arnold implies elsewhere, encourages our best self to develop,
how can it embody that best self before it has developed?[19] And, indeed,
unless we are to write the book off as myth, which Trilling effectively
does, we need a better account of what the best self is, how it relates to
culture, and how to arrive at it. The identification of the state with the
best self already hints at that account since, if this is not merely an empty
gesture, that identification psychologizes the state activity in ways that
may shed light on how Arnold foresees it operating.[20]

Psychologizing is the constant gesture of *Culture and Anarchy*, and attempts to read it in the context of Mill's *On Liberty* or Rousseau's *Social Contract* rather than in the context of the rest of Arnold's critical
theory will, by missing this, constantly ask the wrong questions of the
work. By psychologizing, Arnold can make the process of cultural consciousness productive of itself, thus allowing culture to become an engulfing method of knowing rather than simply a standard that may
be criticized. We may start noticing the psychologizing process by pointing out that the three classes into which Arnold divides the country—
Barbarian, Philistine, and Populace—embody qualities that all individuals contain:

> Since, under all our class divisions, there is a common basis of
> human nature, therefore, in every one of us, whether we be properly
> Barbarians, Philistines, or Populace, there exist, sometimes only in

germ and potentially, sometimes more or less developed, the same tendencies and passions which have made our fellow-citizens of other classes what they are. (*CPW*, V:143)

Not only do we each contain all classes, but each class is itself a partial man. I would like to hold in abeyance for the moment the problem of the Populace for reasons that will become clear. The other two classes Arnold explicitly describes in terms of personality traits. The Barbarians are gracious and mannered but not open to ideas (*CPW*, V:125). The Philistines are self-sufficient and active but smug and without conscious self-direction (*CPW*, V:130). But it will not do to say that since each class is a partial man, the best self is merely a combination. If we link the Barbarian to the Philistine, we will only have a politely smug, self-sufficient ignoramus.

The logical transition from the discussion of the classes and the state to the discussion of the two master forces in the history of society is rather abrupt and unpersuasive, but we know that Arnold's narrative does not move sequentially. Rather, the concepts of Hebraism and Hellenism answer the questions everybody wants to apply elsewhere and inappropriately: my last paragraph's question of how we arrive at a best self, and the question of how this process relates to the workings of authority. The real relationship between the consideration of Hellenism and Hebraism and what has gone before becomes apparent if we link the names with Barbarian and Philistine (again, I note the absence of the Populace and ask that the problem be held in abeyance). One could, of course, create oppositional tendencies out of the pairs Hellene and Barbarian, Hebrew and Philistine, but the linked oppositions suggest that the classes are not in opposition to the social forces but are a degradation of them. This relationship becomes clearer when we find that Hellenism reenacts culture by seeking "to get rid of one's ignorance, to see things as they are, and by seeing them as they are to see them in their beauty" (*CPW*, V:167), while Hebraism reenacts an elevated form of the middle-class desire to identify problems and act to cure them: "Hebraism speaks of becoming conscious of sin, of awakening to a sense of sin" (*CPW*, V:168). Hellenism, then, stands in relation to the Barbarian's thoughtless, external grace, while Hebraism stands in relation to the Philistine's self-sufficiency and self-satisfaction.[21]

By seeing the forces of Hellenism and Hebraism as embodiments of an epistemological process, we can put together how they create the best self. Another constant critical confusion about Arnold is to take these two forces in simple opposition so that, even though he says man needs both qualities, critics presume that this statement is overshadowed by his clear valuing of Hellenism over Hebraism.[22] We can put the workings of the classes together by noticing the basic paradox that culture is identified both as a development of the whole man and also with that aspect labeled Hellenism. This paradox is intensified but also brought to the point of recuperation when we find that Hellenism is also identified with culture's totalizing process:

> Essential in Hellenism is the impulse to the development of the whole man, to connecting and harmonising all parts of him, perfecting all, leaving none to take their chance.
>
> The characteristic bent of Hellenism, as has been said, is to find the intelligible law of things, to see them in their true nature and as they really are. (*CPW*, V:184)

Now both the aspect of development and the aspect of seeing things accurately are, of course, part of culture. By returning to our notion of the critical gaze—in this work expanded to the cultural gaze—we can see how the processes are connected. Just as the gaze upon the object creates knowledge, thus transforming the process of meditation into an action, the Hellenic gaze upon the object will encompass the Hebraistic desire to do and to ameliorate. Thus, by allowing the cultural gaze to occur, or by engaging in it, we transform the degraded elements of Barbarian and Philistine into the elevated whole, which may also be labeled a "best self." In effect, social forces and groups, through Arnold's system of classes and of Hellenism and Hebraism, can be understood to operate just as the critical consciousness operates.

Once we have gotten this far, we can, without much difficulty, see the role that Arnold's history plays as an allegory of various epistemological activities. The description of how Hebraism alone works to allow play to some aspects of the ordinary self by checking others (*CPW*, V:180) becomes an explanation of how an elevated aspect produces the degraded classes by separating instead of harmonizing, by refusing to allow a place for consciousness. The picture of Hellenism, alone in Greece, at ease in Zion, needing the influx of Hebraism (*CPW*, V:168–169) is the historic correlative of the original enclosure of consciousness within Mycerinus's

Lucretian stance, the enclosure Arnold's literary criticism is meant to burst.[23] In effect, literary criticism, expanded into the cultural gaze, not only can now make its process a central social event but can read society through the history of its own development. If *Culture and Anarchy* constantly resists the criticisms that Stephens leveled at "Function of Criticism" and that Frederic Harrison and Henry Sidgwick, among others, leveled at the later text, it is because the concept of criticism has expanded itself to the point that those critiques, in the form of Hebraism, have become part of its process.

I am now ready to deal with the problem of authority and show how its psychologizing works. By putting together various moments in *Culture and Anarchy*, we can see that authority operates with respect to the society over which it presides in the same way that criticism does on its object and Hellenism does on "the intelligible law of things." At the end of the fifth chapter, for instance, Arnold explicitly draws an analogy between the source of authority and the source of harmonious development:

> If we look to the world outside us we find a disquieting absence of sure authority. We discover that only in right reason can we get a source of sure authority; and culture brings us toward right reason. If we look at our own inner world, we find all manner of confusion. . . . What we want is a fuller harmonious development of our humanity, a free play of thought upon our routine notions, spontaneity of consciousness, sweetness and light; and these are just what culture generates and fosters. (*CPW*, V:190–191)

Looking at the second half of the analogy, it is clear that that which culture fosters is also that which culture defines. Nor should this surprise us since the discussion of Hellenism has already indicated that the expansions of the critical gaze allow the process of culture to produce the state of culture, not as a result of circular logic but because the process works to transform its object into a process that its gaze may interpret—to transform it into part of itself. The first half of the analogy, by extension, implies that the culture that is the source of authority will also transform authority into a force capable of operating through cultural consciousness.

Still, authority in its operations is troublesome in *Culture and Anarchy* and, in its operation on the Populace in particular, is a problem on which Arnold's system will founder. To see how he intends authority to operate, though, we may look briefly both forward and back, to an earlier essay,

"The Literary Influence of the Academies," and to a later work, *St. Paul and Protestantism*. In the "Preface" to *Culture and Anarchy*, Arnold refers to the earlier essay as pointing out a problem that the English lack of an Academy produces: provinciality. But in that earlier essay, he notes, he had explicitly refrained from suggesting the institution of an English Academy because that would be a "worship of machinery" (*CPW*, V:234). And, the last paragraph of that essay suggests that the best way to remedy the English lack of an Academy would be simply to be aware of its absence: "Every one amongst us with any turn for literature will do well to remember to what shortcomings and excesses, which such an academy tends to correct, we are liable" (*CPW*, III:257). The essay suggests, in effect, an Academy of the mind, an Academy created by the literary consciousness watching itself for provinciality. But even the very material authority of the Church of England operates the same way in *St. Paul and Protestantism*. There Arnold argues, in a position that the discussion of Irish disestablishment in *Culture and Anarchy* predicted, that historically the church has avoided legislating any doctrine in order that it may leave itself room for free development. It has expelled Puritan provinciality not by legislating against it but by refusing to allow it to be legislated. Again, it protects against the constraints of eccentricity by a watchful gaze that is productive of more and freer consciousness and thought.

But authority does not always seem to work this benignly in *Culture and Anarchy*. The attitude toward the rioting Populace and the repressed passage on how Thomas Arnold would have handled rioting are as familiar as they are disturbing. To get at this anomaly in Arnold's handling of authority, we may first note that the Populace does not fit well into the system of classes and forces I have outlined. It has no elevated correlative as Barbarian and Philistine do in Hellene and Hebrew. More to the point—since that system, one might argue, is my invention—the handling of the Populace does not even parallel Arnold's own handling of the other two classes. When Arnold identifies the mean and the excess of Barbarians and Philistines, he applies to them psychological characteristics, pride and politeness to the one, self-sufficiency and smugness to the other. In the case of the Populace, however, he identifies no characteristic, only the names Odger and Bradlaugh (*CPW*, V:133). He later mentions in passing Harrison's characterization, "bright powers of sympathy and ready powers of action" (*CPW*, V:138), but he really does not take it very far. Insofar as the Populace has any characteristic in Arnold other than being a debased form of the already debased Philistines, that characteristic is simply mindless violence and energy.

Now this is so obviously a stereotype created by class fear that the point of interest seems less to identify it as such and condemn Arnold for it than to consider why that stereotype alone appears in a text that has so thoroughly digested and regenerated, in terms of its own system, all other forms of stereotype.[24] We see the anomaly of the situation in how strangely accurate DeLaura is in identifying Arnold's debt, in his account of the street rioting in *Culture and Anarchy*, to Carlyle's "Shooting Niagara."[25] The parallel is strange, not, I think, because Arnold so frequently disavows Carlyle in *Culture and Anarchy*, but more because, while Arnold shows considerable Carlylean influence, Carlyle's style of narrative is entirely alien to him. Whereas Carlyle is interested in the facticity of event as an important part of the symbology of his narrative, Arnold works not by finding significance in detail but by constantly reading out the structure of his epistemology across large expanses of culture and history. He makes his history through his text, and the accuracy of that history is guaranteed by the strength of the process of consciousness that makes it, not by any density of detail. Thus where Carlyle spends three volumes on the French Revolution, Arnold takes care of all of Western history since the Greeks in a chapter or two. Once we have the basic process, the extensions are quickly comprehensible.

And yet in the face of the rioters, Arnold narrates like Carlyle. This occurs, I think, because, while his system now includes within its meditative consciousness all forms of thought, both the meditative and the practical, Arnold has not yet defined the system in such a way that his text can consume the matter and data of external reality. Arnold does not fear fictionalizing (surely we have seen his willingness to impose his definition of consciousness and the elements therein everywhere else), but his system has not yet expanded to include the relationship of text to referent. In that relationship, he falls back upon the normal conception that texts refer straightforwardly to external things in the world, and thus his cultural system gives him no means for "thinking" the Populace; he can only think *about* them and fall back upon the stereotypes of his class. The tinges of authoritarianism in *Culture and Anarchy* are not, I think, problems with Arnold's elitist notion of culture but, as always, with his not having extended the system quite far enough.

The relationship of the text to its referent differs importantly from the relationship of the narrator to the objects of the narration. In that second area, *Culture and Anarchy* is already encompassed within the system in the same way that I argued "Function of Criticism" was. To extend the epistemology to text and world, though, one has to presume that the text itself, rather than the components of its narrative, can operate like a mind, can think its subject matter. One of Arnold's earliest essays, "On the Modern Element in Literature," provides a model for the text operating in this way.

When originally delivered as a lecture at Oxford in 1857, the essay probably seemed yet another of Arnold's attempts to elevate the ancients. But it was the only lecture of the series in which it had been delivered that Arnold reprinted, and its reprinting in 1869, with a direct reference in the introductory statement to *Culture and Anarchy*, rather changes what looks to be its central point. Look for instance at its definition of "intellectual deliverance," the quality Arnold claims the modern age most demands:

> This, then, is what distinguishes certain epochs in the history of the human race, and our own amongst the number;—on the one hand, the presence of a significant spectacle to contemplate; on the other hand, the desire to find the true point of view from which to contemplate this spectacle. He who has found that point of view, he who adequately comprehends this spectacle, has risen to the comprehension of his age: he who communicates that point of view to his age, he who interprets to it that spectacle, is one of the age's intellectual deliverers. (*CPW*, I:20)

The relationship of this passage to *Culture and Anarchy* is not that hard to work out. An author who finds a "true point of view from which to contemplate" the spectacle of an age will "adequately comprehend" it. In other words, the properly placed meditative gaze will actually encompass the matter of social reality, will comprehend it. Such a view, moreover, by itself serves a prime social purpose. It communicates the age to itself, allows it to know itself, thus delivers it intellectually. This clearly is the type of activity of meditation and social service *Culture and Anarchy* has in mind.

Arnold writes here, though, of minds and objects; the problem of *Culture and Anarchy* was one of texts and referents. But here an interesting thing happens. Arnold discusses in the essay Greek and Roman authors who were or were not adequate to their age. Now he does have some ex-

ternal means of judging whether an age was complex enough for its comprehension within a text to be an act large enough to constitute intellectual deliverance. But, finally, not only his judgments about adequate texts
but also those about complex ages are all formal judgments about texts.
Here, for instance, he compares what he takes to be Thucydides' rational
historian's language with Sir Walter Raleigh's eccentric one:

> Which is the ancient here, and which is the modern? Which uses
> the language of an intelligent man of our own days? which a language
> wholly obsolete and unfamiliar to us? Which has the rational appre-
> ciation and control of his facts? which wanders among them help-
> lessly and without a clue? Is it our own countryman, or is it the
> Greek? And the language of Ralegh affords a fair sample of the criti-
> cal power, of the point of view, possessed by the majority of intelli-
> gent men of his age; as the language of Thucydides affords us a fair
> sample of the critical power of the majority of intelligent men in the
> age of Pericles. (*CPW*, I:27–28)

Had merely a text's adequacy to its age been judged on formal terms, that
would have been a comprehensive enough claim. By making the formal
quality of texts a standard by which we judge the complexity of the age,
however, we give the text global responsibility for how we define its relationship to its age. No doubt, Arnold's judgments on Thucydides and
Raleigh depend to some extent on the representativeness those texts have
for other texts in their age. But finally, texts, by being the evidence,
create the sense of text and age. In other words, the textual gaze upon its
age has the same power of transformation as the critical and cultural
gazes. With this refinement in its system, Arnold's epistemology is freed
from the Carlylean concern with social data. By adequately transforming
his age within his text, he will both create its complexity and offer it intellectual deliverance. This precisely becomes his project in his religious
works.

To trace Arnold's theory of the Bible and that theory's relationship to
the epistemological and narrative structures I have been articulating here
should no longer be necessary. Rather, to conclude this reading of Arnold's
project, I want to discuss one aspect of that theory, the central one of how
we are to take its status, and how Arnold's handling of that question indicates his final expansion of his notion of critical discourse. In *Literature
and Dogma* and *God and the Bible*, Arnold wants to renew his age's sense of

the Bible's value by modernizing its significance. All the supernatural aspects, including any suggestion of a god that has anything like consciousness, he does away with. He asserts, rather, that there is an external force in the world that drives us toward moral action, and this force he labels "God." He then goes further and says that the Jews were the first to recognize this moral force as God and that Jesus renewed and perfected that perception. Consequently the Bible is a uniquely exemplary and thus uniquely edifying spectacle of the worship of this moral force.

There are two major areas of controversy about Arnold's general theory that he was concerned to answer in *God and the Bible*[26] (the attack upon his heterodoxy did not deeply concern him since he assumed that the faith of the majority of his readers had already been irreparably shaken; his task he saw as laying new foundations, and so he had no concern with the old). First, the claim that the existence of an external force that is "not ourselves that makes for righteousness"—that which Arnold labels God—may be externally verified does not seem a much more defensible proposition than that a personal God or a God of love exists. Second, even if such a force did exist, the Bible hardly seems a very important text for that recognition, demanding as it does a massive and doubtful reinterpretation in order even to make the book relevant, much less central, to that recognition.

The noticeable aspect of the first problem is how unnecessary Arnold's notion of experimental verifiability seems and yet how much that notion is the crux of the problem. William Robbins has argued, unexceptionably, that Arnold's mistake was not to argue for a moral force but to assume the manifestation of that force in experiential reality. Had he defined its perception as an ideal one, he would have been on much more solid ground.[27] It is at least true that he would have been on very strong ground with his contemporary, Victorian intelligentsia. But a morality that is an ethical ideal with transcendental groundings gives no special place for the Bible; any example of moral elevation in the face of suffering is as good as any other.[28] For the example of the Bible to be a special one, the Jews in the Old Testament and Christ in the New must have had a historically special perception of that moral reality.

Yet Arnold never really provides any defense of his assertion that the dictates of morality have experimental verifiability; he simply makes it and then remarks that "if any man is so entirely without affinity for [moral truths], so subjugated by the conviction that facts are clean against them, as to be unable to entertain the idea of their being in human nature and in experience, for him *Literature and Dogma* was not written" (*CPW*, VII:231). First, we should note here that one does not have absolutely to believe in the scientific truth of morality in order for the text to work; one need only "entertain the idea." Arnold is asking for the same kind of belief fiction demands. Second, for the person unable even to entertain the idea, the only response Arnold can give is expulsion from the realm of his book. For those, *Literature and Dogma* was not written. But the book can accommodate their absence even if those absent cannot accommodate the book. Their absence is explained by their "subjugation." *God and the Bible* defends *Literature and Dogma* not by justifying or explaining but by engulfing within its system, offering a perception adequate to the spectacle.

Of more importance to Arnold than the status of the force that makes for righteousness, though, is the status of the Bible. Arnold insists, in his introduction, that his purpose is "to restore the use of the Bible to those . . . whom the popular theology with its proof from miracle, and the learned theology with its proof from metaphysics, so dissatisfy and repel that they are attempted to throw aside the Bible altogether (*CPW*, VII:143). Arnold's restoration is based, not on fact, but on interpretation. We see the Bible's value when it "is read aright" (*CPW*, VII:143). In the case of the Old Testament, reading aright shows us, as I said, an exemplary history of a people who perceived God as morality. Now Arnold defends this reading in two ways. When he argues against those who cite constant Old Testament anthropomorphisms, he argues simply that Judaism is a religion that centers around a notion of moral conduct, and its ways of talking about God are related to that. This is at least a tenable interpretation of the Old Testament, but it hardly gives it the special status Arnold claims. Others besides the Jews have had notions of moral conduct more or less imbedded in their religion.

To make the Old Testament special, it must be read in a slightly different way: as a constant drama of the struggle between a people's perception of a truth and the struggle of that truth to emerge clearly, a drama in which, of course, Arnold's reinterpretation takes a part. This drama is not argued for, though, but articulated in passages like this:

> And this native, continuous, and increasing pressure upon Israel's spirit of the ideas of conduct and of its sanctions, we call his intuition

> of the Eternal that makes for righteousness, the revelation to him of
> the religion of this Eternal. Really, we do not know how else to ac-
> count for the evident fact of the pressure, than by supposing that
> Israel had an intuitive faculty, a natural bent for these ideas; that their
> truth was borne in upon him, revealed to him. We put aside all the
> preternatural. . . . We give an explanation which is natural. But we
> say that this natural explanation is yet greater than the preternatural
> one. (*CPW*, VII:220)

This passage transforms the textual interpretation into the important
drama through the evident trope of personification. A historical pattern
of a concern for conduct may not have the special value Arnold wants to
give the Bible. But the struggle of the personified Israel to grasp *his* intuition, the pressure upon *him*, this kind of language creates a psychodrama
of a man whose consciousness is fixed on an object until, finally, working
through his own flawed nature, he understands his perception. It is, of
course, the drama of the critical intelligence and thus the drama of biblical interpretation. It is now, as well, the drama that the interpretation
interprets.

If we ask Arnold so impertinent a question as whether he believes his
interpretation constitutes history or fiction, our answer is likely to partake of the ambiguity of the quoted trope. If we read carefully, though,
we can see both the priority of the interpretation over the event interpreted and the reason for that priority: "In short, the more we conceive
Jesus as almost as much over the heads of his disciples and reporters then,
as he is over heads of the mass of so-called Christians now, . . . all the
more do we make room, so to speak, for Jesus to be a personage im-
mensely great and wonderful; as wonderful as anything his reporters
imagined him to be, though in a different manner" (*CPW*, VI:260–261).
The syntax of the sentence indicates the logic clearly enough. We must
conceive Jesus in a particular way to get him to look a certain way. The
value of doing so is that we then get, not the Jesus his reporters gave
us, but a Jesus we can find wonderful. Interpretation, conception, create
value here.[29]

The value of Arnold's reinterpretation is not merely its usefulness,
though. As I said before, Arnold's history of the Bible is also an account
of the contemporary religious turmoil as he saw it. And he makes clear
the relationship between his text and the *Zeit-Geist*:

> For it is what we call the *Time-Spirit* which is sapping the proof from miracles,—it is the 'Zeit-Geist' itself. Whether we attack them, or whether we defend them, does not much matter. The human mind, as its experience widens, is turning away from them. And for this reason: *it sees as its experience widens, how they arise.* (*CPW*, VI:246)

The interpretation of how miracles are thought to occur and what its observers are really observing thus comments on the state of the age that produced such an observation. Arnold, through his interpretation of the Bible, captures the state of his age within the *Zeit-Geist*. Between the religion his age needs and the religion his interpretation constructs, between the state of the age in which it was written and the method of Arnold's interpretation, Arnold intends a textual correspondence the only evidence of which he offers is the complexity and adequacy of his text and its interpretations. But this, of course, is the textual gaze of "On the Modern Element," the gaze that both comprehends and creates an age's complexity and thus offers it intellectual deliverance. The expansion of Arnold's epistemology is complete. From the critical gaze through the cultural gaze to the textual gaze, Arnold has established a complete adequation. Whether or not adequation is a satisfactory basis for making literary criticism a global discourse, it is at least an entirely coherent one.

Conclusion

Matthew Arnold stands as a kind of terminus to Victorian prose. To extend his literariness, later writers like Pater and Wilde had to make themselves absolute agonists to his role as prophet. As fruitful as that position was, it broke a correspondence between philosophy and literature so complex as to create a prose that constantly resisted the separatist interpretations of either pure formalism or pure intellectual engagement. Our attitudes toward the Victorians have sometimes approached the prejudice that Victorian intellectual history is a contradiction in terms. That may be because both intellectual and literary historians have refused to engage in the kind of literary analysis that is necessary to yield the full complexity of thought in figures like Mill, Newman, Carlyle, and Arnold. Conversely, and far more seriously, the purely literary analysis of Victorian prose writers has been no more satisfactory, and that, I would argue, is because the separation of polemic from literature that those readings assume does not allow them to look for literary shape within the structures that a philosophy articulates and embodies.

Effectively, the readings of this part would allow a reconstruction of this book into a literary history of Victorian prose whose structuring theme would be the development of the genre in terms of its response to the correspondence that was its condition of being: the correspondence between nineteenth-century theories of the structure of consciousness and the structure of nineteenth-century narratives. Within this history, Carlyle's narrative experiments and innovations, in their search for discursive cognates to Carlyle's epistemological theories, would define the genre of Victorian prose and the role of the prose-prophet. The writings of Mill and Newman show the genre of Victorian prose, through this correspondence between consciousness and narrative, engulfing the work of writers whose primary ambitions were perhaps to be philosophers and theologians in more traditional senses but who became prose-prophets as well, perhaps despite themselves but nevertheless in ways we must understand even to understand the way their writing works within its traditional disciplines and discourses. Arnold makes these struggles with the correspondence between narrative and consciousness, between form and philosophy, an explicit theme of his discourse as he uses it both to place himself within the tradition he has seen developing and to expand to conceptual limits the claims to relevance and reference of his own discourse.

The order of this book as it stands indicates, though, the centrality of the structural and methodological analysis in the understanding even of the history of the form. To see the theme of such a history as a development of the correspondence between consciousness and narrative that constitutes the existence of Victorian prose as a form, we must first understand how that correspondence works to structure the form. In such a project, beginning with the attempts of Mill and Newman to preserve discursive divisions allows the analysis that shows how consciousness and narrative come together, how philosophy may be structurally narrativized. Showing how Carlyle and Arnold, figures far more centrally and intentionally prose-prophets, invent, reinvent, and play out the possibilities of that connection, I have been arguing in this part for the relevance for an understanding of Victorian prose of a reading method that begins with a knowledge of the connection between epistemology and narrative.

Gerald Graff has noticed that "whenever I hear anybody talk about reconciling science and literature, I have learned that what is likely to be coming next is some assertion of the fictionality of everything."[30] If one substitutes philosophy—the erstwhile queen of the sciences—for science, to this charge, I can only plead guilty with an explanation. Whether or not philosophy is fiction, I have been arguing here that the texts of Victorian philosophy as they become Victorian prose are narrativized in ways that make the methods of fictive analysis particularly appropriate for handling their ideas. In my lengthy readings of Mill and Newman, I have tried to show how this process occurs and what it tells us about narrative, philosophy, and intellectual history. In this last part, I have turned that knowledge into a methodology. The usefulness of that methodology, and therefore the explanation I attach to my guilty plea, is the readings of Carlyle and Arnold it allows me to offer.

Afterword:
On Using Theory

I have argued in this book for a method of reading Victorian prose, not for or against any particular theory of literature in general. Nevertheless, my argument's deployment of the terms *philosophy* and *literature* as contrasting categories of discourse and its isolation of the moment at which a work passes from one category to another as the one in which philosophic discourse exhausts the methods of argument considered proper to it (strict logical sequence and transparency of reference in its language) owes a considerable debt to that literary theory which has come to be called deconstructionist. I have registered in footnotes the debts my thinking about these categories and their relations owe to the works of Derrida (particularly *Of Grammatology* and "White Mythology") and de Man (particularly his further articulation of Derrida's theory in *Allegories of Reading*). And readers will no doubt note at other specific points in my argument local uses of the theory's methods and terms. Some will also note that I must be misusing, misunderstanding, or diverging from the theory in certain problematic ways since I work through the categories of philosophy and literature to define more adequately Victorian prose as a specific literary genre that occurred at a specific historical period. Deconstruction, in contrast, is usually taken to be fatally corrosive of generic and literary historical definition.[1] In this Afterword, I offer a sketch outlining a justification for my [mis]use of the theory, but a sketch that is also a question: can we remove a theory, or at least this theory, from the context of the debate concerning its ultimate or foundational implications in order to put it to practice for specific ends?

First, though, I must clarify the extent of my divergence from Derrida's and de Man's discussion of philosophy and the literary. The survival in my argument of generic and historical categories occurs because of a more basic divergence from deconstruction in the ways I use the categories of philosophy and literature. Derrida questions a basic opposition between figural language and proper naming, the latter being the root version of a transparent use of language, in order to show how the figural is imbedded in the definition of the proper; and thus metaphor, in the text of philosophy.[2] In an explicit application of this argument to literary theory, de Man calls into question the distinction between grammar and rhetoric in order to show the propriety—so to speak—of literary language within philosophic argument and thus privileges literature as the only discourse aware of its own figurality.[3] If these summaries are simplifications, they are sufficient to show how my divisions between philosophic argumentation and narrative will not fit. Both Derrida and de Man analyze fundamental oppositions and irreducible distinctions, and their reversals and undoings of those oppositions undercut the foundational claims of the discourses those distinctions ground. A contrast between narrative and logical argumentation is in no sense such an irreducible opposition. Indeed, the terms are not logically opposed at all: we usually take the opposite of logic to be nonsense or illogic and the opposite of narrative to be a chaotic mass of unordered events.

Because an opposition between narrative and logic is not sufficiently reduced, it is not worth deconstructing and, strictly, not deconstructible, not because it resists that process but because its undoing would have none of the metaphysical implications that necessitate such an "exorbitant" method.[4] Even if I were arguing that these categories did not exclude each other sufficiently, no aporia calling into question the way we think and interpret would result, and so their undoing would simply be the traditional philosophic process of getting rid of a distinction without a difference. Moreover, nothing in my argument necessarily calls into question any categorical distinction. Deconstruction undoes one of its oppositions by showing that the definition of the normal or prior category—proper naming, grammar, nature—already entails an understanding and thus an implicit inclusion of the category its priority depends on excluding—metaphor, rhetoric, culture. But when, in my analysis of Mill and Newman, I delineate what I take to be contradictions or paradoxes in their philosophy, those problems may well be understood in standard logical terms. Thus the analysis does not corrupt the categories of philosophy and narrative per se. I merely trace the path by which works of Victorian prose move through these categories. The categories of genre and historical period thus survive because no prior concept on which they depend has been dismantled. At this point, I might shelter myself from the theoretical debate by simply claiming that my argument does not rest on deconstructive theory but simply uses some of its terms and concepts for its own purposes.

If this sheltering removed my argument from the context of the theoretical debate between deconstructionists and those theorists concerned to defend the possibility of articulating determinate meanings in texts, it would do so only by leaving both schools in the debate rightfully dissatisfied with the final coherence of that argument. A deconstructionist could criticize it either for misunderstanding the implications of employing deconstructive readings or for insufficiently employing those techniques—in any case, for leaving vital categories in my argument undeconstructed. Were my argument safely under the aegis of a traditional defense of determinate meanings, an attack upon it for being insufficiently deconstructive would not necessarily be a concern. But for those traditionalists, any use of deconstruction corrodes the whole of any argument in which it occurs. Since the theory calls into question all logical argumentation, to use its method at one point calls into question either the validity of that point or of the case as a whole. If I had described the philosophic paradoxes and contradictions I detailed in Victorian prose as local accidents, that would not present a problem for traditionalists. But my debt to deconstruction is more than a matter of using its terms. By describing those problematic moments as necessary and defining ones within the genre, and by using the terms of deconstruction at certain points in my argument, according to traditional theorists I have attempted to define a genre in terms that would cause that definition, and finally my whole case, to evaporate. In effect, both schools in the debate seem to agree that being a little deconstructive is as impossible as being a little pregnant.

Because both schools in this debate argue by being comprehensive rather than exclusionary, in other words, by showing not that the opposed position is wrong but that their own position is prior and contains its supposed opponent, it would be possible to turn my argument's double culpability into a double defense. Derrida has consistently admitted that his method rests on the same metaphysical assumptions it deconstructs, that it works within the system it destabilizes. Therefore, he argues, he says exactly what his opponents say against him but understands better what that saying entails.[5] Further, he does not precisely disprove any theory but simply calls into question any theory's exclusionary ability, ending one of his early important essays by asserting the impossibility of choosing between "the two interpretations of interpretation."[6] But on these terms, what kind of reading would not be deconstructive? No reading can be comprehensively deconstructive since a deconstruction rests on the assumptions it deconstructs, and a consequent deconstruction of a deconstruction would only be aware of this situation without claiming to escape it. Moreover, opposing readings, divergent readings all fall under the rubric of deconstruction, so no reading can avoid being deconstructive. Thus my reading would be deconstructive no matter what I did and insufficiently deconstructive no matter how far I carried the deconstruction. The case of traditional theory is the same in reverse. Taking at his word that Derrida's case rests on the assumptions it deconstructs, traditional theorists argue that, therefore, normal methods of interpretation are prior to deconstruction,[7] which would at best be merely a description of special cases, even if those special cases happened, accidentally, to coincide with all existent texts. Again, by comprehending all arguments, this position disallows itself from excluding any argument. Whether this book were thoroughly deconstructive or not, it would still be thoroughly normal in its assumptions. And like any normal interpretation, its validity would rest on its internal argumentation.

This response is no doubt a glib evasion, but it outlines the more important claims that practical criticism can make when it uses theoretical concepts without attending to the debate surrounding those concepts. Deconstruction has, from its beginning, been an attempt to use concepts in order to evade them, and its claim has always been the intrinsic practical soundness of the evasion. In *Of Grammatology*'s chapter on method, Derrida explains:

> I wished to reach the point of a certain exteriority in relation to the totality of the age of logocentrism. Starting from this point of exteriority, a certain deconstruction of that totality which is also a traced path, of that orb (*orbis*) which is also orbitary (*orbita*), might be broached. The first gesture of this departure and this deconstruction, although subject to a certain historical necessity, cannot be given methodological or logical intra-orbitary assurances. Within the closure, one can only judge its style in terms of the accepted opposi-

tions. It may be said that this style is empiricist and in a certain way that would be correct. It proceeds like a wandering thought on the possibility of itinerary and of method.[8]

Given this methodological opening, a later use of deconstructive terms to wander out of *its* orbit can only seem illicit in the light of a set of rules guarding the theory that not only would be theoretically incoherent but, more important, would run counter to the very gesture that institutes the theory's method. But traditional theory, too, even in its most unyielding claims for the unitariness of truth, has never argued for a unitariness of method. For traditional interpreters, questions of method must always be subsidiary to the validity of the results they achieve. Otherwise, they would not be arguing for the logical necessity of knowing what we mean (the position they claim as their strength) but for some specific method— biographical, generic, historical. And they have always argued that these are only possibilites open to literary criticism. Before M. H. Abrams took the field against deconstruction, he too insisted on eclecticism and the danger of conceiving of one right method:

> Let us imagine a critical language-game, and the form of life that it inescapably involves, which would in fact achieve the goal of certainty that one is tempted to hold up as the ideal of all rational discourse. There would be only one permissible theoretical stance, all the descriptive and normative terms would have fixed criteria of use, and reasoning would proceed entirely in accordance with established logical calculi. . . . If, however, instead of holding up such certainty as an abstract ideal, we realize in imagination the form of life in which such critical discourse would be standard, we find it inhuman and repulsive; for it is an ideal that could be achieved only in a form of political, social, and artistic life like that which Aldous Huxley direly foreboded in *Brave New World* or George Orwell in *1984*.[9]

Tolerance to method, waiting upon the results it achieves rather than trying to legislate it from the outset, must also extend to deconstructive method, by this logic, regardless of the theoretical claims of that method.

In other words, in both deconstruction and various versions of traditional interpretation, at the moment at which the theory establishes its own place, it does so by opening a space larger than itself called something like "methodological experiment." It is at that point where practical criticism may enter and carry away what it needs. In the case of the controversy over deconstruction, this is particularly so because the debate shows every sign of being both endless and unresolvable precisely because each theory can claim with equal validity or lack of it to encompass the other. Ecumenical as this gesture of encompassing might be, it makes any corresponding exclusionary gesture impossible and thus drains the debate of any consequent limitations upon criticism. It is now becoming stylish to argue that theory has no consequences.[10] But literary theory has consequences in just the way every other kind of theory has: it never has the consequences it foresees. One of those consequences has always been the practical criticism it influences and engenders, even despite itself, and regardless of its fortunes in the theoretical debate. If my argument in this book has been persuasive, if the use of deconstructive concepts has led to a more persuasive definition of the workings of Victorian prose, then the problem of the workings of those concepts within the definition may profitably be left to the larger debate to solve. That solution will not affect the status of this work or any other because the value of theory is that it always opens but can never manage to close.

Notes

Introduction

1. For instance, in "Recovering Literature's Lost Ground," in *Autobiography: Essays Theoretical and Critical*, ed. James Olney (Princeton, N.J.: Princeton University Press, 1980), 125, James M. Cox argues that autobiography may renew criticism's interest in "the world of fact," the world he describes as "literature's lost ground," and thus renew its interest in imaginative prose.

2. I stress that these points are a logical sequence, not a necessary chronological or biographical process. The issues I discuss are ones that concerned Mill and Newman throughout their intellectual careers rather than in set stages and at certain times, and I do, from time to time, use later works as a context for earlier ones. My argument entails separating types of discourse, philosophic and narrative, into distinct categories in order to show how, finally, those types of discourse are connected. I would by no means claim that those categories are inherently Mill's or Newman's; their final justification, however, is the understanding they allow of the connections between the philosophies and autobiographies of those writers and, in the last analysis, of the connections between philosophy and narrative in Victorian prose.

3. *The Collected Dialogues of Plato*, ed. Edith Hamilton and Huntington Cairns (Princeton, N.J.: Princeton University Press, 1963), 747.

4. The linkage between any given author's definition of consciousness and the narrative structure of his works is, of course, not deterministic. An author who never gave thought to, or never wanted to justify, definitions of consciousness might experiment with various narrative structures; and in principle, an author aware of and concerned to argue for a definition of consciousness might use a divergent narrative structure. My interest here is to establish the theoretical and working relationship between theories of consciousness and narrative structure rather than to establish a comprehensive, comparative taxonomy. In the light of the theoretical relationship, though, an author whose considered definitions of consciousness and narrative structure diverged would immediately be a case of some interest, both theoretical and practical.

5. Geoffrey H. Hartman's "Romanticism and 'Anti-self-consciousness,'" *Ro-*

manticism and Consciousness, ed. Harold Bloom (New York: Norton, 1970), 45–56, is an excellent discussion of the fear of self-consciousness and the responses to that fear in Romantic and Victorian writers. One can, of course, overstate the fear. As Jerome Buckley has pointed out in his opening chapter to *The Turning Key: Autobiography and the Subjective Impulse since 1800* (Cambridge: Harvard University Press, 1984), 1–19, both the fear of the subjective and the autobiographical impulse were responses of the nineteenth century to the discovery of and fascination with subjectivity. Even if the fear resulted from the fascination, however, the question of why the fear was not more discouraging to Victorian autobiography than it was remains. Thus Avrom Fleishman, *Figures of Autobiography* (Berkeley and Los Angeles: University of California Press, 1983), 112–113, asks that question as well.

6. William Irvine, *Apes, Angels, and Victorians* (Cleveland and New York: World Publishing, 1959), 7. My description of the confrontation follows Irvine's account, 6–7.

7. By contrasting the terms *orthodoxy* and *fact*, I do not mean to suggest that orthodoxy cannot be true, though we still possess enough of the Victorian awe for fact to make such an opposition seem to carry that suggestion. Although fact, as anything that is empirically verifiable, is not synonymous with truth, which may of course involve more than empirics, both Huxley and his twentieth-century commentator, for instance, confuse the two terms.

8. Gerry Brookes, *The Rhetorical Form of Carlyle's "Sartor Resartus"* (Berkeley and Los Angeles: University of California Press, 1972), has noted that readers often saw *Sartor* as spiritual autobiography even before Carlyle had made any autobiographical basis public (4). And in *Natural Supernaturalism* (New York: Norton, 1971), which takes its title from one of Carlyle's chapters, M. H. Abrams classifies it as "a serious parody of the spiritual autobiography which plays with and undercuts the conventions it nonetheless accepts" (130). But its hortatory element has convinced critics like Brookes that it should be treated rhetorically, and its fictional techniques have led a host of critics, most prominently G. B. Tennyson, *Sartor Called Resartus* (Princeton, N.J.: Princeton University Press, 1965), and George Levine, *The Boundaries of Fiction* (Princeton, N.J.: Princeton University Press, 1968), to consider it either as a novel or as approaching the form of the novel. My argument does not necessitate assuming *Sartor* to be one or the other. I am simply responding to its often observed similarity to autobiography and the effects of its ideas upon its form.

9. Thomas Carlyle, *Sartor Resartus*, ed. Charles Frederick Harrold (New York: Odyssey, 1937), 203. Henceforth, this edition will be cited in my text as *Sartor*.

10. For a more detailed discussion of Carlyle's readings and misreadings of Kant, see Rene Wellek, *Immanuel Kant in England* (Princeton, N.J.: Princeton University Press, 1931), 185–202.

11. Both Tennyson, *Sartor Called Resartus* (177–180) and Levine, *Boundaries of Fiction*, (55–57) discuss the role of the Editor as a mediator between Teufelsdröckh's mysticism and empiricist English readers. Both also note that, in the course of the book, the Editor moves closer and closer to his subject in both judgment and style until the identification is all but complete.

12. Irvine, *Apes, Angels and Victorians*, 207. Irvine's remark is given considerable support by the extended and sensitive reading James Olney offers of Darwin's *Autobiography* in *Metaphors of Self: The Meaning of Autobiography* (Princeton, N.J.: Princeton University Press, 1972), 182–202. To a large extent, my argument parallels Olney's position that Darwin's work breaks down as autobiography because his life is not amenable to the kind of scientific observation that was his standard method of procedure. Olney and I differ, however, on one point, which may be minor in terms of Darwin's work but is important in the context of my argument here. Olney argues that, in the service of his science, Darwin effectively destroyed that part of the self that perceives intuitively and that his *Autobiography* was consequently unable to accommodate anything but a narrow vision of himself. I argue that Darwin both believed in an innate self prior to that developed by experiences and explicitly attributed innate qualities to himself. His problem was that scientific observation could record, but not offer any explanation of, those qualities. The importance of this distinction is, of course, that if one erased oneself as completely as Olney argues Darwin did, one could never write an autobiography at all.

13. Charles Darwin, *Autobiography* (New York: Norton, 1958), 21. Henceforth, this edition will be cited in my text as *Autobiography*.

14. John Freccero, editor's introduction, *Dante: A Collection of Critical Essays* (Englewood Cliffs, N.J.: Prentice-Hall, 1965), 5. Fleishman, *Figures of Autobiography*, 7, also notes this problem: that only death can finish a life, that any other point of completion is a fiction.

15. In his recent book, *Fictional Techniques and Factual Works* (Athens, Ga.: University of Georgia Press, 1983), William R. Siebenschuh argues eloquently that there is no necessary opposition between the use of fictional techniques and the presentation of facts and documentary evidence, thus that we can delineate fictional techniques within an autobiography without calling the autobiography fictional. Siebenschuh, however, specifies that he means, by fictional techniques, "stylistic techniques that we normally associate only with fiction or poetry: dialogue, dramatised episodes, sustained narrative or dramatic structure, symbolism, imagery, and heavy dependence on the purely affective dimension of language" (7). It does seem clear that to assume that any works that contain these techniques are fictional is to beg the question of whether using these techniques inherently obstructs the presentation of facts. Narrative historians, for instance, have not generally assumed that, and there is no necessary mutual exclusion between defi-

nitions of "narrative" and of "factual account." As my distinction a couple of pages further on between the definition of "fiction" as a controlling order and that of "fiction" as a representation of imagined events implies, I would agree that one kind of fiction does not, in terms purely of definition, necessitate the other. I also argue, though, below and throughout the book, particularly in my handling in Chapter III of Mill's mental crisis and in Chapter VIII of the problem of rhetoric in the *Apologia*, that there are reasons why one form of fiction leads to another.

16. Edmund Gosse, *Father and Son* (New York: Norton, 1963), 5.

17. Vivian Folkenflik and Robert Folkenflik, in their article "Words and Language in *Father and Son*," *Biography* 2 (1979): 157–174, have also noticed that while the preface to *Father and Son* begins by insisting upon the book as a document, the beginning of the first chapter is highly metaphorical.

18. David Hume, *A Treatise of Human Nature*, ed. L. A. Selby-Bigge (London: Oxford University Press, 1938), 251–253.

19. Ibid., 254–262.

20. Thus E. D. Hirsch, Jr., opens *Validity in Interpretation* (New Haven, Conn.: Yale University Press, 1967) with the warning that his theory will lead to no new interpretive or even methodological insights (x–xi). More recently, Jonathan Culler, in *The Pursuit of Signs* (Ithaca, N.Y.: Cornell University Press, 1981), chap. 1, has bemoaned the way Anglo-American critical desires for new interpretations have obstructed and disabled the growth of our theorizing.

21. This book's argument, particularly its concern for outlining a connection between philosophy and literature that occurs at moments when the usual modes of philosophic discourse break down, clearly owes some of its ideas to deconstructive theory. In particular, Jacques Derrida's seminal analysis, "White Mythology: Metaphor in the Text of Philosophy," in *Margins of Philosophy*, trans. Alan Bass (Chicago: University of Chicago Press, 1982), 207–272, and Paul de Man's *Allegories of Reading* (New Haven, Conn.: Yale University Press, 1979), are central to, though not definitive of, my own thinking about the relationship between philosophy and literature in Victorian prose. Those interested in the ways I use this theory, the important differences between it and my use of some of its elements to my own ends, and the theoretical implications of that use, should consult my afterword. I have reserved that theoretical discussion for a last word because I do not think my argument either depends or rests on that theory, either proves or is an example of it, and thus the discussion of its role is, in certain ways, tangential to my real aims.

Chapter I: The Philosophic Context of Mill's *Autobiography*

1. *Utilitarianism,* in *Essays on Ethics, Religion and Society,* vol. X of the *Collected Works of John Stuart Mill* (Toronto: University of Toronto Press, 1969), 234. Henceforth, this book will be cited in my text as *Util.*

2. A. W. Levi's dating of the periods of composition, in "The Writing of Mill's *Autobiography,*" *International Journal of Ethics* (July 1951): 281–296, as 1853–1854 for the *Early Draft,* 1861 for the rewriting of that draft into the final state in which we have it, and 1869 for the addition of the events of the final third following Harriet Mill's death, has been confirmed by Jack Stillinger, with some minor revisions, in his introduction to the *Early Draft.* The differences between the final version of the *Early Draft* and the completed version of the *Autobiography,* except for the added last third, are not large. Levi characterizes them as "always stylistic" (287).

3. This is, however, precisely the assumption of Mill's psychoanalyzers. A. W. Levi, in "The 'Mental Crisis' of John Stuart Mill," *Psychoanalytic Review* 32 (1945): 86–101, an extremely influential article, bases his conclusion largely on Mill's language. John Durheim, "The Influence of John Stuart Mill's Mental Crisis on His Thoughts," *American Imago* 20 (1963): 369–384, differs from Levi's interpretation, arguing that Mill's education had created a repressive censor through which he filtered his emotions before displaying them, thus breaking down the strength of those emotions; but he uses the same method to arrive at his conclusions. More recently, Bruce Mazlish, in his dual psychobiography *James and John Stuart Mill: Father and Son in the Nineteenth Century* (New York: Basic Books, 1975), has followed both Levi's methods and his conclusions. To be fair, since Mazlish's project is rather larger in scale (he treats Mill's entire life and works), he takes other documents besides the *Autobiography* into account. Nevertheless, his treatment of the mental crisis is largely determined by a rather close reading of that text.

I should clarify that while my objection holds against the psychobiographers of Mill in particular, and against far too many psychobiographers in general, it is not by any means an objection in principle against psychoanalysis or even psychobiography. It is an objection against any naive assumption that autobiographical texts are transparent records of the events to which they refer oddly coupled with the sophisticated Freudian hermeneutic put into play to handle the interpreting, encoding, and distorting processes of the text produced by the psyche in consciousness. In other words, before one can interpret Mill's mental crisis as the distortion of a psychic response, the same logic that led to such an interpretation would necessitate an interpretation of the text that describes that mental crisis as a distortion of a psychic response that led to the writing of the text. To such a fully carried out analysis, could it in principle be completed, my own interpretation of the significance of philosophic context might be a complement, might even be merely further evidence, but could not be an objection.

4. Mill to Harriet, 1 January 1854, *Later Letters of John Stuart Mill 1849–1873*, ed. Francis Mineka and Dwight Lindley (Toronto: University of Toronto Press, 1973), 141–142.

5. Bertrand Russell, "John Stuart Mill," in *Mill: A Collection of Critical Essays*, ed. J. B. Schneewind (Notre Dame, Ill.: University of Notre Dame Press, 1969), finds the logical and metaphysical foundations of Mill's philosophy faulty but sees lasting value in the superstructure of his social beliefs (1–21). Basil Willey, *Nineteenth Century Studies* (London: Chatto & Windus, 1949), finds the contradiction in the value of emotion, coupled with Mill's refusal entirely to reject utilitarian doctrines (141–186). F. R. Leavis, introduction to *Mill on Bentham and Coleridge* (London: Chatto & Windus, 1950), agrees with Willey, noting Mill's attempt to unify Bentham and Coleridge while still remaining tied to the economic and epistemological doctrines of his father (1–38). And Raymond Williams, *Culture and Society* (New York: Harper & Row, 1966) claims that Mill recognizes the value of an intellectual clerisy but leaves poetry and culture as an adjunct to, rather than an integral part of, his view of society (49–70).

6. Michael St. John Packe, *The Life of John Stuart Mill* (New York: Capricorn Books, 1970), 9.

7. James McConnel, "Success and Failure: A Rhetorical Study of the First Two Chapters of Mill's *Autobiography*," *University of Toronto Quarterly* 45 (Winter 1976): 109–122, places Mill's dilemma precisely in his refusal either to quite deny or quite accept his father's education, resulting in a balance of tensions in the *Autobiography*'s prose. My Chapter IV offers a different explanation for that balance.

8. Mill, *Autobiography and Literary Essays*, vol. I of the *Collected Works* (Toronto: University of Toronto Press, 1981), 270. Henceforth, this edition will be cited in my text as *Auto*. Although generally assuming 1854 as the date of composition, I cite the final version to emphasize the importance of the earlier date even for the completed text. Since the Toronto edition has the *Early Draft* and the *Autobiography* printed on facing pages, a citation of the one automatically cites the other. I of course take note of significant differences explicitly. The passage quoted here is part of the *Autobiography* written in 1869 and so not part of the *Early Draft*.

9. Alan Ryan, *J. S. Mill* (Boston: Routledge & Kegan Paul, 1974), 85.

Chapter II: Associationism, Will, and Consciousness

1. Mill to Tocqueville, 3 November 1843, *Earlier Letters of John Stuart Mill 1812–1848*, ed. Francis Mineka (Toronto: University of Toronto Press, 1963), 612.

In English, the passage reads: "I am able to say that I have found peace, since it [his solution to the problem of free will] alone has fully satisfied my need to put in harmony intelligence and conscience, by resting on a solid intellectual basis one's sense of human responsibility. I do not think that any serious thinker may enjoy any tranquility of mind or soul until he has come to some satisfactory solution to this great problem. I have no desire to impose my own solution on those who are satisfied with their's, but I believe that there are many for whom my solution will be, as it has been for me, a veritable anchor of salvation." [My translation]

2. Mill, *A System of Logic*, ed. J. M. Robson (Toronto: University of Toronto Press, 1973–1974), vols. VII and VIII of *Collected Works*, 535. Since these two volumes are paged consecutively throughout, I hereafter give only page references, citing the edition in my text as *Logic*.

3. Eugene R. August, *John Stuart Mill* (New York: Scribner's, 1975), 103.

4. The formulation is the basic model for explaining how associationism can accommodate the ostensibly active capacities of the mind. It thus also solves the problem of explaining attentiveness through association, a problem that Alan Ryan has stated twice is impossible to solve: in *J. S. Mill*, 19, stating, "It is impossible to square the role of the active and critical intellect with the associationist theory of learning," and in his review of Mazlish's *James and John Stuart Mill* in *New York Review of Books*, 29 May 1975, 8, saying, "It is not easy to see how an education based on the associationist psychology of the utilitarians *could* consistently have been the exercise in *analytic* thinking that John Mill describes." In a note to his father's *Analysis of the Phenomena of the Human Mind* (London: Longmans, Green, 1878), II:372–375, expressing his discontent with his father's view that attentiveness to a sensation is a misleading way of saying that the sensation is inherently stronger, Mill allows that one may willfully attend to a thought or a sensation but states that will is ascribable to motivation, which is ascribable, of course, to desires deriving from experience. Since Mill, in this note, is arguing in support of necessity, he does not try to suppress the prior causes of attentiveness or bring it into the service of free will. My later discussion of James Mill's epistemological work and Mill's footnotes cite this edition in my text as *Analysis*.

5. Packe, *Life*, 267. Packe is, of course, not the most acute commentator on Mill's philosophy. Alan Ryan, in *John Stuart Mill* (New York: Random House, 1970), has compared Mill's argument to Hume's famous case for necessity and stated that that case has at times gained "the status of near orthodoxy" (115). Hume argues, like Mill, that believing all human actions are necessarily the result of prior causes does not presume any necessary external coercion or constraint since cause involves only inevitable conjunction. Further, if liberty is defined merely as doing what one wills, such a definition is amenable to an argument in favor of causal necessity as the determining factor in human action since, even if

we do as we will, that does not mean that the will is not caused. Mill thus does use Hume's arguments to take the sting out of the argument for causal necessity and does place himself to some extent in Hume's school of thought. But he goes much further than Hume by contending that a philosophically meaningful sense of liberty involving self-ordination and not simply the ambiguous ability to do what one wills is also consistent with an argument for causal necessity. It is this contention that not only Packe, but Ryan himself, among many other critics of Mill's thought, have found unsatisfactory.

6. Mill, "Coleridge," *Collected Works*, X:125.

7. The need for a percipient is at the root of Ryan's objection that Mill's reality has no spatial extension, in *J. S. Mill*, 224. H. J. McCloskey, *John Stuart Mill: A Critical Study* (London: Macmillan, 1971), 152, objects that possibilities may exist in the absence of sensations and, therefore, of sensors, whereas a definition of matter as sensation depends upon both. All Mill has done, though, is add a contingency clause to sensation. If a tree falls in the forest and no one hears it, we can still say that, had someone been nearby, he *would* have heard it. Thus, though no sensation of sound occurred, the possibility of sensation was there, and therefore, both the tree and the forest exist.

8. As Ryan, *J. S. Mill*, 224, points out.

9. J. P. Day, "Mill on Matter," *Mill: A Collection*, 133, also calls memory and expectation necessary to Mill's theory.

10. Mill, *An Examination of Sir William Hamilton's Philosophy*, ed. J. M. Robson, vol. IX of *Collected Works* (Toronto: University of Toronto Press, 1979), 194. Henceforth, this edition will be cited in my text as *Hamilton*.

11. McCloskey, *Mill: A Critical Study*, 158–159, finds the paradox "unsatisfactory" and concludes that Mill offers "no coherent account of mind." Ryan, *J. S. Mill*, 226, finds Mill's "admission" a "disaster for his whole philosophical system" and, presuming that the fact was "lost on Mill," concludes that "Mill ought to have displayed more alarm that he did." Thomas Wood, *Poetry and Philosophy* (London: Hutchinson, 1961), 168, rather innocently accepts Mill's paradox as ultimate, citing in hushed tones Wittgenstein's "whereof man cannot speak, he must remain silent." As my further argument shows, I think Mill has effectively taken in all of these critics. Robert Cumming, "Mill's History of His Ideas," *Journal of the History of Ideas* 25 (1964): 242, goes further than all of them, stating that when Mill returned to his utilitarian beliefs, he never found a place for self-consciousness. Cumming uses the *Hamilton* passage and another in the footnotes to James Mill's *Analysis* to support his contention. But there is a difference between admitting one has reached an ultimate principle and admitting an inconsistency. All associationists must admit, for instance, that the ability to differentiate between painful sensations and pleasurable ones, so that one will shun the former and desire the latter, cannot be explained experientially. Whatever constitutes the

difference in the two sensations is a given. That does not mean, however, that there is no place for the differentiation of pain and pleasure within associationism.

12. For the purposes of differentiation, "Mill" always refers to J. S. Mill. His father, I refer to as James Mill.

13. Letter to Francis Place, cited in Packe, *Life*, 14.

14. Packe, *Life*, 476.

Chapter III: Examples in Narrative

1. I refer here to critics who place autobiographies in any biographical context at all. In formal readings of autobiographies, it is now quite fashionable to see autobiography as primarily an act of narrative voice rather than referential description. For an account of this development, see my article "Autobiography as Genre, Act of Consciousness, Text," *Prose Studies* 4 (September 1981): 173–175. Although my handling of Mill's *Autobiography* and Newman's *Apologia* has some resemblance and considerable debt to such formal readings, their very formal boundaries do not enable them to consider the discursive movements from philosophy to narrative that is my subject here.

2. Goldwyn Smith, paraphrased by Alexander Bain, *John Stuart Mill: A Criticism* (London: Longmans, Green, 1882), 171.

3. Mazlish, *James and John Stuart Mill*, 291.

4. Alice Rossi, "Sentiment and Intellect," the introduction to John Stuart Mill and Harriet Taylor, *Essays on Sex Equality*, ed. Alice Rossi (Chicago: University of Chicago Press, 1970), 57.

5. Mill to Harriet, circa 1850, in *Later Letters*, 43.

6. Bain, *Mill: A Criticism*, 102.

7. In F. A. Hayek, *John Stuart Mill and Harriet Taylor* (London: Routledge & Kegan Paul, 1951), 64.

8. He could hardly make a claim for her as an active author since, though he asked her at least twice to write parts of works herself (*Utility of Religion* and the section of the *Autobiography* on their relationship that she saw as needed—both requests in the same letter: Mill to Harriet, 20 February 1854, in *Later Letters*, 165–166), she never responded, and there is no evidence of her having done what he asked.

9. The strongest arguments against joint authorship are those of John M. Robson, *The Improvement of Mankind* (London: Routledge & Viegan Paul, 1968), 50–68, and H. O. Pappe, *John Stuart Mill and the Harriet Taylor Myth* (London: Cambridge University Press, 1952). No arguments in favor of anything more than influence have, in my opinion, ever met their objections. In addition to the older positions of Hayek and Packe in favor of joint authorship, the most recent

works on that side of the question are Gertrude Himmelfarb's *On Liberty and Liberalism* (New York: Knopf, 1974) and Rossi's "Sentiment and Intellect."

10. Figured as inspiration and beautiful soul, Harriet comes close in the *Autobiography* to embodying that Victorian cliché, the angel in the house. It is, of course, ironic that Mill, of all Victorians, the author of *The Subjection of Women*, should have reproduced this iconography that one would think more natural to Ruskin's *Sesames and Lilies*. But it is a complex irony. Phyllis Rose, *Parallel Lives: Five Victorian Marriages* (London: Chatto & Windus, 1984), 140, sums up her discussion of the Mills' marriage by saying that Mill "atoned for the subjection of women by the voluntary, even enthusiastic, subjection of one man and portrayed the result as a model marriage of equals." To justify subjection in a marriage of equals, he had to attribute extraordinary powers to Harriet. And Victorians figured women with extraordinary powers as angels and demons, as Nina Auerbach has shown in *Woman and the Demon: The Life of a Victorian Myth* (Cambridge: Harvard University Press, 1982). Thus Mill's feminism, coupled with the special role Harriet plays in the rest of his philosophic exemplification, leads him to a lapse into the Victorian sexual myths he generally resisted.

11. See Richard Rorty, *Philosophy and the Mirror of Nature* (Princeton, N.J.: Princeton University Press, 1979), 322–333, particularly 324.

12. See for instance Paul Fussell's discussion of the war memoirs of Robert Graves and Edmund Blunden in *The Great War and Modern Memory* (New York: Oxford University Press, 1975), 203–220, 254–269, and his perhaps not incidental caveats about war memoirs in general (310–315). Stephen Jay Gould, in *The Panda's Thumb: More Reflections in Natural History* (New York: Norton, 1980), 64ff., in a similar way, determining how Darwin came to his theory of natural selection, discounts Darwin's own account in his *Autobiography*.

13. The *Early Draft* has "speculatively indifferent" in the place of the final version's "theoretically indifferent."

14. Mill, "Wordsworth and Byron" in *Literary Essays*, ed. Edward Alexander (New York: Bobbs-Merrill, 1967), 352.

15. This passage is part of a lengthy section added in 1861.

16. Robert Cumming, in "Mill's History of His Ideas," 240, was the first to notice chronological discrepancies. His central argument about the mental crisis is that, because Mill never found a place for self-consciousness in his later utilitarian psychology, his autobiographical account reveals an activity of reinterpretation from 1828 to 1830: "The 'dull state of nerves' of 1825, which Mill had reinterpreted poetically in 1828 as a mental crisis, became in 1829 and 1830 'a crisis in My Mental History.' It had perhaps undergone the same reinterpretation as the French Revolution and also became one turbulent passage in 'a progressive transformation embracing the whole human race.' If so we would be able to explain why what happened in 1826 did not remain merely a particular episode of the Autumn

but acquired general significance as a distinctive characteristic of an extended period in Mill's mental history, despite the chronological evidence to the contrary" (252). Cumming's shrewdness in breaking through the veil Mill's account throws over the events of 1826–1830 is laudable, and his article deserves far more attention than it has received. I disagree that self-consciousness became a theoretical anomaly for Mill and think that the autobiographical account was designed to support the theory he had developed. I also think that the real activity of reinterpretation occurs much later than Cumming argues. These disagreements, basic as they may be, do not lessen, however, the fact that my argument owes to him the concept of an alternative method of approaching the mental crisis.

17. Professor Francis Mineka informs me that there was a printed record of those who spoke before the society that Mill could have referred to. But it did not supply the kind of detail he gives. If one interprets Mill's claim of memory lapse to refer specifically to his own speeches at the society, one could argue that such a lapse would not preclude the memory of the speeches of others—an argument that does not seem very convincing. Even if the claim of a memory lapse is purely a reference to his own speeches, the import of the paragraph is clearly that Mill was so wrapped up with his depression that, although he could continue his normal life from "mere force of habit," he was largely unaware of what he was doing or what was going on around him. If he "even composed and spoke several speeches" without remembering their content and reception, is it likely that he would nevertheless have sufficiently attended to the debate of others to remember that after twenty-five years?

18. Between the first and last version, there was an intermediate phrasing in the final version of the *Early Draft* that has "before the gloom passed away" in the place of "during the next few years."

19. Bain, *Mill: A Criticism*, 30, 37–38.

20. Packe, *Life*, 79.

21. Mazlish, *James and John Stuart Mill*, 224.

22. Mill to Comte, 15 June 1843, *Earlier Letters*, 584–585: "I have fallen recently into a sort of intellectual, not to say moral, languor that has, for the most part, I think, physical causes. Without any well-defined illness, I am experiencing weak nerves and a chronic, quasi-feverishness, one which I have felt, though, at various earlier times in my life and which I recognize well enough to know that it will not last for long" [my translation].

23. Mill to Carlyle, 22 October 1832, *Earlier Letters*, 128.

24. The *Early Draft* shows two important revisions. Canceled before the final version of the *Early Draft* was the phrase "Probably from physical causes (connected perhaps merely with the time of year)," which occurred before "in a dull state of nerves." Added in the 1861 version was the phrase concerning the Methodist conviction of sin. The direction of revision of this passage was, then, succes-

sively away from an associational explanation and toward an internalized movement. The ultimate result, I think, is to balance the passage even more between the two positions.

25. Carlyle to Jane Carlyle, 24 July 1836, in Hayek, *Mill and Harriet*, 84–85.

26. Caroline Fox, *Memories of Old Friends* (London: Smith, Elder, 1882), I:145–146.

27. Lionel Trilling, *The Liberal Imagination* (New York: Viking, 1950), xii, has Mill's crisis defining "the paradoxical relation" of liberalism to the emotions. More pertinent, we find in Taylor Branch's "New Frontiers in American Philosophy," *New York Times Magazine* (14 August 1977): 13, that the parents of the American philosopher Saul Kripke "tried to check their son's mind gently rather than to push it on, knowing that John Stuart Mill's father had pushed him to emotional breakdown," despite the fact that Kripke's extraordinary talent manifested itself with no outside urging. This incident makes clear that whatever the historical value of Mill's *Autobiography*, it is an enduring myth of the dangers of overeducation.

Chapter IV: Consciousness as a Narrative of Completion in the *Autobiography*

1. The connection dates back at least to Northrop Frye, *Anatomy of Criticism* (Princeton, N.Y.: Princeton University Press, 1957), 307–308. Both Wayne Shumaker, *English Autobiography* (Berkeley and Los Angeles: University of California Press, 1954), and Roy Pascal, *Design and Truth in Autobiography* (Cambridge: Harvard University Press, 1960), discuss similarities in the forms as well. For a recent explicit denial of the connection, see Barret J. Mandel, "Full of Life Now," in *Autobiography: Essays Theoretical and Critical*, 49–72. The most recent and fully articulated defense of the connection is Fleishman's in *Figures of Autobiography*, 1–39.

2. If such a generalization needs documentation, see Barbara Hardy, *The Appropriate Form* (London: Athlone, 1964); Alan Friedman, *The Turn of the Novel* (New York: Oxford University Press, 1966); and Levine, *Boundaries of Fiction*.

3. For Carlyle's remark to his brother upon the work's appearance—"It is wholly the life of a logic-chopping engine, little more of human in it than if it had been done by a thing of mechanized iron"—see Emory Neff, *Carlyle and Mill* (New York: Columbia University Press, 1926), 52. Roy Pascal, *Design and Truth in Autobiography*, has supported this judgment to a modified extent (103–104), and Wayne Shumaker, *English Autobiography*, has warned that the *Autobiography* is wholly an "intellectual history" (148). Of the few who would dissent from Shumaker's view, one is Eugene R. August, who in his article "Mill's *Autobiogra-*

phy as Philosophic *Commedia,*" *Victorian Poetry* 11 (Summer 1973): 143–162, argues that Mill structures his work as a *Divine Comedy* in which Paradise is achieved with the union of poetry and philosophy. Although the argument is often challenging and makes helpful observations about the tone of Mill's narration, it is finally unconvincing precisely because Mill's estimations of the intellectual stance of those around him do not begin to support the emotional and psychological evaluations August wants to see, particularly in the case of Mill's father.

4. Olney, *Metaphors of Self,* 232–259.

5. For a straightforward use of the religious model, see Mrs. S. E. Hanshaw's early review, "John Stuart Mill and Harriet Taylor," *Overland Monthly* 13 (December 1874). Hanshaw argues that Mill was trying to break through his father's atheism to a discovery of God—albeit unsuccessfully. Hanshaw's nineteenth-century religiosity may no longer be fashionable, but if we substitute "utilitarianism" or "rationalism" for "atheism" and "poetry" or "emotion" for "God," much the same argument has been made again and again.

6. John Morris, *Versions of the Self* (New York: Basic Books, 1966), 26.

7. For example, August, "Mill's *Autobiography* as Philosophic *Commedia.*"

8. Levi, "'Mental Crisis.'"

9. *Memoire de Marmontel,* ed. Maurice Tourneux (Paris: Libraires des Bibliophiles, 1891), I:66.

10. Ibid.

11. In "John Stuart Mill's Autobiography: Its Art and Appeal," *University of Kansas City Review* 19 (Summer 1953), Keith Rinehart describes the movement of the book as from "the aegis of one demi-god, his father, to another, his wife," 267.

12. Francis Mineka, "The Autobiography and the Lady," *University of Toronto Quarterly* 32 (April 1963): 301–306; Olney, *Metaphors of Self,* 253; Jack Stillinger, introduction to *The Early Draft of John Stuart Mill's Autobiography* (Urbana: University of Illinois Press, 1961), 27.

Chapter V: The Philosophic Context of the *Apologia*

1. Newman, *Autobiographical Writings,* ed. Henry Tristram (New York: Sheed & Ward, 1957), 5. Henceforth, this edition will be cited in my text as *AW.*

2. Actually, even in this nearly gnomic text, the divisions already exist, if only by implication. In the act of writing down "and now a Cardinal," Newman already implies an importance to the event beyond its recording that makes it worth recording. This document indicates how completely incoherent pure autobiography would be, but also how impossible, since any transcribing into language (and without that how is there any autobiography?) raises all the problems that the divisions of language necessitate.

3. Newman, *Apologia pro Vita Sua*, ed. Martin J. Svaglic (London: Oxford University Press, 1967), 18. Henceforth, this edition will be cited in my text as *Apologia*.

4. John Calvin, *The Institution of the Christian Religion*. I cite the passage from the article in which the correspondence was first noticed: Gordon Rupp, "Newman through Nonconformist Eyes," in *The Rediscovery of Newman*, ed. John Coulson and A. M. Allchin (London: Sheed & Ward, 1967), 210.

5. This belief is held by both Newman's critics and his hagiographers. For the former, Newman wanted an authority as a basis to enforce or at least ratify what he believed in but could not prove. In its extreme form, this was the view of Newman's brother, F. W. Newman, in *Contributions, Chiefly to the Early History of the Late Cardinal Newman* (London: Kegan Paul, 1891). In a less virulent, rather more analytic version, it is held by William Robbins, *The Newman Brothers* (Cambridge: Harvard University Press, 1966). To those more kindly disposed, Newman's desire is for a properly constituted authority to direct him rather than support him. His humility and obedience are thus two of the themes that run through Meriol Trevor's two volumes of biography: *Newman: The Pillar of the Cloud* and *Newman: The Light in Winter* (London: Macmillan, 1962).

6. Strangely enough, this view, like the first, is held by those who are sympathetic as well as by those who are critical (though it is certainly not that of any of the hagiographers). T. H. Huxley, who claimed he could build a "Primer of Infidelity" from three of Newman's works, in *Essays on Some Controverted Questions* (London: Macmillan, 1892), 471, is probably the earliest and most famous of the critics who have felt this way, if we do not count Charles Kingsley's confused approximation of the view. More recently, Owen Chadwick, *From Bossuet to Newman: The Idea of Doctrinal Development* (London: Cambridge University Press, 1957), has depicted Newman as honestly religious but subconsciously skeptical, "stretched on the wrack of doubt," with skepticism "the dead hand which scrabbled at him in the night when his faith was sleeping" (8, 126). David Anthony Downes, *The Temper of Victorian Belief* (New York: Twayne, 1972), 85, finds Newman torn between a "scientific historical sense" and a "personal containment of all knowledge within the peripheries of belief in Christian providence" and states that the conflict "pulled him apart intellectually and personally." Chadwick and Downes essentially replace Huxley's implied charge of hypocrisy with the more sympathetic one of psychological conflict.

Chapter VI: From History to Consciousness

1. Newman, *The Idea of a University*, ed. Martin J. Svaglic (New York: Holt, Rinehart & Winston, 1960), 31.

2. Newman, *An Essay on the Development of Christian Doctrine* (London: Longmans, Green, 1885), 7. Henceforth, this edition will be cited in my text as *DCD*.

3. The belief that religion is mere sentiment or opinion Newman labels "A Form of Infidelity of the Day" in *Idea of a University*, 286–303. Strictly speaking, *DCD* is only an argument for accepting Roman Catholicism rather than Protestantism as the true version of Christianity, not a justification of Christianity itself. But *Grammar of Assent* gets from natural theology to Christianity by much the same kind of historical argument that Newman uses elsewhere to get from Christianity to Catholicism. It is the value of the argument, not its details, that is in question here.

4. Newman, *Apologia*, 101; *Essays Critical and Historical* (London: Longmans, Green, 1885), II:6. The essay in question, "The Catholicity of the Anglican Church," was written in 1839 and appeared originally in January 1840.

5. This summary and much that follows is from the opening chapters of Owen Chadwick's excellent *From Bossuet to Newman: The Idea of Doctrinal Development*. Chadwick discusses on pages 3–4 the dispute I have outlined here.

6. Newman, *Essays Critical and Historical*, II:6.

7. I do not want to suggest that the idea of development sprang full-grown and newly minted from Newman's head. He knew of the Spanish theologians Francisco Suarez and Gabriel Vasquez and their theory of development as a logical movement from premise to conclusion, but he did not know them directly or well. He was aware of the controversy between Bishop Bull and Denis Petau, and F. L. Cross, "Newman and the Doctrine of Development," *Church Quarterly Review* 115 (January 1933): 245–257, has argued convincingly that Newman's movement from Anglican to Catholic was a movement from the Bull to the Petau side of the controversy. Petau's theory of development, however, controversial as it was, represents only the most conservative aspect of Newman's theory.

8. The argument over Newman's use of organic, progressivist theories of history, and his contradiction of those theories, still rages. In Newman's own time, the prevailing view, held by his friend James Mozley (see Chadwick, *From Bossuet to Newman*, 96), as well as by a less sober, anonymous critic in "Mr. Newman: His Theories and Character," *Fraser's Magazine* 33 (March 1846): 253–268, was that Newman was supporting Catholicism by the most liberal of theories, that he was "travelling to Germany by way of Italy" (265). Frank Leslie Cross, in his article "Newman and the Doctrine of Development" *Church Quarterly Review* 115 (January 1933): 245–257, and his book *John Henry Newman* (Glasgow: Philip Allan, 1933), called a halt to all of this, maintaining in the book that "development is conceived as a logical rather than a temporal process . . . we are certainly a long way here from any theory of development as an immanental process" (105–106). This position stresses Newman's view of development as being a result of lan-

guage's various, insufficient attempts to express adequately the unchanging truth of Christianity. It remains a widely held reading of Newman's theory, asserted in no less a place than H. Francis Davis's entry on "Doctrine, Development of" in *A Catholic Dictionary of Theology* (London: Nelson, 1966), II:182–186. The older view has been reasserted in more moderate terms, however, by Chadwick, *From Bossuet to Newman*, 96–119, and by Walter J. Ong, "Newman's Essay on Development in Its Intellectual Milieu," in *John Henry Newman*, ed. Joseph Houppert (St. Louis, Mo.: B. Herder, n.d.), 35. My own view will become clear as the argument progresses, but in short, I think Newman means to offer a limited theory on the order of Davis's and Cross's interpretations but that there are definite dependencies on the more liberal formulations suggested by Chadwick and Ong.

9. Newman, *Fifteen Sermons Preached before the University of Oxford* (London: Rivingtons, 1872), 313. Henceforth, this edition will be cited in my text as *University Sermons*.

10. H. Francis Davis, "Is Newman's Theory of Development Catholic?" in *Blackfriars* 39 (July–August 1958): 315, defends Newman from the charge that, on his theory, "we should be ready to jettison those dogmas which cannot be shown clearly to be developments" by noting his presumption of doctrinal integrity.

11. It seems to be on the basis of this possible reading of Newman that Chadwick, *From Bossuet to Newman*, 95, ends his book with the following inflammatory question: Since it is agreed that "the decree of the Holy Office Lamentabili in 1908" makes it a matter of the faith that revelation ended with the death of the last Apostle, "these new doctrines, of which the Church had a feeling or inkling but of which she was not conscious—in what meaningful sense may it be asserted that these new doctrines are not 'new revelation'?" H. Francis Davis, in his previously cited entry in *A Catholic Dictionary of Theology* and in his review of Chadwick's book in *Downside Review* 76 (Summer 1958): 294–296, answers this question with essentially Newman's question-begging formula: they are not new revelation because Newman thinks they are not because the church says they are not.

12. Newman, *On Consulting the Faithful in Matters of Doctrine*, ed. with an introduction by John Coulson (New York: Sheed & Ward, 1961), 101–102.

13. Ibid., 72.

14. Of course, *On Consulting the Faithful* was directed at Catholic clergy and so could make this assumption. My point, however, is that the epistemological model Newman uses here abandons entirely any notion of development as a positive argument.

15. C. S. Dessain, "An Unpublished Paper by Cardinal Newman on the Development of Doctrine," *Journal of Theological Studies* 9 (October 1958): 331.

16. Ibid., 332.

17. To instance only two of the more rigorous of Newman's explicators, J.-H. Walgrave, *Newman the Theologian*, trans. A. V. Littledale (New York: Sheed & Ward), 89–92, argues that Newman was not concerned with what makes a proposition true but with what leads us to accept it as truth. David Pailin, *The Way to Faith* (London: Epworth, 1969), 172, even more explicitly states that Newman is not concerned with giving faith an objective status.

18. Newman, *Grammar of Assent* (Westminster, Md.: Christian Classics, 1973), 237. Henceforth, this edition will be cited in my text as *GA*.

19. Pailin, *Way to Faith*, 179–180, does recognize this distinction but argues that the use of the term *false certitude*, which should be a contradiction in terms, indicates an inattention to the distinction that betrays Newman's real interest as essentially subjective. Newman, however, in a letter to Meynall, 17 November 1869, in *The Letters and Diaries of John Henry Newman*, (London: Nelson, 1969–1973), XXIV:375, explains that "I have defined certitude as a conviction of what is true. When a conviction of what is not true is considered as if it was a conviction of what is true, I have called it a false certitude." Perhaps this is not the clearest choice of terms, and perhaps the text of *Grammar of Assent* does not make this distinction as explicit as it should. But this statement indicates again how aware Newman was of the space between subject and object and how much his insistence on there being a point at which this space can be crossed was not a movement toward simply ignoring the object.

20. Pailin, *Way to Faith*, 103–104, finds the theory that we may believe what we do not know untenable and therefore argues that assent cannot be unconscious or unexamined. He is then forced into a statement that seems to erase the line between assent and certitude: "Assent is not the unexamined or unconscious affirmation of a statement but the deliberate affirmation of its truth." Because such a revision makes certitude an obviously common occurrence, it destroys even the vestige of tenability to the proposition that serene, assured conviction is likely to be a true certitude. The likelihood of that proposition, after all, rests to a large extent on the rarity of the experience.

21. As Pailin, *Way to Faith*, 254–255, states, this is an extension of real apprehension well beyond the realm an empiricist would normally allow. For a discussion distinctly different from mine of the importance of Newman's theory of real and notional assents and apprehensions to the *Apologia*, see Olney, *Metaphors of Self*, 202–232.

22. Pailin, *Way to Faith*, 187–188, with some reservations, and A. J. Boekraad, *The Personal Conquest of Truth According to J. H. Newman* (Louvain: Nauwelaerts, 1955), 270–271, with complete approval, ratify this contention.

23. *The Philosophical Notebook of John Henry Newman*, ed. Edward Sillem (New York: Humanities Press, 1969), II:22. The first volume of this work is Sillem's

General Introduction to the Philosophy of John Henry Newman; the second, the notebooks themselves.

24. *Philosophical Notebook*, II:23.

Chapter VII: Belief as Example

1. For a discussion of the composition of the *Philosophical Notebook* and its relation to that period of time, see Sillem, *Philosophical Notebook*, I:68–71. In addition to the *Notebook*, of the eighteen entries in his journal (reprinted in *AW*, 209) that Newman marks as attempts to begin *Grammar of Assent*, dating as far back as 1846, nine are dated between 1859 and 1864.

2. Letter to Edward Badeley, 15 January 1864, in *Letters and Diaries*, XXI: 18–19.

3. Martin J. Svaglic's "Why Newman Wrote the *Apologia*," in *Newman's "Apologia": A Classic Reconsidered*, ed. Vincent Ferrer Blehl, S.J., and Francis X. Connely (New York: Harcourt Brace & World, 1964), 1–25, covers in far greater detail much of the same background that I have been discussing. Svaglic also believes that Newman was using the controversy to achieve a reason for the defense he had wanted to make before the controversy had started. But, of the above letter, and the way events turned out, he concludes that the coincidence of Kingsley's accusations with Newman's desired grounds was "one of those special providences Newman loved to chronicle" (11). I think my discussion of Newman's pamphlet indicates that this is more nearly a case of God helping those who help themselves.

4. Letter to Badeley, 8 March 1864, in *Letters and Diaries*, XXI:73.

5. *Apologia*, 345. All of the pamphlets and other materials relevant to the controversy are reprinted in Svaglic's edition of the work and are cited from that text.

6. I follow here G. Enger's argument about the use of the term in *Apologia pro Charles Kingsley* (London: Sheed & Ward, 1969), 118–120.

7. In fact, Kingsley was not as explicit about this accusation as perhaps Newman might have hoped. He suggests the possibility of Newman's having been a secret Romanist in a snide parenthetical remark (*Apologia*, 366), but he never makes the accusation directly. Newman is forced, in his "True Mode of Meeting Mr. Kingsley," to use Kingsley's objections to terming "Wisdom and Innocence" "Protestant" as his entry into the question of his covert Romanism, another mark of how much he wanted that subject raised.

8. At this point critics might ask what would happen if one did not have an early theory that one converted from. But a conversion necessitates that at some level one does have such a theory. That theory may not be as fully articulated as Newman's Tractarian theory, but if one converts, by definition one must convert

from one set of beliefs, or at least one set of attitudes, to another. To the extent that those beliefs or attitudes are found wanting, they must then be seen, even if only in retrospect, as having been a theory.

9. Newman, in *University Sermons*, 234, claims at a key point that "the safeguard of faith is a right state of heart." J. M. Cameron, *The Night Battle* (London: Catholic Book Club, 1962), 216, discusses this moment as presenting not arguments but intuitions. To the extent that Cameron is right, Newman's summary of his position is clearly misleading.

10. For a more detailed discussion of this aspect of the relationship between the *Apologia* and the *Grammar*, see Robert A. Colby, "The Structure of Newman's *Apologia pro Vita Sua* in Relation to His Theory of Assent," *Dublin Review* (Summer 1953), 140–156. An updated version of the article appears in David J. DeLaura's Norton critical edition of the *Apologia*, 465–480.

11. The first full-scale defense of this theory is by Cross, *John Henry Newman*, 130–145. Walter Houghton, *The Art of Newman's "Apologia"* (New Haven, Conn.: Yale University Press, 1945), 95–106, essentially agrees, though he argues that, since Cross's information comes from the *Apologia*, Newman is not fictionalizing but only changing the emphasis slightly. In fact, by extracting the connotations of Cross's use of the word *resentment* and concentrating on the theoretical implications of the condemnation of Tract 90, we can see the same theory in defenders of Newman such as Walgrave, *Newman the Theologian*, 318, and John Beer, "Newman and the Romantic Sensibility," in *The English Mind*, ed. Hugh Sykes Davies and George Watson (Cambridge: Cambridge University Press, 1964), 201.

12. *Letters and Correspondences of John Henry Newman*, ed. Anne Mozley (London: Longmans, Green, 1891), II:286.

13. Newman, *Discussions and Arguments* (London: Longmans, Green, 1891), 6–9.

14. *Letters and Correspondences*, II:345.

15. This is the claim of Houghton, *Art of Newman's "Apologia"*, 102.

16. David J. DeLaura, *Hebrew and Hellene in Victorian England: Newman, Arnold and Pater* (Austin and London: University of Texas Press, 1969), 314.

17. *Philosophical Notebook*, II:171.

Chapter VIII: Consciousness as a Narrative of Reflection in the *Apologia*

1. A quick list of discussions of esthetic form or rhetorical skill in the *Apologia* would include Leonard W. Deen, "The Rhetoric of Newman's *Apologia*," *ELH* 29 (June 1962), 224–238; Sister Mary Baylon Lenz, "The Rhetoric of Newman's *Apologia*," in *Newman's "Apologia": A Classic Reconsidered*, 80–104; Martin J.

Svaglic, "The Structure of Newman's *Apologia*," *PMLA* 67 (March 1961), 140–156; and of course Houghton's book, *Art of Newman's "Apologia."* There are many others. My point here is sufficiently demonstrated by the far more frequent occurrence of words like "structure," "rhetoric," and "art" in titles of works on Newman's *Apologia* than in those of works on Mill's *Autobiography*.

2. Paul de Man's use of the terms *grammar* and *rhetoric* as replacements for the opposition of form and content, his discussion of the implications of the opposition of rhetoric and grammar, and his construction of that opposition in *Allegories of Reading* (New Haven: Yale University Press, 1979), 1–16, all indicate that the suggestion that rhetorical power is deceptive, implicitly if not logically opposed to straightforward meaning, is more than just a Victorian notion.

3. Houghton, *Art of Newman's "Apologia"*, 12.

4. See, for instance, Edwin Muir, *The Structure of the Novel* (London: Humanities Press, 1928), 23f., also cited recently by Roger Henkle, *Comedy and Culture* (Princeton,: N.J. Princeton University Press, 1980), 76, who uses the distinction in a discussion of comic fiction. Commonly the distinction occurs in the form of a division between narratives of plot and those of character. Although narratives centering on character need not be static even if they de-emphasize external action, and Robert Scholes and Robert Kellogg discuss techniques of character development in their chapter on character in *The Nature of Narrative* (New York: Oxford University Press, 1966), 160–207, even they reestablish the distinction implicitly at other points (see 207, 232).

5. Olney, *Metaphors of Self*, 226.

6. Lenz, "Rhetoric of Newman's *Apologia*," 85.

7. In his *University Sermons*, 21–23, Newman explicitly argues that while an unmediated awareness of one's own intuitions leads to a knowledge of God and of the basic truths of Natural Religion, to achieve the fullest knowledge of religious truths, one needs the historical event of revelation and the external objectification it supplies.

8. Thomas Vargish, *Newman: The Contemplation of Mind* (London: Oxford University Press), 179.

9. William E. Buckler, "The Apologia as Human Experience," *Newman's "Apologia": A Classic Reconsidered*, ed. Blehl and Connely, 70.

10. For a more detailed reading of this passage, see Michael Ryan, "The Question of Autobiography in Cardinal Newman's *Apologia*," *Georgia Review* 31 (Fall 1977), 695–696.

11. For Derrida's analysis of erasures, additions, and compensations in Rousseau, see *Of Grammatology*, trans. Gayatri Chakravorty Spivak (Baltimore: Johns Hopkins Press, 1976), 141–165. To say that Newman recognizes the dilemmas Derrida's analysis opens is only to say what Paul de Man says about Rousseau, though, in *Blindness and Insight* (New York: Oxford University Press, 1971), 102–141, and not to argue that Newman transcends that problematic situation.

12. Hugo M. Achaval, "Theological Implications in the Apologia," *Newman's "Apologia": A Classic Reconsidered*, ed. Blehl and Connely, 140.

13. Joseph L. Altholz, in "Newman and History," *Victorian Studies* 7 (March 1964), 297, describes the conversion as "an experience in history," the result of the historical researches that also led to the *Essay on Development*; and Trevor, in *The Light in Winter*, 333, identifies the theory of development as "the great unifying idea" behind the *Apologia*.

14. For early reactions to the *Apologia*, including this and other mixed responses, see Vincent Ferrer Blehl, "Early Criticism of the *Apologia*," in *Newman's "Apologia": A Classic Reconsidered*, ed. Blehl and Connely, 47–63.

15. Levine, *Boundaries of Fiction*, 244.

16. Lionel Trilling, *Sincerity and Authenticity* (Cambridge: Harvard University Press, 1971), particularly chap. I.

17. Deen, "Rhetoric of Newman's *Apologia*," 229.

Chapter IX: Reading Victorian Prose

1. Newman, *Idea of a University*, 20.

2. Ibid., 94.

3. Newman, *University Sermons*, 150.

4. "Mill's Diary: Selections," *Mill's Essays on Literature and Society*, ed. J. B. Schneewind (New York: Collier, 1965), 348.

5. For such articles on Mill and Newman, see my notes through the book. For the treatment of Arnold, see A. Dwight Culler, "No Arnold Could Ever Write a Novel," *Victorian Newsletter* (Spring 1966): 1–5, as well as the notes to the Arnold chapter. For Carlyle, see Janet Ray Edwards, "Carlyle and the Fictions of Belief," *Carlyle and His Contemporaries*, ed. John Clubbe (Durham, N.C.: Duke University Press, 1976), 91–111.

6. John Holloway, *The Victorian Sage* (New York: Norton, 1965), 10.

7. Although this may sound like the absence of literary theory, it was explicitly argued for by A. Dwight Culler in "Method in the Study of Victorian Prose," *Victorian Newsletter* (Spring 1956): 1–4.

8. Holloway, *Victorian Sage*, 9.

9. George Levine, "Nonfiction as Art," *Victorian Newsletter* (Fall 1966): 6.

10. Ibid. 2–3.

11. George Levine and William Madden, introduction to *The Art of Victorian Prose*, ed. idem (New York: Oxford University Press, 1968), xvii.

12. That there is a connection, if not precisely what the connection is, critics of Victorian literature are starting to realize. David DeLaura, "The Allegory of Life: The Autobiographical Impulse in Victorian Prose," *Approaches to Victorian Autobiography*, ed. George Landow (Athens, Ohio: Ohio University Press, 1979):

333–354, and John Reed, *Victorian Conventions* (Athens, Ohio: Ohio University Press, 1975), 400–439, both point to the use Victorian writers make of their memory to form archetypal patterns or myths that convey their sense of certain issues or the important aspect of certain historical periods. Neither writer, however, really discusses what this transformation of consciousness into literature involves.

Chapter X: Experience Teaching by Philosophy

1. Both Albert LaValley, *Carlyle and the Idea of the Modern* (New Haven, Conn.: Yale University Press, 1968), 118, and Tennyson, *Sartor Called Resartus*, 84, for example, see *Sartor* as a basis for the rest of the writing, involving a simple outward turning, a use of the same "method and style" (according to Tennyson) adapted to different topics. And Rene Wellek, in *Confrontations* (Princeton, N.J.: Princeton University Press, 1965), 34, argues that Carlyle's "philosophy is clearly formulated in [*Sartor*]; and it is no exaggeration to say that every fundamental idea found its expression in this final effort to sum up the convictions of his youth."

2. As Wilhelm Dilthey, in "*Sartor Resartus*: Philosophical Conflict, Positive and Negative Eras and Personal Resolution," trans. Murray Baumgarten and Evelyn Kanes, *CLIO* 1 (June 1972): 54, was perhaps the first to realize, "Carlyle's entire predisposition inclined him towards a very personal historiography, for the understanding of which we must turn to his philosophical writing."

3. All references to Carlyle's works, unless otherwise noted are from the American variant (New York: Scribner's, 1903–1904) of the Centenary edition (London: Chapman & Hall, 1896–1901) of *The Works of Thomas Carlyle*, ed. H. D. Traill, henceforth cited in my text as *Works*, with a roman numeral for the volume, an arabic numeral for the page. Citations of *Sartor Resartus* continue to refer to the Harrold edition cited in n. 9 to my introduction.

4. See Tennyson, *Sartor Called Resartus*, 82, for an account of this projected history.

5. This passage is the best refutation of the frequent argument that Carlyle thought "that the philosophy must emerge from the facts and not vice versa," as Louise Merwin Young puts it in *Carlyle and the Art of History* (Philadelphia: University of Pennsylvania Press, 1939), 25. Young specifies this view as a later one, but, as I show, Carlyle's sense of the priority of philosophy does not change.

6. The relationship between Carlyle's Puritan roots and his experimentation with German philosophy has been much debated. Although the issue is only tangent here, my position is closer to Charles Frederick Harrold's in *Carlyle and German Thought 1819–1834* (New Haven: Yale University Press, 1934), which contends that the German philosophy was an incompletely understood overlay for the Puritan beliefs Carlyle felt needed new buttressing, than it is to A. Abbot Ikeler's

in *Puritan Temper and Transcendental Faith: Carlyle's Literary Vision* (Columbus, Ohio: Ohio State University Press, 1972), which argues that the contradictory evaluations of literature in Carlyle derive from the contradictions of concomitantly held German philosophy and Puritan belief.

7. For a discussion of Carlyle's rejection of Scottish Common Sense philosophy, see Harrold, *Carlyle and German Thought*, 21–22.

8. This depiction, of course, starts with the chronologically confused reception of a text completed in 1831 but not published in England in book form until 1838 (there had been an American book publication in 1836 and an abortive serial publication in *Fraser's* in 1833–1834), after the popularity of *The French Revolution* prepared for the second, more popular reception. More recently, though, very acute critics of *Sartor* such as Tennyson in *Sartor Called Resartus* and Levine in *Boundaries of Fiction*, both of whom are very sensitive to the fictive strategies of the work, have still ended up stabilizing the text prematurely, as I argue below.

9. Recent examples here are Peter Glassman, "'His Beautiful Edifice of a Person': *Sartor Resartus*," *Prose Studies* 2 (1978): 25–40, and Geoffrey Hartman, *Criticism in the Wilderness* (New Haven, Conn.: Yale University Press, 1980), 48–50 in particular. To Victorianists, some of the extravagance of these critics' conclusions almost needs no commentary, which may be unfortunate because the reaction to that extravagance effectively denies a proper consideration of the aptness of many of the important revisions of received ideas that their close readings lead to. An important exception to the problematic readings mentioned in this note and the last is Janice L. Haney's "'Shadow-Hunting': Romantic Irony, *Sartor Resartus* and Victorian Romanticism," *Studies in Romanticism* 17 (Summer 1978): 307–333. Haney both attends to, indeed focuses on, the primacy of the interpretive activity in the text and accommodates the text's attempts to direct that activity, suggesting, in her terms, that *Sartor* uses social activity to modulate Romantic irony as Romantic irony modulates Romantic allegory (327–333). Her agreement with all these critics in treating the text as enclosed, uncontaminated by context, however, creates important differences between her treatment and mine.

10. See Tennyson, *Sartor Called Resartus*, 157–173, and Levine, *Boundaries of Fiction*, 65–68.

11. See his chapter "Structure," 160–162, 168–169, 175, 185–187.

12. This identification is one of the features of Carlyle's philosophy that seems most to appeal to many modern critics. It is the basis for recent studies connecting him with Marxist and existential thought, such as Phillip Rosenberg's *The Seventh Hero: Carlyle and the Theory of Radical Activism* (Cambridge: Harvard University Press, 1975), and Eloise M. Behnken's *Thomas Carlyle: "Calvinist without Theology"* (Columbia: University of Missouri Press, 1978), as well, of course, as LaValley's *Idea of the Modern*.

13. Why would Carlyle virtually end *Sartor* on this note of failed interpretation, of textual opacity? There is considerable evidence, after all, that Carlyle in-

tended *Sartor* as a definitive turn from his review writing toward his desired role as an influential, ameliorative voice on the English scene. If "Characteristics" were not there to re-create opacity from another direction, one might suspect either that *Sartor* had gotten away from Carlyle or that I had finally outdone Teufelsdröckh's interpretive resourcefulness in creating and destroying significance. But "Characteristics" does, as I show, seem to confirm this failed conclusion. As an explanation of intention, one can only note the notoriously complex and frustrated compositional and publishing history of *Sartor*. The book was frequently rejected by publishers, was heavily rewritten, was a dismal failure in its first magazine appearance, and was not published in book form in England until 1838, when Carlyle's other works, particularly the *French Revolution*, had made the reputation *Sartor* was supposed to. Carlyle's awareness that he had not found the form for his prophecy (remember he could not know that it would come to be taken as one of his key texts) could thus easily have found its way into this text and have led him to the alternative attempt of "Characteristics."

14. "Characteristics" is both an underinterpreted and, for that reason, a misinterpreted essay. Although criticism of *Sartor* has come to recognize its convolution, comments on "Characteristics" still respond flatly to it as a simple series of declarative statements. Thus LaValley, *Idea of the Modern*, 62, sees in it an exemplification of Carlyle's weakness as a systematic philosopher, and Ikeler, *Puritan Temper and Transcendental Faith*, 140, labels it Carlyle's most clear manifestation of his Puritan prejudices. I would hardly want to argue either that Carlyle is as rigorously systematic as, say, Kant, or that there is no Puritan element to his thought. I do contend here, though, that "Characteristics" is as deliberate, careful, and convoluted as *Sartor* and deserves far more careful treatment than it has received.

15. One ought to remember in reading Carlyle that before the doctrine of Fact arose, in *Sartor*, Carlyle had described facts as useless without interpretation (203) and tended to value Fantasy (217, 219–220, 222) instead. Nor does identifying Fantasy with Kant's reason, as Harrold does (*Sartor*, 220, n. 1), change my point that Carlyle seems clearly to take the word in its usual as well as in its specialized sense. Keeping in mind these passages as the background for Carlyle's historiography becomes particularly important in the discussion below of Carlyle's use of facts.

16. Hayden White, *Metahistory* (Baltimore: Johns Hopkins University Press, 1973), 147–149, has explained succinctly and clearly this idea of pulling from the chaos of history a philosophic truth reflective of the historian more than of the history. Since White does not deal with the attack upon this process in "On History" or with the fear of the consciousness that such an act entails in "Characteristics", however, he both starts and stops here in his discussion of Carlyle's historiography.

17. J. A. Froude, *Thomas Carlyle: A History of His Life in London* (New York: Scribner's, 1884), for instance, believes that Carlyle's histories replace philosophy with fact and that it was his "special gift" to "bring dead things and dead people actually back to life . . . with every feature he ascribes to them authenticated, not the most trifling incident invented" (IV:173).

18. Hill Shine, *Carlyle's Fusion of Poetry, History and Religion* (Port Washington, N.Y.: Kennikat, 1967; reprint of University of North Carolina Press, Chapel Hill, 1938), 37–56, marks Carlyle's valuing social accuracy and facticity as the bridge that led him from poetry to history. More recently, Janet Ray Edwards, "Carlyle and the Fictions of Belief," *Carlyle and His Contemporaries* (Durham, N.C.: Duke University Press, 1976), 91–111, also argues that the connection between Carlyle's histories and fiction is the way he treats facts vividly, even though accurately. Indeed, one would be hard put to find a critic of Carlyle who does not agree.

19. But see Wellek, *Confrontations*, 109, who notes that Carlyle had no notion of how to interrogate his documentary sources.

20. The stubbornness of the belief that Carlyle was interested in facts for their vivid concreteness is perhaps best exemplified in Young's use in *Art of History* of precisely these passages to exemplify Carlyle's "process of particularizing the individual" (150–153). That these passages are vivid I would certainly not dispute. To see them as particularizing or making concrete anything but the process of gazing upon a fact, though, takes its own kind of act of interpretive will.

21. In a different context and to rather different ends, David DeLaura, "Ishmael as Prophet: Heroes and Hero-Worship and the Self-Expressive Basis of Carlyle's Art," *Texas Studies in Language and Literature* 11 (Spring 1969): 706, notices Carlyle's penchant for merging his voice with a variety of others to form "a single energizing force."

Chapter XI: The Gaze within the Text

1. Relating Arnold and Newman constitutes a minor industry of its own in Victorian studies; likewise Arnold and Carlyle. David DeLaura's importance to the field is well enough indicated by the fact that he has produced the major work detailing each of these relationships: *Hebrew and Hellene in Victorian England* definitively and exhaustively establishes the first, while "Arnold and Carlyle," *PMLA* 79 (1964): 104–129, is still the best treatment of the second. More recently, Peter Alan Dale, *The Victorian Critic and the Idea of History* (Cambridge: Harvard University Press, 1977), reshuffles the names to declare a central esthetic line stretching from Carlyle through Arnold to Pater, reserving Newman and Mill for another tradition (12). Meanwhile, Lionel Trilling has discussed the relationship between *Culture and Anarchy* and Mill's "On Liberty" in *Matthew Arnold*

(New York: Columbia University Press, 1949), 259–265, and Edward Alexander's *Matthew Arnold and John Stuart Mill* (New York: Columbia University Press, 1965), is a comprehensive comparison of the two.

2. To draw yet another connection, one might say that Arnold's relation to Victorian prose is analogous to Nietzsche's relationship to German philosophy. They both saw the linguistic density of ostensibly transparent discourses and proceeded to make that density a central concern of their philosophies. For an exemplary treatment of Nietzsche in this vein, see Paul de Man, *Allegories of Reading*, 79–131.

3. Trilling so completely makes Arnold's prose earnest that he asserts that what he calls Arnold's dandyism ended with the poetry, although he allows him a continued elegance (*Matthew Arnold*, 33). DeLaura, in *Hebrew and Hellene*, likewise finds the charge of aestheticism leveled at Arnold not a just one (70). William Madden, *Matthew Arnold: A Study of the Aesthetic Temperament in Victorian England* (Bloomington: Indiana University Press, 1967), on the other hand, makes the continuity of Arnold's aestheticism from his poetry through his prose the central thesis of the book, and Dale, *Victorian Critic*, 168, essentially agrees.

4. All the critics cited above ultimately formulate some version of this position, though they tend to weight either the esthetic or the social aims more highly, depending upon their slant. Critics who explicitly formulate the combination as central to Arnold include Patrick J. McCarthy, *Matthew Arnold and the Three Classes* (New York: Columbia University Press, 1964), 29–30, and Raymond Williams, *Culture and Society* (New York: Harper & Row, 1966), 115–116. A. O. J. Cockshut, *The Unbelievers* (New York: New York University Press, 1966), 65, describes the combination as "the heart of George Fox and the manners of Lord Chesterfield." Terry Eagleton, *Criticism and Ideology* (London: NLB, 1976), 107, has perhaps the best label, though, calling it an "aestheticized sociology."

5. Holloway, *Victorian Sage*, 202, opens his chapter on Arnold by quoting the letter and does so precisely to argue in that chapter for the tone as a rhetorical device, a way of persuading the reader.

6. Arnold, *Complete Prose Works*, R. H. Super, ed. (Ann Arbor: University of Michigan Press, 1960–1977), V:115. All further references to Arnold's prose are to this edition, henceforth cited in my text as *CPW*. This quotation occurs in Arnold's summing up of the criticism of his first chapter, "Sweetness and Light," in its first appearance as an article in *Cornhill*. All of the criticisms of that chapter are of the same kind.

7. Sidney Couling, *Matthew Arnold and His Critics* (Athens: Ohio University Press, 1974), 4, quotes Max Muller to that effect.

8. See Dale, *Victorian Critic*, 102–103, for a discussion of Arnold's "Lucretian stance," modern critical definition of it, and response to it.

9. Couling, *Matthew Arnold and His Critics*, 115–116, attacks Arnold for the contradictions and presumptions involved in judging Colenso from the perspective of literary criticism. But he clearly sees this to be a subsidiary problem with the essays rather than the central concern I am arguing that it is.

10. Trilling's account, *Matthew Arnold*, 208, of Colenso acting out a Voltairian joke catches the right tone.

11. Not explicitly, however. In *Culture and Anarchy*, he uses Colenso as an allusion to characterize Hepworth Dixon (*CPW*, V:206), but clearly implies the discursive distinction of religion and science. In *God and the Bible*, Arnold distinguishes himself from Colenso in having provided a positive criticism rather than a negative one (*CPW*, VII:147, 377–378), but this distinction ultimately also depends on the division of discourses in "Function of Criticism" since Arnold more or less assumes all negative criticism to be scientifically accurate and proceeds to what literature will tell us about religion.

12. Edmund Burke, *Works and Correspondence* (London: Francis & John Rivington, 1852), IV:591. Arnold italicizes the passage.

13. Arnold's use of Burke may have something to do with the strange attraction Burke held for nineteenth-century liberals. John Morley wrote two books on him, in 1867 and 1879. Gladstone read him constantly during his dealings with Ireland in the 1880s. And, in a lighter vein, the shallow liberal, Lord Fawn, uses him as a club to browbeat his sisters' governess, Lucy Morris, in Anthony Trollope's *The Eustace Diamonds*, chap. VII, while Trollope manages at the same time to show that he has read Burke too.

14. My account of this controversy, though not my interpretation of its theoretical significance, generally follows and is drawn from Couling's explanation, *Matthew Arnold and His Critics*, 145, 153, 158.

15. Quoted in Couling, *Matthew Arnold and His Critics*, 158.

16. Ibid.

17. DeLaura, in "Arnold and Carlyle," 106, 107, finds this narrowness in the case of Carlyle.

18. Frederic Harrison, "Culture: A Dialogue," reprinted in *Culture and Anarchy*, Ian Gregor, ed. (New York: Bobbs-Merrill, 1971), 277.

19. Trilling, *Matthew Arnold*, 254.

20. Sheldon Rothblatt, *The Revolution of the Dons* (New York: Basic Books, 1968), 116–131, has noted Arnold's psychologizing of the state, but since he attributes this to Arnold's own feeling of alienation, he assumes that the book embodies Arnold's confused psyche rather than that Arnold constructs a coherent model of how he thinks the state-as-mind would work.

21. If the identification of the Hebraistic sense of sin with middle-class demands for active meliorism seems not that close, turn back to Arnold's quoting of

Frederic Harrison's criticism of him as holding up the pouncet-box of culture while "death, sin, cruelty stalk among us" (*CPW*, V:116). The awareness of sin sets off the desire for reform.

22. One result of seeing the forces in opposition is the fiction that in moving from *Culture and Anarchy* to *Literature and Dogma*, Arnold was recognizing the need for Hebraism in English society as well. But Arnold did not start writing like Carlyle. As DeLaura argues in *Hebrew and Hellene* (174), the mixture was always there, and it was always there, I think, because the Hellenistic process always contained Hebraism.

23. In this context, Richard Jenkyns's criticism, in *The Victorians and Ancient Greece* (Cambridge: Harvard University Press, 1980), 272, that Arnold gets his history wrong becomes, to say the least, trivial and the criticism that Arnold confuses cultural and moral criteria (266, 273) equally derives from a failure to see how the epistemological process works.

24. Williams, *Culture and Society*, 125, has noticed that Arnold's application of authority to rioters is an anomaly in the book rather than an indication of culture's elitism.

25. DeLaura, "Arnold and Carlyle," 118–119.

26. The bulk of the book defends his reading of the authorship and implications of the Fourth Gospel from the attacks upon it of German textual criticism. Since he prefaces this defense, however, with the quite accurate contention that his theory of Christianity is independent of his view of the Fourth Gospel's historicity, the extended argument about that Gospel is not relevant here.

27. William Robbins, *The Ethical Idealism of Matthew Arnold* (London: William Heinemann, 1959), 129–130.

28. Thus Robbins exemplifies Spinoza and Christ in the same breath (129), precisely what Arnold does not want to allow.

29. This is not quite the same as Park Honan's contention, in *Matthew Arnold: A Life* (New York: McGraw-Hill, 1981), that Arnold admits he might be wrong in his speculation (368–369), since not correctness, but the adequacy of conception to need, is at issue here.

30. Gerald Graff, *Literature against Itself* (Chicago: University of Chicago Press, 1979), 15.

Afterword

1. M. H. Abrams, "Rationality and Imagination in Cultural History: A Reply to Wayne Booth," *Critical Inquiry*, 2 (1976): 458, argues that "if one takes seriously Miller's deconstructionist principles of interpretation, any history which re-

lies on written texts becomes an impossibility." J. Hillis Miller, "The Critic as Host," *Critical Inquiry*, 3 (1977): 439, rather airly responds, "So be it." But Derrida argues, in *Of Grammatology*, 159, that because the impossibility of separating the signifier from the signified is "historically articulated," deconstruction may work within writing to question it. This dependence on perceiving a historical effect may make Miller's response too dismissive.

2. Derrida, "White Mythology," particularly 230–245 (see Introduction, n. 21).

3. De Man discusses grammar and rhetoric in *Allegories of Reading*, 3–19, while his central argument for literature as self-deconstructing and therefore a privileged discourse is "The Rhetoric of Blindness" in *Blindness and Insight*, 102–141.

4. The term is Derrida's to describe his attempt to exit the orbit of Western metaphysics in *Of Grammatology*, 157, 161–162.

5. In "Limited Inc abc," *Glyph*, 2 (1977), a reply to John Searle's critique of an earlier essay, Derrida notes that he has quoted all of Searle's essay in his own response (245), implying, as he does throughout, that he has incorporated Searle's position within his argument. He also, earlier, implies the reverse, that Searle has understood the earlier essay because he has reproduced the effect of it in arguing against it (176–177).

6. Jacques Derrida, "Structure, Sign and Play in the Discourse of the Human Sciences," in *Writing and Difference*, trans. Alan Bass (Chicago: University of Chicago Press, 1978), 292–293.

7. Graff, *Literature against Itself*, 193, argues that deconstruction's dependence on logocentrism implies logocentrism's truth. Wayne C. Booth, "M. H. Abrams: Historian as Critic, Critic as Pluralist," *Critical Inquiry*, 2 (1976), says that he "finds the possibility of having . . . a deconstructive history exhilirating" (439), but he also stipulates that it would be "plainly and simply parasitical on"—thus subsidiary to—"the work of people like Abrams, whose solidity, even when rejected as obvious or dull, is relied upon in every act of deconstruction" (441).

8. Derrida, *Of Grammatology*, 161–162. The play on "orbit" relates back to Derrida's labeling of his method as "exorbitant."

9. M. H. Abrams, "What's the Use of Theorizing about the Arts?" in *In Search of Literary Theory*, ed. Morton W. Bloomfield (Ithaca, N.Y.: Cornell University Press, 1972), 53–54.

10. Stanley Fish argues this position at length in "Consequences," *Critical Inquiry*, 11 (1985): 433–458, drawing out the implications of the arguments in Steven Knapp and Walter Benn Michaels, "Against Theory," *Critical Inquiry*, 8 (1982): 732–742.

Index

.